T0342322

Illusions of Influence

MODERN AMERICA

A series edited by

Barton J. Bernstein and David M. Kennedy

Illusions of Influence

THE POLITICAL ECONOMY OF

UNITED STATES–PHILIPPINES

RELATIONS, 1942–1960

NICK CULLATHER

Stanford University Press

Stanford, California 1994

Stanford University Press
Stanford, California
© 1994 by the Board of Trustees of the
Leland Stanford Junior University

Printed and bound by CPI Group (UK) Ltd,
Croydon, CR0 4YY

CIP data appear at the end of the book

Stanford University Press publications
are distributed exclusively by
Stanford University Press within
the United States, Canada, and Mexico.

FOR MY FATHER

Preface

Work on this book began in 1986, shortly after the EDSA revolution overthrew the dictatorship of Ferdinand Marcos, and concluded as the last American troops left Subic Bay in 1992. The end of the special relationship between the Philippines and the United States offered an occasion and an opportunity to study its inner workings. Newly opened collections of state and diplomatic papers in Manila are unique in Southeast Asia for their scope and accessibility to scholars. I am grateful to Mrs. Fe Angela M. Versoza for introducing me to these collections, and to Alex Calata and the Philippine-American Educational Foundation for funding my research.

My teachers at the University of Virginia and fellow Fulbrighters in Manila listened patiently to my ramblings about what I had found and lent structure to my ideas through their comments and criticisms. I wish to thank Robert McMahon, Jim Rush, William Taylor, Brian Balogh, Paul Hutchcroft, and Jerry Burns for their help. Melvyn Leffler's advice and friendship over the past eight years made this book possible, and I am especially grateful to him. I am also thankful to Lewis Gleeck and Robert Ferrell for reviewing the final manuscript. The remaining errors are my own.

On an orthographic note, I have used diacritical marks in the Philippine manner—avoiding accents on vowels—in spelling names and places. Thus "Jose" and "Garcia" are spelled without accents, but "Osmeña" includes a tilde. The g at the end of "Malacañan," the name of the Philippine presidential palace, was purged amid the nationalist reforms of the mid-1950s. For consistency, the modern spelling is used throughout.

N.C.

Contents

8 pages of photographs follow page 144

Abbreviations

The following abbreviations are used throughout the text and the notes:

CCS	Combined Chiefs of Staff
CED	*Current Economic Developments, 1952–1954: Foreign Relations of the United States Microfiche Publication*
CIA	Central Intelligence Agency
CINCPAC	Commander in Chief, Pacific Forces
CNO	Chief of Naval Operations
DDRS	*Declassified Documents Reference System*
DSDF	Department of State Decimal Files
ECA	Economic Cooperation Administration
ECAFE	United Nations Economic Commission for Asia and the Far East
ECEFP	Executive Committee on Economic Foreign Policy
FBIS	Foreign Broadcast Information Service
FRUS	Department of State, *Foreign Relations of the United States*
HMB	Hukbong Mapagpalaya ng Bayan (or Huks)
HRAF	Human Relations Area Files
JCS	Joint Chiefs of Staff
JPS	Joint Planning Staff
JUSMAG	Joint United States Military Advisory Group
NAC	National Advisory Council on Foreign Economic Policies

NSC	National Security Council
OCB	Operations Coordinating Board
OHC	Office of High Commissioner to the Philippine Islands
OIR	Office of Intelligence and Research, Department of State
OPD	Operations Division, Department of State
PHILCUSA	Philippine Council on United States Aid
RG	record group
UNRRA	United Nations Relief and Rehabilitation Administration
UP	University of the Philippines
USAFFE	United States Army Forces, Far East
USNA	United States National Archives

Illusions of Influence

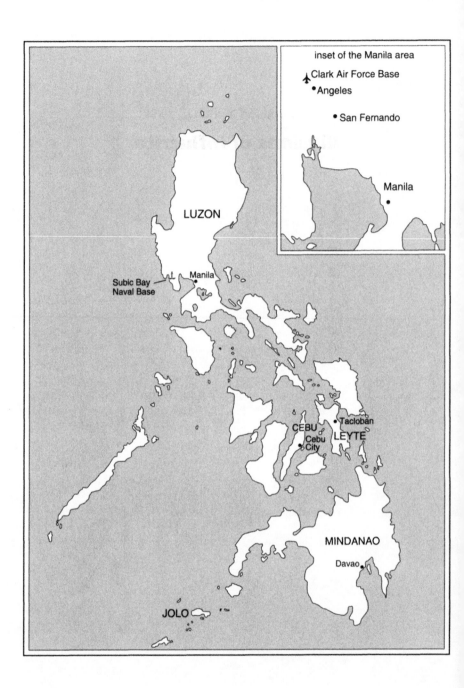

inset of the Manila area

Clark Air Force Base
Angeles

San Fernando

Manila

LUZON

Subic Bay
Naval Base

Manila

CEBU
Cebu
City

Tacloban
LEYTE

MINDANAO

Davao

JOLO

Introduction

As Typhoon Diding ripped across central Luzon on June 25, 1991, a lava dome burst atop Mt. Pinatubo, spewing a column of ash and pyroclastic debris ten kilometers into the air. Residents of Manila, shaken from their homes by earthquakes, emerged under a sky blackened at midday, streaked by lightning, and raining white mud. It looked like the end of the world. That day, Pinatubo and Diding destroyed the two largest U.S. overseas military installations, Clark Air Force Base and Subic Bay Naval Base, smothering them under a snowy blanket of ash and mud. A week earlier, thirty thousand Americans had evacuated the bases. As their final act, guards had detonated ammunition stores, raining rocket fragments on towns ten miles away.[1]

Filipinos recognized that the destruction of the bases meant the end of the special relationship between their country and the United States. For Americans, Philippine House Speaker Ramon Mitra explained, the bases were "the most important thing in the Philippines. We asked them before about their being champions of human rights, their investments here. But these are nothing when compared to their military bases here." Three months after the eruption, the Philippine Senate reluctantly confirmed the demise of the relationship, voting 12 to 11 to reject a new treaty on military bases. Senate President Jovito Salonga declared the vote a "shining chapter in our history." Reviewing his government's dealings with the United States over the previous 45 years, he observed that "the trouble really is that sometimes we wanted freedom and independence without threat and without tears."[2]

Scholars have drawn other conclusions. Few have been willing to concede that the Filipinos exercised much freedom within the relationship. As the title of one study, *In Our Image,* suggests, writers tend to depict the Philippines as a country that surrendered its identity to the cultural, economic, and military domination of the United States. Historians describe U.S. control as "neocolonial," a form of domination that served the needs of American manufacturers and investors. Philippine nationalist scholars contend that the chief function of U.S. military bases was to protect investments. Studies on hegemony and dependency emphasize how the United States used military and economic power to draw postcolonial states into the world capitalist system. These studies raise important questions about how relationships between the United States and its client states function, what their results are, what keeps them going.

The U.S. experience with the Philippines provides a window on collaboration and resistance within a client relationship. The United States deployed its full array of instruments of influence: trade links, investment, military bases, propaganda programs, covert action, lending, and aid programs. "It was in the Philippines," according to Gabriel Kolko, "that U.S. policies in the Third World, with their complex tensions and ambitions, rhetoric and interests, were revealed most clearly both in theory and practice." Despite this concentration of power, U.S. officials found that Filipinos thwarted their development plans, harassed American businesses, diverted aid, restricted trade, and made military bases the target of nationalist attacks. Culture and political economy undermined collaboration. Areas where the two governments could cooperate steadily shrank. Yet, despite frustrations, the relationship continued until a natural disaster and the end of the Cold War finished it, and the two sides parted with reluctance.[3]

The Philippines is commonly cited as an example—often the preeminent example—of the successful application of U.S. pressure on a Third World country. The United States, many observers agree, was able to coax and coerce Philippine regimes to satisfy its military needs, protect its business interests, and go along with its plans for reform. Nationalist historians in the Philippines accept the conventional dependency analysis that the relationship constituted a pact of class domination between elites in both countries bent on exploiting Philippine land and labor. American studies take a variety of approaches, but all uniformly accept U.S. officials' own assessment of their influence on Philippine events. But how well did U.S. officials understand developments in the Philippines? How often did their needs coincide with those of their clients, whose economic interests often yielded to cultural and national imperatives? How can the influence of the United States be measured without taking into account domestic Philippine pressures that might have muffled or amplified its effect on policy?[4]

Special relationships defy reduction to the simplistic assumptions made about them. Postcolonial leaders made choices about how to accommodate their class and national interests within constraints imposed by the world system. Few chose the extreme options, abject collaboration or all-out resistance. Most found ways to work around, subvert, or deflect U.S. power and the power of core economies. Their decisions reflected a mixture of political, economic, and cultural imperatives. An economic interpretation of U.S. motives fails to comprehend the multiplicity of interests at stake in the Philippines and Southeast Asia, a region that absorbed little investment and supplied a negligible portion of the needs of American industry. Hidden within this complexity are clues about the values and interests motivating leaders on both sides.

Alliance with the United States affected all Filipinos, and the present book attempts to discern how U.S. military and aid policies ripple through a society, affecting its leadership, economy, minorities, cities, and countryside. Filipinos constructed a unique economic system, crony capitalism, that depended on privileged access to United States markets, aid, and multilateral lending. The designers of this system used it to preserve the economic and political power of a traditional, landed elite against challenges from ethnic minorities and new classes created by industrialization and urbanization. U.S. policies made crony capi-

talism possible, but could also threaten it. Filipinos learned how
to prevent those policies from interfering with their plans, to use
the strategic value of their country as leverage, to create room for
autonomous action. In trying to steer U.S. policy along lines advantageous to themselves, Filipinos found nonconfrontational resistance—foot-dragging, noncompliance, deception—more effective than outright
defiance. Sociologists describe the use of passive resistance by oppressed individuals and groups, but it is not often recognized as a
feature of international relations. Filipinos gave this method a
central position in their dealings with the Americans, stalling
programs, diverting resources, and widening the gap between
American perceptions and Philippine realities. Political and economic frailty turned into strength at the negotiating table, as
Philippine leaders compelled U.S. officials to compromise to
make up for their own weaknesses.[5]

Philippine leaders did not see themselves as obstructionist or
deceptive, nor did they regard their actions as tactics in an adversarial relationship. They constructed their own interpretations of U.S. goals and policies and fit their aspirations into this
vision. When policies seemed ungenerous or demanding, they
saw them as out-of-character and responded by reinterpreting
them, implementing them in ways that accommodated Philippine interests, or seeking officials who represented the "true"
American position. They expected the United States to live up
to standards of fairness, loyalty, and generosity. In effect, they
imagined an alternate United States and conducted diplomatic
relations with it.[6]

The militarization and compartmentation of postwar foreign
policy made the United States susceptible to Philippine manipulation. In the decentralized executive of the national security
state, Philippine representatives had more room to maneuver,
more forums for appeal. Policies might originate in the State Department, but they could also come from the Defense, Interior,
Commerce, or Treasury department, from the National Security
Council, from special missions, or from multilateral agencies
like the World Bank. They seldom came from Congress. The lack
of congressional scrutiny after 1947 insulated policy from Amer-

ican business and agricultural interests that might have objected to crony capitalism, and pushed strategic and geopolitical considerations to the fore.

The preeminent importance of U.S. strategic interests allowed Philippine leaders to turn the relationship to their advantage and expand their autonomy, as Salonga put it, "without threat and without tears." The United States compromised its commitment to a global economic policy based on liberal nonpreferential trade and betrayed American business interests in order to protect its strategic stake. Keeping the bases as bargaining chips entailed sacrifices for Filipinos, but they placed a higher priority on the economic advantages of the alliance. The two sides struck a bargain that allowed Filipinos to preserve and modernize their patrimonial political system, protect developing industries from foreign competition, and remove key sectors of the economy from the control of aliens and ethnic minorities. In return, the United States kept its military bases.

These were the terms of the bargain, but both countries reached for more. United States officials never surrendered hope that they could make the Philippines a model of democratic development, a showcase of the advantages of cooperation with the West. Filipinos continued to try to coax from the United States the generosity they believed their sacrifices deserved. Amid disappointments, each side clung to its illusions.

ONE

From Colony to Client State

In the early morning darkness of December 8, 1941, an aide awoke the U.S. high commissioner to the Philippines, Francis B. Sayre, with news that Japanese planes had attacked the Hawaiian Islands. Hours later, bombs fell on airfields north of Manila. In the following days, Sayre's aides burned documents as Philippine and American forces under General Douglas MacArthur retreated to prepared defenses on the Bataan Peninsula and the fortress island of Corregidor. On December 24, MacArthur ordered Sayre and other officials to evacuate Manila, and early in the afternoon a limousine bearing Commonwealth President Manuel Quezon pulled up in front of the high commissioner's residence, grandly situated between Manila Bay and the city's central park. Offshore, Quezon's steam yacht, the *Mayon*, rode at anchor, awaiting the Philippines' most prestigious refugees. As the officials and their families hurried to board, they left behind a city that would never again be called without irony "the pearl of the Orient."[1]

When Corregidor fell five months later, Philippine and American leaders had already begun to think about the design of postwar relations between the two countries. Ironically, the Japanese attack committed the United States to return to the islands, reversing a process of withdrawal that had been under way for seven years. The war gave U.S. officials and Quezon's government time to devise a new relationship under which the Philippines would enjoy political independence but the United States would retain a substantial military and economic stake in the islands. Reinventing the Philippines as a client state required U.S. and

Philippine leaders to order their priorities through a bureaucratic contest waged in three arenas: the U.S. Congress, the executive branch, and the Philippine government-in-exile. Debates in Washington settled the competing claims of security and economic policies, budgets, and social reform. They decided the shape of the future Philippines, the limits of sovereignty, the diversity of its economy, the nature of its leadership.

The United States had come to the islands in 1898, when Commodore George Dewey's Pacific Fleet sank a Spanish flotilla in the opening battle of the Spanish American War. Filipino revolutionaries, seizing a chance to rekindle their smoldering rebellion, overran garrisons throughout the islands and established a republic led by General Emilio Aguinaldo. The Philippine Republic controlled nearly all of the archipelago outside of Manila, but President William McKinley and the U.S. Senate ignored Aguinaldo's government when they chose to purchase the islands as part of a settlement with Spain the following year.[2]

The United States annexed the Philippines to gain a haven for naval forces patrolling the China coast, to assure access to the lucrative China trade, and to fulfill an imagined obligation to "uplift and civilize" Filipinos. Democratic congressmen warned that American labor and agriculture would suffer from Filipino competition. They argued that the islands could not be defended, and that the imperial enterprise would drain the treasury. The administration felt strongly enough about its Philippine mission to silence the opposition with offers of patronage, but America's venture in colonialism rested on an unstable consensus that could be overturned when the Republicans lost control of Congress.[3]

Before Filipinos could be civilized, they had to be subdued. Aguinaldo's forces held out for three years at a cost of 20,000 lives, and resistance continued sporadically for a year after his capture. The indifference of the peasantry and the defection of a substantial portion of the educated urban elite hastened American victory. Aguinaldo failed to articulate nationalist aspirations in a way that would mobilize the support of tenants and farm workers. Peasants wanted freedom from both alien and upper-class oppression, but Aguinaldo's pronouncements aimed at an elite audience. His officers had to coerce assistance from peasants, and the rebellion never enjoyed mass support. The American military government exploited this weakness, encouraging collaboration with promises of education, autonomy, and commercial opportunity. On July 4, 1902, Theodore Roosevelt declared the end of the war.[4]

The American colonial government concentrated on fiscal stability, democratization, and conservative social engineering. The post of governor-general was a stepping-stone to high office for Republicans, and a political banishment for Democrats. Appointees of both parties sought to reduce the costs of colonial rule while expanding American influence through investment, schools, and the creation of institutions after the American pattern. A colony-wide school system taught Filipinos English and gave them a common tongue for the first time. In 1907, the elected Philippine Assembly gathered a new generation of leaders to Manila. Two years later, the Payne-Aldrich Tariff opened American markets to Philippine products, chiefly sugar, and attracted investment to the islands. The growing community of American traders organized a chamber of commerce, laid a railroad across central Luzon, and built a summer resort in the mountain town of Baguio.[5]

Unwilling to accept the islands as a permanent possession, Congress restricted American ownership of Philippine land, and the islands attracted few settlers. The American colony consisted of schoolteachers, administrators, missionaries, soldiers, and traders. These Manila Americans hoped to join the islands to the United States permanently, but fears of racial impurity and foreign entanglements diluted Congress' imperial enthusiasm. Pledging eventual independence for the islands, colonial officials undertook to instruct Filipinos in the habits of self-government.[6]

The colonial government fostered Filipino leadership and gave it substantial autonomy. U.S. officials stressed the development of electoral politics as the core ingredient of democratic government, overlooking the benefits of a strong, professionalized civil service. Elections strengthened the power of the feudal elite and solidified patron-client ties. Political parties became patronage machines at the service of wealthy families. Divided into electoral districts contested by rival clans, the peasantry had little voice, and national politics came under the sway of flamboyant operators who appealed to elite constituencies.[7]

By the early 1930s, Quezon had emerged as the islands' preeminent political operator. An officer in Aguinaldo's army, he had surrendered to American forces in 1901 and had gone to prison, then to law school. He had befriended American officials, who helped him get into politics as a provincial governor in 1906. Elected to the National Assembly the following year, he eventually became majority leader. He duelled for supremacy with Sergio Osmeña, political chieftain of Cebu, emerged victorious, and thereafter embraced Osmeña as an ally. In 1916, Quezon engineered the passage of the Jones Act, guaranteeing eventual independence for the islands, and established himself as a champion of Philippine nationhood. He thereafter used nationalism to advance his political fortunes while remaining fearful of the strains that would be placed on his leadership if the Americans did depart.[8]

Quezon established his political dominance as the United States reduced its political and economic stake in the islands. The Philippines had severe problems, but the American administration and Congress took an increasingly detached view of the commonwealth's slow economic growth, its military insecurity, and its feudal power structure. By the early 1930s, Congress had decided the islands were a strategic and economic liability, and the United States should get out.

Congress was right. Militarily and financially, the colony was a losing proposition. During the 40-year occupation, in which the United States spent over a billion dollars to govern and defend the islands, the rich trade promised by turn-of-the-century imperialists failed to materialize. U.S. private investment in the 1930s amounted to some $200 million, or only about 1 percent of total overseas investment. The portion of national income derived from the Philippines, according to one estimate, totaled "at most a very small fraction of one percent." Strategically, the islands were indefensible. U.S. military plans called for the Army and Navy to flee in the event of attack. By the beginning of the administration of President Franklin D. Roosevelt, U.S. officials wanted to free themselves of these burdens, and began seriously to consider Quezon's demands for independence.[9] U.S. farm and labor interests led the drive for independence legislation. Sugar and dairy lobbies and the American Federation of Labor argued that Americans lost jobs and income to Philippine competition. The military, anxious to withdraw from the unstable Orient, raised no objection. The onset of the Depression lowered farm prices and spurred Congress to act in 1933, when it passed the Hare-Hawes-Cutting Independence Act, but Quezon thwarted its enactment in hopes that a new U.S. administration would grant more generous trade concessions. At a time when India's nationalists languished in jail, the Filipinos were holding out for better terms.[10]

The following year, Quezon accepted the modest improvements of the Tydings-McDuffie Act, which gradually cut trade links over a decade in which the Philippines would be a self-governing commonwealth. Philippine legislators drafted a constitution, and the electorate chose Quezon to be the first president. In the United States, the act appeased both imperialists and their opponents in Congress with an equivocal clause permitting the United States to retain naval bases while working for the "perpetual neutralization" of the islands. The Navy, however, had no plans to stay. In theory, the act should have diversified the Philippine economy by phasing out the sugar quota, but after the first quota reductions and tariff increases became effective in 1941, nothing changed. Landowners considered industry too risky, and kept their money in real estate. Quezon's government had no plans for diversification, and no idea where its revenue would come from after 1946. Philippine legislators petitioned the United States in May 1941 to suspend further quota reductions, a move that might have been a prelude to a general reconsideration of the independence issue. As Japanese armies massed on Formosa, 50 miles to the north, members of the Philippine elite looked to independence with dread, knowing they would lose both their livelihoods and their protector.[11]

Quezon had reason to fear the withdrawal of American power. He sat at the pinnacle of an old and traditional social structure sorely tried by its encounter with twentieth-century capitalism. As the colonial regime came to an end, each of the three Philippine social groups—the landowning elite, the large peasantry, and the small Chinese middle class—witnessed the erosion of traditional privileges and anticipated a future of economic decline and social conflict.

Quezon presided over a government of landed lawyer-politicians, the scions of wealthy *mestizo* (racially mixed) families who had dominated their respective provinces since Spanish times. In the early twentieth century, the colonial administration had reconciled itself to this elite's powerful influence over the mass of Filipinos. Governor-General William H. Taft had discovered that the elite had placed the peasantry into "a kind of quasi slavery called *caciquism.*" He found the paternalistic landowners, or *caciques*, morally lacking, "prone to yield to any pecuniary consideration, and difficult persons out of whom to make an honest government." Nonetheless, he admitted, "we shall have to do the best we can with them." Before Taft convened the Philippine Assembly, geographic and linguistic separation had prevented dominant families from acting collectively. A Filipinized government, with a budget for public works, a national lending bank, and authority to appoint mayors and local officials, drew the caciques to Manila and made them a national oligarchy. The small American administration could do nothing without the elite's help. But as one Filipino historian has observed, the oligarchy resisted selectively, giving the Americans a free hand in military and educational affairs but little influence in the economic and social fields.[12]

The oligarchy prospered under the American regime. The United States provided a lucrative market for the products of Philippine haciendas: coconut, abaca (Manila hemp), and, above all, sugar. By 1933, two-thirds of the export income for the Philippines came from the sale of sugar in the United States, a trade that directly or indirectly supported six million of the country's 14 million people. In the 1920s and 1930s, sugar made the oligarchy rich, and it provided the bulk of the colonial government's revenue. Output grew, not because productivity improved, but because more land was brought under cultivation and hence under the control of caciques. Share tenants cleared and planted land in return for loans of seed and tools, a relationship strengthened by Filipino traditions of ritual kinship and mutual obligations, known as *utang na loob*. In the Philippines, a country balkanized by geography and language, such ties were important, and naturally carried over into politics. American schoolteachers observed that even the youngest children, choosing sides for games, knew their social ranks and deferred to their superiors.[13]

The oligarchy had internal divisions, but these were softened by rules of deference and, after 1934, by the mediation of Quezon. Members of the elite tied to the sugar industry, the "sugar bloc," had interests that differed from those involved in other types of planting or in manufacturing. The sugar bloc was divided between millers and planters, each group with different preferences in legislation. In the rush to enlarge their land holdings, planters ran up heavy debts to millers and government banks. They favored measures to expand credit and increase their share of the sugar earnings. Millers opposed credit expansion and leaned toward protectionism.[14]

Racial distinctions accentuated political and economic differences between caciques. Mestizos came in two kinds, white (usually Spanish) and Chinese (often distinguished by the suffix *co*, as in "Cojuanco"). The "white" Soriano and Elizalde families, heavily invested in manufacturing, were more protectionist than the sugar bloc and disagreed over trade legislation with advocates of planter interests like Osmeña and Benigno Aquino, both of whom had Chinese blood. Andres Soriano and his partner, Manuel Roxas, owned an investment, trading, and manufacturing conglomerate that included the San Miguel brewery and Philippine Air Lines. They joined ranks politically with Joaquin Elizalde, owner of the largest sugar *central*, La Carlota, and of investments in rum distilleries, ropemaking spindles, and an assortment of light manufacturing and trading ventures. Elizalde identified Osmeña as his political adversary, calling him "el Chino," and deprecating him as "a conservative Chinese burgher." All members of the mestizo elite, white or Chinese, united behind Quezon, the only leader who seemed capable of continually enlarging the fund of spoils and of distributing it equitably.[15] Quezon knew the rules of *utang na loob*. He practiced politics patrimonially, exercising power by personal mediation and dispensation, and acting to enlarge his personal power and to frustrate potential rivals. The oligarchs trusted him to settle their disputes, to protect the sugar earnings, and to deal with the United States. In return, they granted him enormous discretionary powers over political, economic, and military affairs. American officials worried about Quezon's tendency toward dictatorship, but the oligarchs knew such a tendency would always be restrained by culture, by what one scholar has described as "the complex structure of alliance and affinity, of rite and blood relationships." Nonetheless, the Philippines in the 1930s was a one-party state. Quezon's "unipersonal" government gave itself broad executive powers in the constitution of 1935. In 1941, in the face of external threats from the Japanese and internal threats from peasant insurrection, Philippine legislators granted the president nearly absolute power.[16]

Cacique power rested unsteadily on the labor and electoral support of the largest class, the peasantry. In the 1930s, the patrimonial system that thrived among the rulers in Manila disintegrated in the countryside. As the quantity of new land available for cultivation dwindled, landlords had less use for the growing tenant populations on their estates. Many of the younger caciques, educated at Iowa State College or the University of Illinois, hired overseers and attempted to replace their traditional obligations to their tenants with a rationalized, contractual relationship. The peasants, or *taos*, had not shared in the prosperity of the 1920s. As one official observed, the tao "benefitted the least from the economic advantages of the American connection." While the urban Filipino enjoyed Asia's highest standard of living, the tao lived at subsistence level. He regarded his landlord's favors— loans of rice and tools, the privilege of gleaning harvested fields— as essential to survival, hence as a right. But landlords had less respect for the peasants' traditional rights, granted fewer favors, and, increasingly, evicted tenant families. Disputes between peasants and landlords became more frequent, particularly in the part of central Luzon just north of Manila, where roads, infrastructure, and commercial agriculture were more developed.[17] Overseers attempting to enforce contracts with tenants often encountered resistance, occasionally even mob violence. In 1931, several hundred tenants captured and looted a provincial capital. The American vice-governor noted that the peasants rebelled "chiefly against 'caciquism,' agrarian oppression, and Constabulary abuses." Outbreaks became larger and better organized. In 1933 and 1934, the publisher of an oppositionist newspaper, the *Sakdal*, organized a peasant movement that supported land redistribution, tax abolition, and immediate independence. On the night of May 2, 1935, seven thousand Sakdalistas attacked 14 towns surrounding Manila. The Constabulary quickly suppressed the rebellion, but the scale of the uprising and rumors of Japanese support panicked Quezon's government.[18]

Quezon initiated a "social justice" program of cosmetic reforms and appealed to landlords to deal mercifully with tenants, but taos continued to organize to protect their rights. Tenants in central Luzon joined peasant unions and voted for socialist and communist candidates. They also continued to fight. "By the latter half of the 1930s," according to one account, "scarcely a week would pass without a major incident of agrarian discontent." In 1939, Quezon responded with a "mailed fist" policy that militarized central Luzon and put hundreds of peasant activists in jail. By 1941, seven provinces in central Luzon were under virtual military occupation. Colonial officials believed that only the lack of arms prevented the taos from overthrowing cacique rule. In 1941, the Philippines teetered on the brink of class warfare.[19]

Between, yet apart from, the two classes of Filipinos, the ethnically Chinese middle class occupied a social and legal limbo. The Chinese population, always substantial, increased dramatically under colonial policies designed to trap refugees migrating to California. Within days of Manila's capture by American forces in 1898, military authorities had extended exclusion laws to the Philippines. Thereafter, the Philippines became part of an American defense-in-depth against Chinese immigration. Colonial administrators had encouraged the illegal entry of thousands of Cantonese and Fukienese migrants. Without documents, the immigrants could journey no further, much to the satisfaction of American traders. Businessmen considered Chinese laborers efficient and tractable, and admired the willingness of Chinese merchants to carry wares up malarial rivers and into mountain fastnesses. By official accounts, the Chinese population increased from 40,000 in 1898 to 117,000 in 1939, when it accounted for over 70 percent of foreigners in the islands. The illegal status of the Chinese frustrated attempts at an accurate count, however, and the actual community may have been triple that number.[20]

More impressive than its size was the growth of the Chinese community's economic power and its simultaneous separation from Filipino culture. Forced by law and status into an entrepreneurial role, Chinese merchants by the 1930s dominated internal commerce and retail trading, from rural shop stalls to city department stores. They owned three-quarters of the rice mills in the Philippines, conducted 70 to 80 percent of the retail trade, controlled the lumber industry and private lending institutions, and in most rural areas offered the sole source of credit. To keep this powerful minority compliant and happy, the colonial government sponsored separate civic and social institutions—Chinese chambers of commerce, hospitals, schools, and clubs—encouraging a process one historian calls "retro-assimilation." By the 1930s, a son born to a Filipino-speaking Chinese family would likely learn Chinese in a Chinese school, go to work for a Chinese firm, marry a woman from the mainland, and in a single generation separate himself and his family from Filipino culture.[21]

Filipinos, whose every transaction passed through Chinese hands, grew to resent the symbiotic relationship between their colonial rulers and this alien class, which grew more populous, more wealthy, and more foreign with each year. The National Assembly tried to restrict Chinese economic activity by law, but the U.S. Supreme Court banned legal discrimination in 1924. In 1931, anti-Chinese rioting broke out in San Pablo, 50 miles southeast of Manila, and quickly spread to the capital. Filipinos

looted and burned stores and killed several shopkeepers before
the Constabulary restored order. Anti-Chinese sentiment united
caciques and peasants. Legislators accused the Chinese of usury,
of tax evasion, and of conspiring to paralyze the country with a
rice embargo.[22]

In the 1930s, a growing nationalist movement argued that unless the Philippines obtained independence, the Americans
would allow the Chinese to take over. Young leaders like
Elizalde and Manuel Roxas organized anti-Chinese leagues and
gained a political victory in Article XII of the Philippine Constitution of 1934, which prohibited the "disposition, exploitation,
development, or utilization" of Philippine land or resources by
foreigners. To prevent new industries from falling into Chinese
hands, Quezon's government chartered state corporations, which
soon included banks, textile and flour mills, utilities, railroads,
and factories making shoes, iron, and cement. Although they
could count on the modest support of Vice President Osmeña,
the Chinese enjoyed little sympathy among Philippine leaders,
and they feared that independence for the Philippines would
bring confiscations and harassment.[23]

Of the three Philippine social classes, only the peasants readily
welcomed independence. Among the elite, nationalist and anti-
Chinese arguments competed with the obvious advantages of
keeping trade and defensive links. An ambivalent leadership
slowly reconciled itself to an independence forced on it by the
United States. "Filipino sugar fears full independence," an American journalist observed. The loss of the U.S. market would have
"severe and possibly fatal" consequences. Filipinos also feared
Japanese expansionism and the "threat of racial extinction" from
an influx of Chinese refugees. Quezon wanted a perpetual do-
minion status for the Philippines, "a partnership in commerce
and defense." "It is our fate," he told his friend Roy Howard, "to
have to depend on some big nation." But Quezon could not back
away from an entire career of nationalist agitation, at least not
in public.[24]

The Japanese attack on December 8 reversed the process of
American withdrawal from the Philippines. Once the United

States committed itself to defeating Japan and occupying the whole of the Pacific, the Philippines changed from a strategic liability to a vitally important asset. The reversal of the strategic equation reopened the trade issue, and required the Roosevelt administration to take more than an abstracted interest in the Philippines' thorny domestic problems.

The war ended talk of a neutral Philippines. When Congress had first considered legislation setting in motion a timetable for Philippine independence, the question of military bases divided both American and Philippine officials. The legislation's sponsor, Senator Harry Hawes, along with Osmeña, the Philippine negotiator, proposed to retain American installations in the islands. The State, War, and Navy departments decided to oppose bases as expensive, unnecessary, and probably provocative. Concern that Japan might regard the U.S. presence as a preparation for war caused military planners to recommend a complete withdrawal to Hawaii. Quezon, seizing a chance to embarrass Osmeña, also opposed retention, arguing that foreign army bases insulted Philippine nationhood. The president objected less to naval bases, since the Navy had seldom interfered in Philippine domestic affairs during the 1920s, at a time when the Army commonly did.[25]

The final 1934 legislation ceded Army property to the Philippines following independence, left the question of naval bases open to later settlement, and enjoined the United States to work toward the "perpetual neutralization" of the new republic. The Navy set up a board to decide if it should have a Philippine base and where it should be. Six years later, the panel produced a plan for a single base on the tiny, remote island of Jolo, far enough from Japanese bases on Hainan and Taiwan to avoid the appearance of a threat. It was never built.[26]

Quezon rested his hopes on the plans prepared by his military adviser, Douglas MacArthur. MacArthur had come to the Philippines shortly after he graduated from West Point in 1903. His father, General Arthur MacArthur, had served as military governor of the islands in the years 1900–1901, sharing power uneasily with Governor-General Taft. Owing partly to his father's experience, the younger MacArthur resented the colony's civilian officialdom and consorted instead with the Philippine elite, particularly Soriano, Elizalde, Roxas, and Quezon. After distinguishing himself in World War I, MacArthur became one of the Army's rising stars, but he was never far from controversy. Whenever prudence required his absence from Washington—as it did twice in the 1920s—Quezon furnished a suitable assignment. After leading federal troops against bonus marchers encamped in Washington in 1932, the general accepted Quezon's offer to return to the Philippines and organize an army.[27]

MacArthur drafted an ambitious plan that called for a citizen army of 10,000 men capable of meeting an invasion at the beaches. It contradicted the U.S. Army's War Plan Orange, which was based on a more realistic appreciation of American weakness in the western Pacific. Orange called for American and Philippine troops to retreat to Bataan, a narrow peninsula across the mouth of Manila Bay, where they would resist to the "last extremity."[28]

The southward advance of Japanese forces caused U.S. military authorities to modify their plans in an attempt to deter an attack on the Philippines. In late 1941, as Japan amassed forces in Taiwan for a push into Southeast Asia, General George C. Marshall, the Army chief of staff, reinforced United States forces in the Philippines and ordered a buildup of long-range bombers in the Philippines to threaten Tokyo with direct retaliation. The 340 B-17s never arrived, but Marshall's untested assumption that Philippine-based air forces could deter aggression in Asia survived to inspire the planners of America's postwar defense.[29]

The battles of Bataan and Corregidor played out as planned. After an abortive attempt to stop the Japanese from landing troops, MacArthur ordered a retreat to Bataan. Eighty thousand American and Philippine troops held the peninsula's craggy terrain through the spring of 1942. On March 11, MacArthur left for Australia, and on April 9, Bataan fell. Corregidor lasted until May.[30]

The Philippines figured into the earliest U.S. postwar base plans. In December 1942, Roosevelt asked the Joint Chiefs of Staff to select sites for air bases to be used by an "international police force" that would preserve peace after the defeat of the Axis. Frank Knox, the secretary of the navy, instructed the Joint Chiefs' strategic survey committee to study as well the related subject of postwar air bases for United States use. After weeks of grappling with its vague instructions, the committee ventured a document predicting the shape of the postwar world. After the Japanese surrendered, the planners predicted, the allied nations would enforce peace, singly or jointly, in three zones of responsibility: Britain and the Soviet Union would police Europe, Africa, and the Middle East; the United States would have sole responsibility for the Western Hemisphere; and the Big Three, assisted by China, would keep peace in the Far East. The planners recognized a potential for friction among the policing powers, especially in zones of divided responsibility, like Asia. To meet its obligations in the Far East, and for its own defense, the United States would require "a line of naval and air bases west from Hawaii to and including bases in the Philippines and Bonins."[31]

Although the strategic survey committee paid lip service to collective security, the derision that crept into the planners' descriptions of the international police force revealed how little faith they placed in it. Skeptical about the utility of international organizations, the army and navy officers who led the committee urged the United States to look first to its own defense and that of the Western Hemisphere and "our position in the Far East." Establishing sovereignty or long-term rights over bases of "obvious importance" to national defense, they concluded, should be a primary war aim.[32]

Bases on the far shores of the Pacific would be obviously important to the survey committee because of the planners' belief that leaps in war-making technology would soon leave the United States exposed and vulnerable. H. H. Arnold, the commanding general of the Army Air Forces, pointed out that super-heavy bombers and rocket bombs could strike with "a sudden devastation beyond any 'Pearl Harbor' experience or our present power of imagination to conceive." The United States must meet an attack with equally revolutionary methods of defense, he warned, and it must meet it as far as possible from United States territory. In future wars, the adversary who acted first would strike with such force that his opponent would be unable to recover. Distant bases would not be points at which to receive attack, but staging grounds for preemptive assaults against the enemies of the United States. "Our territorial security cannot be defended," Arnold admonished, "without denying or threatening the air base areas from which hostile air attack might be launched." The Navy, too, foresaw a preemptive role. If the world knew the United States would use its fleet "*before and not after* a series of Munich conferences," one admiral explained, "the personal following of any future Hitler would be limited to a few would-be suicides."[33]

The planners gave little thought to who the future adversary might be. Indeed, it seemed beside the point, for the danger arose not from any particular nation, but from changes in the technology of war. On the few occasions when planners mentioned a likely enemy, they named Japan, and occasionally the Soviet Union.[34]

Military planners devised a scheme for a chain of distant bases to deter attack and to serve as jumping-off places for preemptive strikes. At the center of the chain, barring the western approaches to the United States, stood the Philippines, its northern flank protected by a base in the Bonin group and its rear by bases in the Marianas, Caroline, and Marcus groups and the island of Palau. These subsidiary bases and trusteeships would protect America's principal Pacific outpost. By November 1943, the Philippines had become a central feature of America's postwar defense.[35]

Philippine leaders had also reconsidered their future security. Four days after fleeing Manila, Quezon decided that the Philippines needed American bases. In a bunker on Corregidor, he told Osmeña that a "lesson of this war" was that the Philippines "cannot escape the necessity of accepting" American protection. After arriving in Washington, commonwealth officials pestered the administration for postwar security guarantees in return for "a generous lease of strategic air and naval bases." On April 27, 1943, when a bedridden Quezon again urged Undersecretary of State Sumner Welles to accept airfields and naval bases in his country, Welles replied that the Army and Navy favored the idea, but made no move to close the deal. U.S. officials were in no hurry to negotiate before they had finished their plans.[36]

That changed in July 1943, when the Japanese premier, Tōjō Hideki, announced his country's intention to declare the islands independent. Jose P. Laurel, Quezon's former minister of justice, began to organize a Philippine government under a new constitution. To deprive the enemy of a propaganda coup, Philippine and United States officials now urged Roosevelt to issue a similar declaration. Secretary of War Henry Stimson, fearing Filipinos might join the Japanese in the defense of the islands, called on Quezon in early September and urged him to support legislation to accelerate independence. Stimson, a former governor-general of the Philippines, wanted the United States to promise independence upon the expulsion of the Japanese, but another former governor-general, Supreme Court Justice Frank Murphy, wanted independence granted immediately to prevent the Japanese from exploiting Philippine nationalism. With Quezon's support, Senator Millard Tydings introduced an independence resolution, touching off a fusillade of criticism from Stimson, Secretary of the Interior Harold Ickes, and newspaper columnists. All agreed that the Philippines could not have independence without first granting military-base rights to the United States. "What will we do," asked Walter Lippmann, "if this 'independent' government exercises its sovereign right to oust us entirely from the Pacific?" Lippmann called the Philippines the "strategic center" of U.S. defense, a truth so clear that "a Filipino who does not see that is not fit to govern an independent state." The Tydings resolution forced Pentagon officials to defend their still-incomplete postwar plans.[37]

Quezon initially refused to back away from the Tydings resolution, threatening to "go Jap" rather than accept less than immediate independence. But before long he relented and took a leading role in drafting a substitute bill. On October 10, Stimson, Tydings, Ickes, Undersecretary of the Interior Abe Fortas, and Samuel Rosenman, counselor to the president, gathered around Quezon's bedside at the Shoreham Hotel to discuss a new joint resolution. Rosenman recalled the conference as "among the most dramatic episodes of my years in Washington." Quezon was "tensely holding on to life, determined to carry on in the cause to which he had dedicated his whole career." Replying to Rosenman's question about military reservations, the Philippine president acknowledged that his country's security still needed to be balanced against the demands of national pride. "If you yourselves include that provision," he warned, "the independence of the Philippines will be like that of Manchukuo. Let me ask you to put it there. I shall assume responsibility." Desiring American military protection for the Philippines, Quezon had every reason to be happy with the new bill allowing independence to be granted after the two governments had agreed on a list of bases to be leased to the United States. Accompanying legislation established an interdepartmental panel, the Filipino Rehabilitation Commission, to settle postwar trade and reconstruction issues. In a public statement on August 14, a month before the Japanese officially granted independence to Jose P. Laurel's government in Manila, Roosevelt declared that in the view of the United States, Quezon's administration held "the same status as the governments of other independent nations."[38]

The independence scare moved the Philippines to the top of the military planning agenda. As independence legislation awaited congressional action, Pentagon officials hastily drafted lists of prospective base sites. The Navy dusted off its 1940 plan for a base at Tutu Bay on the island of Jolo and added to it a list of seven subsidiary bases forming a ring around the archipelago. Army Air Force planners devised a scheme for two clusters of heavy bomber bases, one in the south, near Cagayan on the island of Mindanao, and the other to the north, on the central Luzon plain. A ring of fighter bases would guard the approaches to the main base areas. The Joint Chiefs of Staff received and immediately rejected this slapdash proposal shortly after Tydings withdrew his motion for immediate independence. The Joint Chiefs recognized the plan as an antique, dating from the days when the United States kept Philippine bases to defend the Philippines rather than to project power against a potential attacker. Forces were to be positioned not in the south, to shorten lines of supply and retreat, but in the north, to strike suddenly and without warning against adversaries in Eurasia and Japan. The United States, Admiral William D. Leahy observed, would "not again be placed in the position of having to defend the Philippines." Rather, the bases would be "essential to any action that we might have to take against Japan before the defense of the Islands would again become necessary." In January 1944, Leahy asked Roosevelt to defer choosing sites until the military drafted new plans.[39] Although the flurry of activity over the independence issue accomplished nothing of propaganda value, it set the ground rules for the postwar relationship. When the Office of War Information proposed to have bombers drop copies of Roosevelt's August 15, 1943, speech announcing the American position on Philippine independence, MacArthur declined, suggesting that matchbooks bearing his own picture be dropped instead.[40] Nonetheless, the Tydings legislation had several important effects. The United States now clearly would retain military bases after the war. Roosevelt's statement granted "practical independence" to the Philippine government-in-exile, a status the Quezon administration would test during the approaching debate on trade policy. The Filipino Rehabilitation Commission opened discussion within and between the two governments on the question of postindependence economic relations. Finally, the bill permanently joined the three issues—security, independence, and trade—at the heart of the postwar relationship.

Although the State and Treasury departments crafted most of America's postwar foreign economic policies and built the formidable Bretton Woods institutions to carry them out, the Interior Department developed postwar economic plans for the Philippines. The Philippine policy contradicted the guiding principles of what the State Department called "the United States' global policy for the expansion and liberalization of world trade." The United States found this contradiction embarrassing as it negotiated with Great Britain and other powers for a new world trade order based on multilateralism, reduced tariffs, and the elimination of discriminatory trade barriers. The Department of the Interior prevailed over the multilateralists, thanks to the emphasis it placed on the importance of the strategic relationship, its influence in Congress, and the support of the War Department. Its proposals occupied a middle ground between the liberal internationalist stance of large manufacturers and the State Department, and the protectionism of powerful agricultural interests.

Interior Department officials spent the war years preparing to bring Philippine trade legislation before Congress. From 1939 until the Japanese invasion, the department administered the commonwealth's economic and foreign affairs through the Office of the High Commissioner in Manila. High Commissioner Francis Sayre was evacuated from Corregidor in February 1942 and returned in April to Washington, where he resigned, leaving it to his advisers, Richard R. Ely and Evett D. Hester, to establish a wartime office. In August, Roosevelt placed the office under the Interior Department and charged it to undertake "an immediate inquiry" into postliberation economic problems. The acting interior secretary, Fortas, asked Hester and his staff of five to draft trade and rehabilitation legislation to be introduced in Congress as early as 1943. For the next three years, the Office of the High Commissioner considered itself an economic arm of the Philippine government, representing the commonwealth at the Bretton Woods conference and at the United Nations Relief and Rehabilitation Administration conference in Atlantic City, developing plans for a new currency, supervising the finances of the government-in-exile, and planning for postwar rehabilitation.[41]

Before the Second World War, the Philippines depended on the United States as a market for its agricultural products and as a source of manufactured goods and investment capital. Already the largest foreign buyer of Philippine goods when the islands were annexed in 1898, the United States increased its share of trade until, by 1938, it consumed four-fifths of the goods leaving Philippine ports. The colony exported tropical commodities: sugar, abaca, coconut oil, copra, tobacco, lumber, and pineapple. The largest export, sugar, went entirely to the United States, as did almost all of the coconut products and pineapple. A few goods—tobacco, copra, lumber, and abaca, a rope fiber prized for its toughness—sold in Europe and Japan, as well as the United States. Filipinos owned the land that produced these goods, but foreigners, Chinese and Americans, owned the canneries, sawmills and centrals that processed them for export. Americans owned a third of the sugar centrals, half the coconut refineries, over half of the sawmills and rope-making spindles, and the only pineapple cannery. American investment was concentrated in processing, mining, and public utilities.[42]

Hester considered the sugar industry the most "troublesome" sector in the Philippine economy. It provided the bulk of the national income while subjecting labor to intolerable conditions. Tenants on sugar haciendas, according to the Agriculture Department, lived "in debt continually, often with little knowledge of their indebtedness," a condition that allowed landowners to work them "to extremes." The average Filipino drew his income from a parcel of land one-quarter of the size required to feed a single American. "The future prevention of unrest," an official commission warned in 1938, would hinge on the government's ability to eradicate the "traditional and deep rooted abuses" of the land tenure system. Conflicts between landlords and tenants could only be aggravated by the war, which would return the Philippines, according to Hester, "to a barehanded stage of subsistence farming and primitive craftsmanship."[43]

Hester and his staff expected no reforms from the Philippine government. They feared that relinquishing sovereignty "prematurely" would surrender power to an autocratic elite dedicated to preserving the hacienda and its abuses. One staffer in the Office of the High Commissioner called Philippine politics "jefe democracy," a system in which a powerful clique "could give the word and overnight change entire national attitudes." The Philippine constitution gave the elite latitude to shape the government to suit its interests, and Hester warned that the independent Philippines could be "a representative republic, a socialistic state, a corporate state, or a temporary but renewable dictatorship." Quezon's government already showed a propensity toward the latter two. The Interior Department knew through the FBI that important commonwealth officials belonged to the pro-Franco *falange*. "There can be no doubt that Andres Soriano, Finance Minister in Quezon's Cabinet is a falangist," Ickes wrote in his diary. "I believe that the Resident Commissioner, Elizalde is also. There is more than a little doubt about Quezon himself." Hester told Ickes of falangist plans to "take over" after the war and how admirers of fascist corporate states had already managed to place a large portion of the Philippine economy under the control of state enterprises.[44]

The huge state sector, which before the fall of Manila comprised 41 major government enterprises involved in banking, sugar, cement, warehousing, shoes, textiles, and railroads (to name only a few), served the Philippine elite in several ways. It kept new concentrations of economic power subordinate to the political power of the caciques, and checked the growing financial clout of the Chinese minority. But restrictions aimed at the Chinese also affected American investors. The Philippine constitution prohibited foreign ownership of land and exploitation of natural resources. American businessmen believed this and other provisions for expropriation of industries would be used to evict companies from the islands. In 1939, the largest corporation in the islands, the Pacific Commercial Company, sold out, and other firms prepared to follow suit. Hester believed that after the war the Philippine government would be receptive to investment, but only temporarily. The present government, he felt, would willingly exempt Americans from the constitution in exchange for favorable trade terms.[45]

Interior Department officials rested their hopes for reforms on restoring the influence of American firms, which might act as a liberalizing and incorruptible counterweight to the native elite, and on retaining key economic levers (currency and tariffs) for the United States. They aimed to use capital to democratize as well as to rehabilitate the Philippines. New industries and diversified agriculture would, they hoped, give Filipinos markets other than the hacienda in which to sell their labor, and create sources of wealth and political muscle other than land. Hester's solution involved diverting sugar land into the production of rice, corn, and other crops for domestic consumption, and fostering light industry, such as the manufacture of soap and cement, two industries with substantial U.S. investment. American capital, he believed, could also restore utilities, communications, and transportation networks destroyed by the war.[46]

The Interior Department's rehabilitation and trade proposals gave special protection to American capital and admitted a diminishing quota of Philippine sugar to the United States without duty, thus assuring a steady flow of tax revenue for the Philippine government. These provisions drew on Hester's understanding of the Philippine experience between 1935 and 1941, when U.S.-imposed quotas on several commodities diverted some investment into mining and other new ventures. In time, Hester claimed, the importance of agricultural exports would decline relative to the economy as a whole. The fixed quota would limit the growth of commodity agriculture and foster new industries free from the unrest and backwardness of the hacienda. The key to the plan was gradualism. The Philippine government relied on the revenue it received from commodity export taxes, especially the tax on sugar. Too rapid a conversion would bankrupt the government, with disastrous consequences for social stability and investor confidence. Although Hester's plan sought to liquidate the sugar industry eventually, the sugar bloc preferred it to the alternative. Under existing legislation, the sugar trade would be terminated in 1946.⁴⁷

Most members of Quezon's cabinet had ties to the sugar industry and favored the Interior Department's gradual approach. Roosevelt encouraged Quezon to turn postwar planning for the Philippines over to the State Department, but after consulting with Fortas and Secretary of State Cordell Hull, the Philippine president found the Interior Department more sympathetic to the Filipinos' desire to avoid changes that might disrupt their social structure. He never afterward wavered from that position, but one member of his cabinet fought alone for three years to loosen the Interior Department's grip on his country's future. The Philippine resident commissioner, Joaquin Elizalde, pressed Quezon to exercise the "practical independence" promised in Roosevelt's speech. To Elizalde, Hester's plan seemed designed to help his political rivals in the sugar bloc and allow American manufacturers to challenge Philippine industry. In February 1944, with the encouragement of dissenting Interior Department officials, Elizalde urged Quezon to declare "semi-independence" by creating a Department of Exterior Relations and National Economy and giving it authority to devise alternate plans for reconstruction. "Interior can do little for us now," he advised. "Consider the advisability of working our own salvation independently and having the State Department handle our affairs and our fate."⁴⁸

Elizalde envisioned a trade policy that would tap markets in Asia and Latin America and reduce dependence on the United

States. His proposed department would survey Central and South American markets, review trade treaties in force, and organize a foreign service. The new policy would require closer cooperation with the U.S. Department of State and, Elizalde hoped, diminish the commonwealth government's reliance on the Interior Department. Quezon greeted the idea coolly, postponing action until the Tydings bill had passed. Undaunted, Elizalde tried his plans on State Department officials. Replying a month later, Secretary of State Hull drew a line on precisely how far "independent status" extended. He reminded Elizalde that the United States, not the commonwealth government, acted for the Philippines "in all matters concerning foreign relations." The State Department would not allow the commonwealth to open diplomatic relations with other countries. Hull suggested instead that the Filipinos establish an office to advise the State Department. Elizalde drafted orders creating an exterior relations department and placing himself at its head. Quezon, irked at his subordinate for having provoked Hull, buried the orders in a file.[49]

Quezon's death on August 1, 1944, finished any hope for a break between the commonwealth government and the Interior Department. A long-standing hostility, fed by racial animosity, stood between Elizalde and Quezon's successor, Osmeña. At their first meeting, Osmeña accepted the idea of a department for national economy and suggested that Elizalde resign as resident commissioner to head it up. Believing Osmeña intended to shelve him, Elizalde refused to be in the cabinet unless he was retained in both posts, whereupon the president dismissed him. "It was obvious," wrote Elizalde, "that President Osmeña wanted to place the whole matter of rehabilitation in the hands of Mr. Hester and the Department of the Interior." This was also obvious to Hester, who found Osmeña "more liberal and less amenable to falangist influences."[50]

The Interior Department urged its position on the Filipino Rehabilitation Commission, the panel of nine Filipinos and nine Americans established in 1944. Hester had "far more knowledge of the subject than any other member of the Commission," according to an observer, and his recommendations would be "the basis of most future discussions." The commission included the chairmen of the House and Senate committees on territories, Senator Tydings and Representative C. Jasper Bell. Bell, a former municipal official from Kansas City, had advanced his career through loyalty to local boss Thomas Pendergast. In 1932, Pendergast rewarded Bell by favoring his congressional candidacy over that of presiding judge Harry S. Truman. Although he had played little part in the Philippine policy debates of the 1930s, Bell's chairmanship placed him in a decisive position on the Rehabilitation Commission.[51]

The commission's chief job was to decide between the Interior Department's plans and those developed separately by the State Department. In March 1945, Assistant Secretary of State William L. Clayton, Jr., prepared a policy statement on postwar Philippine trade. Clayton had just endorsed the "Economic Charter of the Americas," pledging the United States to eradicate obstacles to trade between nations, particularly discriminatory obstacles. His policy on Philippine trade affirmed the charter's principles, and he viewed quota arrangements as "inconsistent" with the U.S. policy of reducing trade discrimination.[52]

Clayton's statement echoed earlier pronouncements on U.S. war aims. The Atlantic Charter committed the United States and Great Britain "to further the enjoyment by all states . . . of access, on equal terms to the trade and the raw materials of the world." The internationalists in Roosevelt's administration considered security and liberal trade inseparable, an idea captured in Hull's slogan, "If goods don't cross borders, soldiers will." By 1944, the "expansion and liberalization of world trade on a multilateral, nonpreferential basis" had become a fixed star by which the State Department steered policy. The Treasury and Commerce departments, too, backed the multilateralist line and assisted in designing the World Bank and the International Monetary Fund to carry the policy into practice. They had strong backing from business groups—like the National Foreign Trade Council and the National Association of Manufacturers—representing industrial and exporting industries. The multilateralist policy could claim the committed support of three cabinet departments, a large and influential business sector, and the president of the United States.[53]

The State and Interior departments squared off in June 1945 at a meeting of the Executive Committee on Economic Foreign Policy before an audience that included nearly every government agency concerned with postwar planning.[54] Although the clash ended in stalemate, it allowed each side to count its backers among the interested departments. Clayton placed before the panel a plan he felt other decolonizing powers could emulate. It avoided absolute quotas and swiftly phased out preferences, setting Philippine goods on equal terms with other imports entering American ports within 15 years of independence. An escape clause allowed the United States to revoke even these privileges if necessary to implement a global agreement. The plan phased out preferences faster than the Interior Department wanted to, and eschewed Hester's quotas. Discussion in the executive committee quickly turned to the issues raised by these two differences: how much of a jolt the Philippine economy could withstand, and how much damage one exception would do to U.S. foreign-trade policy. One point aroused no disagreement, but nonetheless remained central to the discussion: the importance of the Philippines as a postwar military ally.[55]

Fortas contended that strategic and foreign-policy considerations required a gentle adjustment to nonpreferential trade. Clayton's plan would cause chaos, he argued. It would dry up foreign investment and present to Filipinos "a choice between political dependence and economic disaster." Should other colonial governments follow suit, many colonies would choose to remain dependent rather than sever economic ties to the mother country. The Filipinos, he warned, building to his best argument, would be driven into alliances with other powers, alliances that would threaten the military bases on which the United States depended for its safety. "The economic security of the Philippines," Fortas declared, "is vital to the military security of the United States."[56]

Undersecretary of War Robert P. Patterson had supported this argument in a letter to the executive committee earlier that month. "From a military standpoint, it is obvious that policies should be avoided which would cause economic or political penetration of the Philippines by other powers," he cautioned. The greatest danger was that "the Philippine economy may come to be complementary to those of Japan and Russia." The trade program should assure, he observed, that the Philippines would continue to rely on the United States, and that the islands would not be forced to endure sudden shocks "which honest and effective management cannot cope with." The Navy endorsed his statement. Military representatives at the meeting declined to state which proposal best served national security, but they carefully noted Fortas's remarks on the bases.[57]

Woodbury Willoughby of the State Department challenged the assumption that eliminating preferences would shock the Philippine economy. The sugar industry, he admitted, would be substantially curtailed, but Clayton's plan would redirect resources into commodities that could compete successfully. There was a "tendency for U.S. capital to withdraw from the Philippines," an inevitable consequence, he maintained, of independence. In support, the Treasury Department's spokesman pointed out that the islands were already in chaos and suggested that the committee concentrate on the type of economy it wanted to emerge from the inescapable postliberation disorder. "From the point of view of military security," the spokesman contended, the diversification that would result from elimination of preferences was better than "an economy dependent on one or two chief products." The Commerce Department representative agreed and proposed eliminating all preferences and rehabilitating the Philippines with foreign aid. None of the other panelists wanted to apply multilateralism strictly. Most agreed with Ben Dorfman of the Tariff Commission, who confessed that "the economic advantage of the preference plateau can be easily exaggerated, but the Filipinos want it, we can accede without appreciably affecting our basic position, and to do so would promote friendliness."[58]

Even Clayton's plan tried to soften the hardships multilateral competition would wreak on a fragile economy. The security and economic interests of the United States, a State Department report affirmed, "demand not only free access and trade in Southeast Asia, but also a rising standard of living there." Internationalist rhetoric admitted no contradiction between these goals, but grappling with the Philippine problem forced the State Department to face the possibility that achieving a multilateralist order might cause incomes in some countries to sink, and defeat the efforts of the United States to win friends in the developing world. Interior and State department officials agreed that applying multilateralist policy strictly would cause Philippine wages to drop to the level of the world's poorest countries. They differed only on the nature of the compromise necessary to assure stability. As the Philippine resident commissioner, Brigadier General Carlos P. Romulo, remarked, "Differences of opinion have not been over the necessity for preferences, but over their character and duration." Even some within the State Department felt Clayton had not compromised enough. "It's not likely," an official in the Philippine Division observed, that a lone case of discrimination would have a major effect on the total world commerce picture. "It is clear that the collapse of the Philippine experiment from whatever cause will sacrifice virtually all of the goodwill" the United States had earned in Southeast Asia.[59]

The multilateralism of the Roosevelt and Truman administrations bore scant resemblance to Ricardian free trade. Even the staunchest proponents of multilateralism, Clayton and Secretary of Commerce Henry Wallace, denied they were classical "free traders," insisting during congressional testimony that they favored protectionism when it could prevent serious injury to a domestic industry.[60] Instead, administration officials agreed that prosperity led to international harmony. Multilateralists advocated *freer* trade as the best means to achieve prosperity, while acknowledging that protectionism had a role in special cases. A committee on cartel policy headed by Treasury Undersecretary Dean Acheson enumerated four such conditions in November 1944: to aid national defense, to conserve scarce commodities, to protect public health and morals (by, for instance, restricting trade in narcotics), and to ameliorate "cases of acute crisis" caused by foreign competition. Clayton agreed that the first and possibly the last of these conditions applied to the Philippines. Preferences could be allowed under these circumstances, but they should last no longer than necessary (until 1949, he thought) and should be applied in a nondiscriminatory manner. Absolute quotas, limiting the total amount of Philippine sugar that could enter the United States, did not qualify.[61]

Disagreement between the Interior and State departments deadlocked the Rehabilitation Commission. Clayton urged the members of the commission to bear in mind the policy of the United States to eliminate the global "network of preferences and other trade discriminations." "Whatever we do in regard to United States–Philippine trade relations," he warned, must not "embarrass us in carrying out that policy." Hester replied by pointing out the irony of erecting trade barriers in order to promote free trade. Tariff discrimination need not contradict the State Department's objectives, he argued. If preferences were a quid pro quo for military bases, free trade, and investment rights, other nations could not complain unless they offered identical concessions. He had warned the commission to expect State Department opposition, but he believed his own views would prevail in a Congressional debate.[62]

MacArthur's recapture of the Philippines created an urgent need to break the deadlock on rehabilitation aid and planning. On October 20, 1944, United States troops and Filipino guerrillas began the liberation of the Philippines on the island of Leyte. On February 27, 1945, Osmeña reestablished the commonwealth government in Manila. Ickes urged Roosevelt to restore civil administration under the high commissioner's office as quickly as possible, but MacArthur and his supporters in Congress resisted the appointment of a commissioner. Stimson wanted a counterweight to MacArthur's civil authority and helped persuade Truman, who became president in April 1945, to restore the office. In July, President Truman sent the leading candidate for the job, War Manpower Commissioner Paul V. McNutt, to Manila.[63]

McNutt found Manila in ruins. A month of savage fighting had razed four-fifths of the capital, and with it nearly all of the country's modern industry and cultural, educational, and commercial institutions. On the main boulevards, crowds of U.S. and Philippine soldiers, guerrillas, prostitutes, peddlers, and beggars jostled among shacks propped on the broken remnants of once-great buildings. Manila, in the words of one resident, "presented the appearance of some hellish fair or carnival against a background of ravage and ruin." As McNutt met with MacArthur's aides, relief officials were only beginning to discern the fearful magnitude of destruction in the countryside. The Philippines had lost 65 percent of its cattle, hogs, and chickens, 25 percent of its plows and farm tools, most of its irrigation systems and rice mills, 80 percent of its motor vehicles, and 70 percent of its animal carts. Relief workers found three of every four rural people dressed in rags or bark, and entire provinces where nakedness was "the rule rather than the exception." Almost half the *carabao*, the sole source of farm power other than human labor, had been killed for meat. Planting of rice and corn was down by 40 percent, and with chronic shortages of fertilizer, bags, tools, and transport, only a fraction of the yield could reach market. Officials predicted mass starvation unless the United States could send help in time.[64]

McNutt returned to Washington and told the president of the devastation he had witnessed. A popular ex-governor of Indiana, once considered Roosevelt's rival for the presidency, McNutt possessed unique qualifications for the top Philippine job, having already served in the post and having maintained simultaneous friendships with MacArthur and Truman. The president granted him "unprecedented powers in regard to the Philippines," Clayton's aides complained.[65]

Philippine officials respected McNutt's influence, and the appointment finished Elizalde's plan to shift the commonwealth government's support from the Interior Department to the State Department. The former resident commissioner had become campaign manager and Washington representative for Osmeña's opponent, Roxas, who by late 1945 had a commanding lead in the presidential race that would end in April 1946. Elizalde urged Roxas to support the State Department's position, but Roxas considered McNutt's support essential to winning rehabilitation aid, which he saw as more urgent than trade legislation. Roxas also opposed the State Department's plan, believing export industries would recover too slowly to benefit from declining quotas. "It seems McNutt represents the administration," he advised Elizalde.[66]

The appointment of McNutt as the new high commissioner ended the work of the Rehabilitation Commission and gave the Interior Department a powerful advantage in the approaching congressional debate on trade. In speeches in Manila and Washington, McNutt championed policies developed by the Interior Department, urging agricultural reform on Filipinos and promising opportunity to American business. The "kind of feudalism" that "has dominated the life of the average land worker," he proclaimed, "must be progressively eradicated." He relied on investment to solve agrarian problems. A rehabilitation policy aimed at forestalling unrest must recognize "that capital must be attracted here, that investments must be safeguarded and savings encouraged." Eliminating preferences while armed rebels roamed the countryside, he warned, would plunge the Philippines into civil war. "It does not seem humanly possible," he told Truman, for the government "to cope with the coincidence of political independence, sharp downward revision of economic standards, budgetary bankruptcy, and rehabilitation."[67]

Hester and Ely had served under McNutt previously in Manila, and the three men agreed on the high commissioner's trade and rehabilitation agenda. Just two weeks after taking office, McNutt and Hester drafted a trade bill and gave it to Representative Bell, who introduced it in the House on September 24. It provided for 20 years of preferential tariffs, absolute quotas on Philippine goods entering the United States, restrictions on the autonomy of the Philippines in trade dealings with third countries, and special legal protection for American citizens and corporations in the Philippines. Clayton's office produced an alternate bill that Tydings introduced on October 18, 1945. Based on the executive committee's plan, it called for a 22-year adjustment period, during which duties on Philippine exports entering the United States would rise by 5 percent a year to reach the full duty by 1968. Until then, the Philippines would enjoy an advantage in American markets, but there would be no absolute quotas, no restrictions on economic sovereignty, and no special breaks for Americans doing business in the Philippines. Tydings's bill, however, had little chance of getting a hearing. Revenue bills originate in the House, which ignored Tydings's draft.[68]

Despite reservations, Philippine leaders rushed to support the Bell bill. All major political factions considered a quick trade bill that would restore prewar conditions as nearly as possible essential to arresting the slide into anarchy. Amid the hyperinflation caused by abundant dollars and scarce goods, one newspaperman, Renato Constantino, observed that Filipinos were beginning to turn against independence as "the government stands helplessly by, unable to cope with the situation." Osmeña urged haste, assuring Truman that the Bell bill had his endorsement. Roxas pledged McNutt his backing, but complained privately that "neither the Tydings nor Bell bill is completely satisfactory" since both contained declining preferences. McNutt's "ideas of what the Philippine bill should contain do not exactly correspond with ours," Romulo, the Philippine resident commissioner, admitted, "but a frontal attack on his position would hurt rather than help our cause."[69]

Philippine leaders preferred dependency and bilateralism to equality and economic sovereignty. Osmeña and Roxas agreed that an ideal trade act would allow a renewable 20-year period of "free trade" in which Philippine agriculture and industry could resume its prewar pattern. Roxas and Osmeña had strong ties to sugar interests, but there is little reason to think that a leadership of a different class composition would have behaved differently. Peasant leaders did not disagree with the administration on the basic features of an ideal trade regime. When the Philippine Congress debated the trade issue in June 1946, the Democratic Alliance, a bloc of socialist and communist congressmen, favored continued bilateral free trade, objecting only to conditions that restricted Philippine autonomy over domestic planning, conditions Roxas and Romulo also found objectionable. The Philippine leadership's preference for 20 years of free trade, a more prolonged dependency than the United States was willing to grant, aroused few objections at home.[70]

Bell and McNutt argued their case in Congress by emphasizing the magnitude of the destruction caused by the war and the advantages of diversification. They offered preferential, bilateral trade as a less costly alternative to rehabilitation aid, and stressed the long-term advantages to the United States of a bilateral relationship. McNutt recalled the desolation he saw driving from the Manila airfield to the high commissioner's residence: "A heartbreak as far as I was concerned. Too many missing faces, too many missing places." Bell declared that "the Japanese destroyed substantially everything that man has done in the Philippines," leaving the United States with only two choices: it could "open the Treasury and pour millions" into rehabilitation, or it could offer the kind of trade relief that would make it possible for Americans and Filipinos to do business together. Pointing to section 17 of the bill, the "parity" clause, which gave Americans "the same rights as to property, residence, and occupation as the citizens of the Philippines," Bell recommended his bill as a "businesslike" alternative to handouts. He offered a way to bring prosperity to both the Philippines and the United States, "prosperity in the years to come such as has seldom been dreamed of, in my humble opinion."[71]

Pressure from industries and agricultural groups played only a minor role in the debate on the Bell bill, leaving the stage to the bureaucratic actors. Early in the House hearings, committee members demanded to hear some industry testimony, and McNutt produced J. S. McDaniel, secretary of the Cordage and Twine Industry Council, who admitted under questioning that he had not seen the bill. Harry Hawes, lobbyist for the Philippine sugar industry, worried that Cuban sugar interests would influence the debate. "Cuba has expanded her trade to an enormous degree," he told Roxas, "and with a powerful lobby will try to hold it." But the threat never materialized. Amid a global sugar shortage, both Cuban and domestic producers enjoyed strong demand and high market prices that reduced their objections to Philippine competition.[72]

The major concessions to business in the Bell bill were the parity and currency provisions, designed to make American capital feel at home in the Philippines. These clauses helped firms with potential rather than actual investments in the Philippines. The American Chamber of Commerce of the Philippines, which represented the prominent trading firms in the islands, strongly opposed special privileges for Americans, believing nationalist resentment would counteract any putative benefits; but businesses anticipating future investments in the Philippines lobbied for parity and other investment incentives. In October 1945, the Standard Vacuum Oil Company proposed a clause exempting American firms from Philippine constitutional restrictions on foreign business. The Philippine-American Chamber of Commerce, a New York-based group of industrial and banking giants, most of which had only "nominal or indirect connections" to Philippine business, persuaded McNutt to include it in Bell's legislation.[73]

On the third day of hearings, Tydings brought consideration of the legislation to a halt by warning the Ways and Means Committee that the administration was divided over whether to endorse the bill. The committee's chairman, Robert Doughton, who had fought earlier battles for multilateralism, refused to take further action without an endorsement from the White House. President Truman had at different times assured Tydings and Bell of his support; now both legislators asked for a verdict. Rosenman told Truman that he had a cabinet dispute and suggested that he "have Ickes, McNutt and Will Clayton come over and you definitely tell them what kind of tariff legislation you prefer."

The president met with McNutt, Tydings, Bell, Fortas, Clayton, and the secretary of state, James Byrnes, on November 13, 1945.[74] They struck a compromise that became House Resolution 5856. It allowed duty-free trade for eight years. Beginning in 1954, duties would increase at the rate of 5 percent annually over 20 years, with imports above quota subject to full duty. The proposal placed absolute quotas on two items, sugar and cordage, for 28 years. Truman also approved a separate rehabilitation bill providing $625 million for public works and $400 million for individual damage awards, disbursed under United States supervision. The bulk of the rehabilitation funds, Bell and McNutt made clear, would come from revenue generated by the revived sugar trade. The new legislation, Romulo reported to Manila, "contained many of the amendments we proposed, and was, from our point of view, much more favorable."[75]

For the multilateralists, the White House meeting was a clear defeat. The compromise established a preferential trading system lasting 28 years. It contained absolute quotas, to Clayton "the most vicious of trade restrictions." It gave Americans special legal rights in the Philippines, and gave the United States president veto power over Philippine monetary policy. Clayton believed the new bill would embarrass the United States in future negotiations with other governments, and invite criticism from nationalists and imperialists around the world.[76]

Having defeated the multilateralists, the bill's advocates next faced a challenge from domestic sugar interests and Secretary of Agriculture Clinton Anderson, who felt the trade bill would impede comprehensive legislation to control sugar imports. Anderson managed to arrange for the hearings to be postponed until after Christmas to allow his department to study the issue. Ickes asked Truman to intervene, reminding him of the urgency of the Philippine situation. Romulo succeeded after several meetings in pacifying Anderson, who withdrew his objection. At a meeting on January 29, 1946, Truman asked his cabinet to support the bill, and his assistant followed up by asking each department to approve a statement affirming that "an abrupt change in the long-existing trade relations would unduly shock the economy of the Philippines." The State Department refused to capitulate, however, and agreed only to the "basic principles" of the legislation.[77]

State Department witnesses continued to grumble as Congress concluded its deliberations. The House committee did not report until March 27—just three months before Philippine Independence Day—and the bill proceeded to the Senate Finance Committee. Clayton told senators that absolute quotas were "wrong" and that the bill would sabotage trade negotiations with Britain. He particularly objected to a clause, unique in trade legislation, banning renegotiation for five years. "Is it not conceivable," Senator Albert Hawkes ventured, that McNutt and his allies were "trying to do something special in connection with . . . the Philippines?" The Senate panel approved the bill in four days, with only a minor reduction in the sugar quota.[78]

As the Finance Committee put the finishing touches on the trade bill, the Senate Banking Committee, meeting just down the hall, approved a $3.75 billion loan to Great Britain. The administration and Congress brandished the loan as a weapon against the "economic aggression" of bilateral trade agreements that perforce "put the weaker nation at the mercy of the stronger." The contradiction attracted the attention of the press and highlighted the unusual nature of the Philippine bill. "To recognize just how unique these pieces of legislation are," the *Christian Science Monitor* noted, "it is only necessary to recall that preferential trade relations with foreign governments completely contradict American policy."[79]

Secretary of State Byrnes reluctantly advised Truman to sign H.R. 5856, but urged him to make clear that some portions would require later revision. The new interior secretary, Julius Krug, objected that "demagogues and irreconcilables" in the islands would use the proposed statement to thwart the bill's enactment by the Philippine legislature. On April 30, 1946, President Truman signed the Philippine Trade Act and issued a statement calling it an "unprecedented plan of preferential trade relations." Although discriminatory trade was "alien to the policies of this administration," he admitted, the catastrophic condition of the Philippine economy—"itself unprecedented"—justified extraordinary steps for its rehabilitation. To assure the Philippine legislature's compliance, the Rehabilitation Act, signed the same day, withheld war-damage payments pending approval of the trade agreement by the Filipinos. Congress and the White House brushed aside the State Department's protest against this "coercive expedient," an unnecessary prod to the Filipinos, who considered the arrangement the best they were likely to get. Although disappointed by Truman's approval of the bill, State Department officials believed they could repair the damage later.[80]

The multilateralists had been handicapped during the congressional debate. Legislative procedure gave Bell the initiative, and the State Department's arguments, which stressed diffuse global objectives, were less appealing than the promise of low-cost rehabilitation and a stable, prosperous military ally. Many congressmen wanted to show gratitude for sacrifices made by the Filipinos during the war. As a result, the bill passed unanimously in both houses. The president, too, wanted to appear generous and assure that a vital military ally would become prosperous and stable. McNutt's arguments, bolstered by the consensus among administration officials on the strategic importance of the Philippines, strongly influenced Truman's decision. The United

States, it was felt, could give in without badly compromising its position, and by doing so could earn Philippine friendship. The kind of compromise the Interior Department offered—between domestic (in this case, strategic) objectives and multilateralist goals—was the kind to which Congress and the president were accustomed.

Even the staunchest multilateralists applied a double standard when it came to protecting domestic industry from foreign competition. In the Philippine case, officials simply extended that double standard to cover a client state. The Philippines rated special treatment because of its standing as a military ally. U.S. officials had been ready to terminate the special trade relationship with the Philippines until they decided to keep military bases there. Once Army and Navy planners declared Philippine bases vital to the safety of the United States, they necessitated a reexamination of the entire bilateral relationship.

Four years after Sayre's flight from Manila, the United States had become reentangled with the Philippines. Administration officials would now be deeply involved in the Philippine problems they had been anxious to leave behind in the 1930s. Pentagon officials' interest in naval and air bases required that the Philippines remain in the economic orbit of the United States, safely protected from the bumps and jars of international capitalism. American investors benefited from this policy, but they did not instigate it. Philippine leaders seized the chance to obtain the autonomous but dependent relationship Quezon had wanted. Free from external economic and military threats, they could continue to rule their private fiefs and profit from their privileged access to the world's richest market. But restoring the Philippine economy and state proved more difficult than the promoters of the 1946 trade act had suggested. The dilapidated social structure Quezon had abandoned in 1941 had collapsed. Four years of warfare had left Filipinos hungry, bitter, and armed.[81]

TWO

Factionalism and Its Advantages

The postwar Philippine government enjoyed none of the cohesion of its prewar predecessor. The delicate political equilibrium of the 1930s depended on the presence in Malacañan Palace of a president the caciques could trust to apportion largesse fairly and leave them unmolested in their rural domains. Quezon was an original. Not of the oligarchy, he ruled on its behalf, gathering to himself tremendous personal power while leaving local authority alone. As peasant unionism and insurgency grew, he responded by enlarging the Philippine Constabulary and making cosmetic agricultural and "social justice" reforms. The oligarchy, through its representatives in Congress, gratefully accepted his leadership and coalesced into a disputatious but deferential retinue that lived by the doctrine *tayo tayo*, "just among us." None of Quezon's successors possessed his ability to unite the elite. Neither Osmeña nor Roxas could tame Congress, reestablish patrimonial authority, or put together a military and reform program to beat the Huks.[1]

In their state's weakness, Philippine leaders found leverage that helped them in dealing with the United States. Historians criticize the Truman administration for having imposed onerous trade and defense arrangements on a prostrate ally, and accuse Philippine leaders of lacking "the intellectual and attitudinal equipment" to resist; but Philippine leaders bargained more skillfully than their critics admit. The government's infirmity, its internal divisions and lack of funds, compelled Truman to yield to Philippine wishes on issues related to trade and the bases. The 1946 trade act opened the Philippines to American imports and prohibited protectionist controls. Within a year, the State and Treasury departments reversed course, encouraging the Philippines to exclude American goods and impose controls to avert bankruptcy. Philippine negotiators were able to maneuver U.S. officials into acceding to nationalist demands on the 1947 bases treaty, relinquishing desirable sites in Manila, and allowing Philippine courts more jurisdiction over U.S. troops than Britain or Spain enjoyed.[2]

A stronger Philippine government might have done worse. Leaders obtained concessions by presenting themselves as mediators between the United States and uncontrolled political and economic interests. Deadlock in the Philippine Congress constrained U.S. policy, prompting Washington to cede greater economic authority to the Philippine president.

The regime's weakness was no ploy. Prisoner to its powerful clients, the Philippine state employed its new powers to satisfy particularistic demands, and dissipated its resources through corruption. Osmeña and Roxas tried to rally support with nationalist appeals and largesse. At each turn the regime gained enemies and plunged deeper in debt. By 1948, it was headed for self-destruction.

In his most famous photograph, MacArthur is depicted splashing ashore on Leyte, jut-jawed and determined, his eyes scanning the destruction wrought by U.S. forces on the morning of October 20, 1944. To his left can be seen the aged and less resolute figure of Osmeña, whose solemn expression betrayed his misgivings about joining the invasion. President Osmeña knew that by accompanying MacArthur he risked converting his administration into "a sort of puppet government for the military." Harold Ickes, the interior secretary, warned him not to go, that without funds or authority he would be at MacArthur's mercy. Osmeña explained, however, that he could not disappoint the Filipino people. "They might even think," he said, "that I was afraid."[3]

Four days after the landing, MacArthur summoned Osmeña to the ruined capitol at Tacloban and proclaimed the civil government restored. None of the photographs of this event show Osmeña. All eyes were on MacArthur, who made his declaration and sped away in a jeep, leaving the president, according to one witness, "standing alone and confused, not knowing which way to turn."[4]

In the following months, the president would find his fears justified. Osmeña wanted to restore Quezon's centralized one-party state, but the social structure that had supported the prewar regime had splintered. While Osmeña struggled to unite the country under his leadership, MacArthur thwarted his every move. Within three months the general and his powerful Filipino allies isolated Osmeña and formed a shadow government around Roxas, a former aide to MacArthur and a high official in the Japanese-sponsored republic. The struggle between Osmeña and Roxas produced a faction-ridden state unable to check either the rebellious peasantry or the destructive avarice of the elite.

Osmeña's government lacked the ingredients of a patrimonial state. Most importantly, it had no money. In Quezon's time, sugar revenue had flowed through the government to local caciques in the form of patronage and largesse, while political allegiances and votes had flowed back toward the top. The U.S. invasion disrupted these channels, distributing hundreds of millions of dollars directly to Filipino employees. Compared to people in the world's other war zones, Filipinos had buying power. Throughout 1945, American-made goods came in as fast as ships could unload them (60,000–120,000 tons a day), and Filipinos paid cash. Osmeña had neither the technical nor the political ability to capture these dollars in taxes, and the United States offered no financial aid to the regime. Four-fifths of the commonwealth's prewar treasury remained impounded in the United States until Congress released it in late 1945. Quezon had spent the remainder on relief supplies. Without patronage, Osmeña could muster little support outside of his retinue in Manila.[5]

The commonwealth government existed largely on paper. Without funds, staff, or offices, Osmeña had to fashion a government from scratch. Disrupted communications and transport made it impossible to impose centralized authority. The war continued for eight months after Osmeña's return. Large areas remained under Japanese or U.S. Army control. Not one ton of interisland shipping remained afloat. Bridges, telegraph lines, and railroads were out. Air transport did not resume until November 1945, mail service until mid-1946.[6]

The local elites on whom Quezon's authority had rested were in no position to help Osmeña. Many were in jail. Others found their local authority challenged by new political rivals, guerrilla leaders, and armed peasants. Ickes's plans to prosecute collaborators robbed Osmeña of the elite's support. The Interior Department placed a high priority on purging collaborators, and Ickes instructed Osmeña to recruit only untainted officials, a policy that proved unrealistic. Nearly every experienced politician had worked for the Japanese. "The guerrillas," according to one reporter, "got only the second and third string boys." The Japanese had cultivated the caciques and had attempted, through them, to control the countryside. Laurel's administration had included most members of the prewar government, and many who had avoided public service employed their talents as war profiteers. After reestablishing the commonwealth in Manila in February 1945, Osmeña found he could neither staff his administration with the few innocent officials available, nor persuade Ickes to modify the policy. Moreover, punitive actions against collaborators widened the rift between Osmeña and the elite.[7]

After the capture of Manila, U.S. counterintelligence agents filled Bilibid and Mutinglupa prisons with 6,000 suspected collaborators. The prison roster, according to one officer, read like the Manila social register. In the countryside, guerrillas imprisoned landlords or prevented them from returning to their estates. Those who avoided detention often found they had lost their property and social position. After sharing a cell block at Mutinglupa with senators Claro Recto, Jose Yulo, and Benigno Aquino, as well as industrialist Vicente Madrigal, Quentin Paredes, the political chieftain of Abra, returned home to find a guerrilla leader in charge of his province and his home in ruins; "Gone were the chandeliers, the carpets, the silver, the crystal, the china . . . collected during a lifetime of gracious living." Preoccupied with personal misfortunes, members of the elite could spare nothing for Osmeña, whom many blamed for their predicament.[8]

The collaboration issue divided the elite, but not neatly. Those who had not collaborated during the occupation often had relatives who had. Osmeña's son was a war profiteer. Some collaborators had hedged by helping the guerrillas. Most notoriously, Roxas had served simultaneously in the Laurel cabinet and as a guerrilla general. Some cacique politicians (usually those out of office in 1941) had joined the resistance. Tomas Confesor, defeated by one of Roxas's political allies in 1940, became a guerrilla leader; after the war, he was an outspoken proponent of purge trials. But not all loyalists shared Confesor's enthusiasm. Osmeña tried to put the issue aside, fearing its potential for factionalism. His fear became a reality in April 1945, when MacArthur "liberated" Roxas.[9]

Roxas and other members of Laurel's cabinet crossed Japanese lines on April 16 and turned themselves over to the U.S. Sixth Army. MacArthur's headquarters reported that the cabinet had been captured but that Roxas had been "freed." Army intelligence officers considered Roxas among "the guiltiest of the puppets," all the more reprehensible because of the double game he had played. When Osmeña objected to Roxas's special treatment, MacArthur explained that he knew Roxas personally and could vouch for his loyalty.[10]

The two men were old friends. Roxas had led the conservative, Spanish-mestizo faction with which MacArthur had aligned himself in the 1930s, a clique that included Elizalde and Roxas's cousin and business partner, Soriano. In February 1942, the three men had engineered the transfer of half a million dollars from the Philippine treasury to MacArthur's personal account in a New York bank, and may also have protected the general's secret investment in a Philippine gold mine. MacArthur perhaps repaid these debts by exonerating Roxas. The Roxas family paper, the *Manila Daily News*, hailed the decision. MacArthur, according to his biographer, placed "his stamp of approval on Roxas as a Filipino patriot and United States Army officer and freed him to launch his campaign for the presidency of the Philippine republic."[11]

MacArthur shared his Spanish-mestizo friends' dislike for the man they called "El Chino." "I can't work with Osmeña," he told a visiting congressman. Throughout 1945, he undercut Osmeña's attempts to consolidate control, taking credit for favorable developments and blaming Osmeña for supply bottlenecks and the decision to cut guerrilla pay. The final stroke came when MacArthur pushed the president to reconvene the prewar legislature, an action designed to discredit Osmeña with his supporters in Washington while giving Roxas a forum for attacks on the administration. Fourteen of the 22 surviving Philippine senators had collaborated. Seven were in jail. Over a third of the House faced prosecution. To achieve a quorum, collaborators would have to be included, in clear violation of Ickes's order. When the Congress met in June, it named Roxas senate president, voted itself four years of back pay, and set about obstructing Osmeña's program. Ickes, who opposed collaborators but had no plan for getting rid of them, threatened reprisals against Osmeña and inadvertently helped Roxas. In August, MacArthur departed for Japan and released the remainder of the imprisoned collaborators, an act widely interpreted as a blanket amnesty. Roxas initially had everything to fear from the collaboration issue, but he managed to turn it to his advantage. The issue undercut Osmeña's support both in the Philippines and in Washington.[12]

The uncertain date of the presidential election—scheduled for November 1945, then moved to April 1946—stretched the campaign season to a year. In the first months, Roxas seemed to have all the advantages: MacArthur's reflected glory, access to the Elizalde and Soriano fortunes, and the loyalty of most of the elite. On July 12, 1945, the *Star Reporter* declared, "Osmeña Dead Politically." Roxas laughed off Osmeña's offer to join a unity ticket and began formulating policies, bargaining with U.S. officials, and cutting deals as if his election were merely a formality. But Roxas, like Osmeña, badly overestimated the oligarchy's resilience. The caciques were divided and threatened in their local strongholds. Roxas's challenge strengthened forces that would subvert unity for years to come.[13]

Roxas's candidacy enabled popular guerrilla leaders to challenge local political bosses. As U.S. troops pushed into the provinces, they replaced governors and mayors with guerrilla commanders. Young men of modest means and varied backgrounds assumed offices once reserved for landowners. Some, like Ramon Magsaysay and Ferdinand Marcos, used this opening to gain national prominence. Deferential to power, these "new men" posed little threat to the cacique system, but they posed an immediate threat to individual caciques, who found themselves running against war heroes. A two-party race enabled guerrillas to establish rival machines. In the past, national politicians had assembled a slate by choosing the leaders of preeminent local factions. Roxas now had to choose in each district between rival factions headed by old politicians and new men. In a volatile, unfamiliar political climate, winners were difficult to predict, and each choice alienated powerful constituencies and individuals.[14]

Roxas had no constituency in central Luzon, where peasant guerrillas had eradicated cacique politics. Organized peasants and communist mayors had united in 1942 in a popular anti-Japanese, antilandlord political and military movement called the Hukbalahap. The Huks controlled the countryside, abolished rents, and redistributed land. Three years later, they established local governments up to the provincial level. When U.S. troops entered central Luzon in early 1945, they came as invaders rather than as liberators. "There were no American flags in sight, no cries of 'Mabuhay, you come, Joe,' " said one officer. "These were not America-loving Filipinos." MacArthur made hesitant efforts to disarm the Huks and replace their leaders, but recognized that suppressing the movement would start a war. Huk organizers followed troops into Manila and established a trade-union federation, the Committee on Labor Organizations, which soon claimed 80,000 members. In mid-July, the union, the Communist party, and the Huks united in a popular front, the Democratic Alliance, which called for immediate independence, prosecution of collaborators, and protection for peasants' and workers' rights. On January 11, 1946, the Alliance endorsed Osmeña. That same day, U.S. Army intelligence reported that the Democratic Alliance was gathering strength and would heavily influence the coming election.[15]

As his lead narrowed, Roxas tried to turn racial animosity against his opponent, calling Osmeña a "Chinese puppet" and a "mandarin." In early 1946, Roxas's newspapers printed Chinese-baiting editorials, and Roxasista crowds chanted anti-Chinese slogans. These tactics had little effect in the rural areas, where anti-Chinese feeling was weaker, and they united the wealthy Chinese community behind Osmeña. Chinese retailers Albino and Alfonso Sycip backed the president with their daily newspaper, the *Courier*, and 1.5 million pesos.[16] Characteristic of Philippine politics, neither party had an ideological coloration. Osmeña's Nacionalista party drew supporters from both the right and the left, assembling a motley coalition of reformers, Muslims, old politicos, and sugar barons. Osmeña could count on his allies in the sugar bloc and politicians from the southern islands. Roxas gathered much of the old oligarchy, some of the "new men," and local officials who had served the Japanese. Both parties contained collaborators and guerrillas. The candidates' views on national issues had little effect on their support, which was built on alliances with local machines. Faction *liders* based political calculations on local opportunities and their chances for preferment under various regional and national candidates. Such alliances were unstable. Senator Jose Zulueta's faction changed sides twice during the campaign.[17]

Both candidates touted their influence in Washington. Nacionalistas argued that the United States would cut aid to a Roxas government. Roxas played up his connection with MacArthur. U.S. officials were divided: the State and Interior departments favored Osmeña, and High Commissioner McNutt backed Roxas. McNutt saw Roxas as the more "chauvinistic" candidate, who would drive a harder bargain on the bases and trade, but he considered Osmeña too weak to rule effectively. Neither candidate wanted an endorsement per se. Rather, each wanted to be seen as able to influence U.S. policy on behalf of Philippine interests. After months of occupation, voters wanted a president who would deal sternly with the Americans. The 38,000 occupying troops had worn out their welcome. Undisciplined GIs provoked hundreds of "incidents" daily, with civilians often ending up dead. U.S. Army vehicles comprised a fifth of Manila's motor traffic, but caused half of the traffic deaths. In January 1946, thousands of GIs rioted to protest delays in demobilization. The mob rampaged through Manila, looting stores and homes. Filipinos demanded protection, and criticized Osmeña for being too diplomatic. Osmeña, in turn, accused Roxas of toadyism.[18]

Roxas's victory on April 26, 1946, produced no return to consensus politics. Winning by a slim 8 percent margin, Roxas lacked a mandate decisive enough to command Congress's respect. He carried only half of his congressional slate. Osmeña's coalition won ten of the 21 Senate races, and over a third of the House seats. The Democratic Alliance took seven of the eight house seats in central Luzon. Roxas's control of Congress was nearly as weak as Osmeña's had been. He would need to cater to the interests of nearly every member to push through even routine legislation.[19]

Congress began obstructing legislation a few weeks later by stalling the "parity" amendment to the constitution. A condition of the Bell trade act, the amendment granted American investors the rights and privileges of native-born Filipinos with respect to conducting business. Some of Roxas's backers favored the amendment (Soriano had acquired U.S. citizenship during the war), and the new president agreed that if the Americans had wanted to exploit the Philippines, "they would have done it while they owned the country." But influential industrialists, nationalist legislators, and the Democratic Alliance condemned parity as the act of an ungrateful and overbearing ally. Editorialists accused Roxas of selling out to American business. Liberal congressmen put up a feeble defense. "If we face the facts, we have to admit that we are only relatively independent," Senator Lorenzo Sumulong observed. "We lost some of the attributes of absolute independence the moment we agreed to the United States having bases here."[20]

Interior Department officials had designed the parity measure to satisfy potential investors, like the Standard Vacuum Oil Company, and to give Congress something to show for the trade and rehabilitation acts, which many members considered extravagant; but parity was a disaster for U.S. policy. American trading firms opposed it, knowing it would only arouse a nationalist backlash. The State Department considered it insulting and unenforceable. Congressman Bell, chairman of the Filipino Rehabilitation Commission, told the Filipinos that parity gave them a chance to rebuild. "You don't need a dribble of American capital here," he said. "You need a lot of it." McNutt placed a stipulation in the rehabilitation act requiring the enactment of parity before war-damage payments over $500 could be disbursed. Amending the Philippine constitution required two-thirds majorities in both legislative houses and a national plebiscite. The issue excited anti-American feeling in the Philippines before and during negotiations on military bases and placed extraordinary political demands on Roxas's new administration.[21]

To push the parity amendment through Congress, Roxas resorted to tactics that provoked a militant response. In May 1946, Liberal congressmen expelled seven members of the Democratic Alliance on trumped-up charges of vote fraud. Even the Supreme Court, which upheld the action, observed that it had more to do with parity than with fraud. The expulsion gave the Liberals the margin they needed to push the amendment through Congress. Alliance congressmen returned to central Luzon to reorganize Huk units against the government. "That was the final provocation," according to one journalist. "The Huks dug up their World War II arms and central Luzon once again became a battleground."[22]

A troubled and divided Philippines gained independence on July 4, 1946. In a colorful outdoor ceremony in Manila's central park, United States and Philippine officials marked the birth of a nation. As the red, blue, white, and yellow Philippine flag passed the Stars and Stripes on its way to the masthead, a great cheer rose from the crowd. In a radio message, Truman promised "a new partnership." Carpenters had spent weeks making the capital presentable for the ceremony, but no last-minute slicking could hide the hulking, ruined buildings. A man in the crowd told a reporter, "Yes, we are getting our independence, but it will take so many years to rebuild our country. Perhaps it can never be done." "Their economy is disrupted, their treasury empty," observed the *Washington Post.* "Indeed it is probable that the whole economy of the country must be radically altered." But, the editorial continued, the islands had become "more necessary than ever to our Pacific defenses," assuring that the relationship would be as close as it was before.[23]

Between March 1945 and March 1947, the United States elaborated plans for Philippine bases, selected sites, and concluded

agreements with Osmeña and Roxas. To project power north-
ward into Asia, and to take advantage of facilities built for the
invasion of Japan, planners chose permanent bases on Luzon,
close to Manila, rather than on the smaller, less populous southern islands preferred by prewar planners. Philippine leaders were
anxious to strengthen military ties to the United States, but to
mollify domestic critics they drove hard bargains on issues of jurisdiction, economic rights, and the choice of sites. Limited resources and Philippine recalcitrance compelled U.S. military officials to reevaluate the strategic importance of Philippine bases.

Decisions made late in the war committed the United States
to bases in and around Manila.. MacArthur received instructions
in March 1945, with his forces still fighting on Luzon, to construct bases for further attacks against Japanese targets. The di-
rective emphasized that strikes against Borneo and the Dutch
East Indies would originate from bases elsewhere, and that the
Philippine airfields would support operations against Japan itself.
The Joint Chiefs told MacArthur to deploy the bulk of his air
forces "initially in North Luzon and the central Luzon plains."
Three weeks later, the Joint Chiefs asked the general to determine sites for permanent installations. Under the Tydings resolution, the U.S. president could declare the Philippines indepen-
dent as soon as the Japanese were expelled, and Osmeña asked
Stimson, the secretary of war, for an early bases agreement in order to hasten independence and improve his political prospects.
Tydings, too, pushed for an agreement, warning Truman that,
"Filipino politics being what they are," obtaining a treaty would
only grow more difficult. MacArthur knew Philippine leaders
would object less to bases far from Manila, and he urged the Joint
Chiefs to choose a site in the Visayas, but the Pentagon's instructions ruled this out. Sites "should be considered not merely
as outposts, but as springboards" from which forces could be pro-
jected against potential enemies. They should require few improvements, and be large enough to stage "a force of five divisions and eighteen air groups simultaneously." Only the Luzon
facilities qualified.[24]

Philippine officials, anxious to sign an agreement, did not ask
the Americans to limit their choice of sites. Stimson complained

that the Navy wanted "options on practically all of the harbors in the Philippines," and that the Army wanted almost as much. On May 14, 1945, Osmeña and Truman signed a "preliminary agreement" fulfilling the conditions of the Tydings resolution and containing a list of sites to be used as a basis for treaty talks after independence. The Navy chose 14 major ports, and the Army selected 24 airfields. The agreement put the bases question aside for a year during the debate in the United States over the Philippine trade act and the Philippine presidential campaign.[25]

Roxas held strong views on the security of the weak, impoverished nation whose leadership he assumed in April 1946. Like most of his countrymen, he feared a repetition of the recent ordeal. The threat of a resurgent Japan or another Asian hegemon overshadowed the danger of American military expansion in the Pacific. In late 1946, when the Soviet Union opposed American moves in the United Nations to obtain "strategic trusteeships" in the central Pacific, the Philippine delegate, Romulo, considered defending the Pacific islanders' right to self-determination, but Roxas ordered him to support the United States. "It is more to our interest," he told Romulo, "to have the United States retain its present strategic role than [it is] to United States continental interests."[26]

In forming a position on the bases, Roxas consulted Philippine military and political leaders. He found a "small but growing" faction opposed to the bases. Some of these men sought to complete the separation between the two countries; others wanted to avoid the strains "a large body of alien troops, possessing special privileges of immunity to our laws and sometimes inconsiderate of our rights," would place on the most important bilateral relationship their country had. Many in this latter group believed a "succession of incidents" would spoil the special relationship between the two countries. Retail and manufacturing interests worried about economic competition from black-market goods imported by the military and sideline businesses operated by GIs.[27]

Roxas disagreed with many of these views, but his political weakness required him to take them into account. He told Elizalde that he considered bases "desirable from a Filipino viewpoint," and he listed advantages: enhanced security, a strong bilateral tie to the United States, and "material benefits, in the form of dollar expenditures and employment." Members of the antibases faction who feared a souring of U.S.-Philippine relations were overhasty, Roxas believed. When incidents threatened friendly relations, a new arrangement should be negotiated, but not before.

Nonetheless, the president recognized the danger alien troops posed, and he would not accept an agreement that might produce friction later on. Two issues particularly disturbed him. First, the United States would probably ask that its soldiers be exempted from Philippine criminal jurisdiction, "an arrangement which can be interpreted as extraterritoriality," the symbol of imperial contempt for Asian law. Second, the U.S. Army valued its large complex at Nichols Field and Fort McKinley in Manila. Aware of Manilans' resentment of the army presence, Roxas decided the installation had to be moved. To help obtain these concessions, he retained Breed, Abbott, and Morgan, a New York law firm whose litigator, Allan A. O'Gorman, had worked for the Tabacalera cigar monopoly.[28]

In the first round of negotiations in May 1946 in Washington, Roxas pushed the United States to give ground on the jurisdiction issue and to relinquish economic benefits from the bases. He opened talks with a generous promise of cooperation, then laid down two stipulations. He would not submit to extraterritoriality, or to the presence of foreign troops near populated centers. He then returned to Manila, leaving negotiations to the lawyers. Laying aside the location issue, the United States presented a draft agreement modeled on the current treaty with Britain regarding military bases. The Filipinos rejected it, stressing their chief objection to "full and exclusive extraterritorial jurisdiction over all offenses, wherever committed, by members of the United States armed forces" or civilian employees. The Filipinos asked the United States to assume liability for damages caused by military personnel, to obtain permission before letting third parties use the bases, and to forego mineral rights on base lands. The War Department insisted that retaining jurisdiction over off-duty troops was essential if the bases were to be useful. They proposed a clause limiting extraterritorial jurisdiction to offenses "punishable under the Articles of War," but the Filipino team's lawyers dismissed this change as cosmetic, since the articles included all types of crime. The State Department urged the Pentagon to yield the point. The British agreement "had not worked well in practice" and needed revision. A third draft permitted U.S. jurisdiction only over crimes committed within the base, and met Philippine demands on liability, third-party use, and mineral rights. It also subjected American personnel to Philippine income tax on outside earnings.[29]

To allow direct conversations between McNutt and Roxas, U.S. officials moved the talks to Manila in July, a decision they soon had reason to regret. In the rumor-filled capital, negotiations turned into a sequence of public denials, with McNutt and Roxas repudiating reports that the United States would rule the entire Manila port area and that an impasse had halted deliberations. As in Washington, Roxas let others do the talking. He worked out a Mutt-and-Jeff routine with his chief negotiator, Vice President Elpidio Quirino, with the latter playing the obstinate heavy while Roxas affected sympathy for McNutt's position. McNutt reluctantly accepted a complicated jurisdiction formula that gave the Philippines more authority over U.S. troops than other host nations then enjoyed.[30]

McNutt made no headway on the location issue. The Army firmly opposed surrendering its two best-equipped installations, McKinley and Nichols, feeling it could not afford to replace them. Roxas complained that the bases furnished a "constant source of friction with the civilian population and a convenient object of attack" by nationalists. Dean Acheson, who was now undersecretary of state, urged the War Department to give up its Manila installations, to no effect. To defuse the issue and allow Roxas time to campaign for the parity plebiscite, McNutt suspended talks, provoking another wave of rumors about deadlock. Roxas blasted Filipino critics and the Soviet newspaper *Pravda*, which assailed the "new forms of alien political, economic and military bondage" being tested in the Philippines.[31]

Animosities stirred by the parity issue disrupted the bases talks. The plebiscite campaign lasted from late 1946 until March 1947, running concurrently with the bases talks. Newspapers attacked Roxas for being soft on Americans. The debate put Mc-Nutt on the defensive, forcing him to answer charges of imperialism and ingratitude. The amendment won a low-turnout plebiscite by a four-to-one margin, but the vehemence of the elite's anti-American reaction surprised United States officials, leading them to reconsider their chances of obtaining treaty concessions.[32]

Officials in the State, War, and Navy departments acknowledged by November 1946 that Philippine opposition would prevent them from getting the agreement they wanted. Army Chief of Staff Dwight D. Eisenhower began privately to examine the idea of withdrawing U.S. forces from the islands. He asked MacArthur for his views. In the 1930s, Eisenhower had observed with skepticism MacArthur's efforts to prepare a Philippine defense. A decade later he had even stronger misgivings about the likelihood that the Philippines would become the "stable, well-organized and intently loyal ally" needed to make the bases worthwhile. "Such a development," he told MacArthur, "is beyond the expectation of logic." In the meantime, maintaining troops in the islands would keep the United States "constantly in hot water. Financially and militarily, the cost will probably outweigh any ensuing advantages." MacArthur agreed that bases would have little value without "a completely voluntary and untrammeled acceptance by that country of the resulting situation," but he advanced two objections to a pullout. Removing troops could "leave a vacuum which well might be filled by other and hostile influences." Moreover, Philippine bases comprised part of a global plan, and the Army should consider the damage the loss would do to overall strategy. Eisenhower agreed, but believed that if the Navy stayed, the Army could withdraw without upsetting global strategy.[33]

Domestic concerns strengthened Eisenhower's case for retrenchment. The Pentagon had scant money for military construction in the Philippines. Congress and President Truman's Council of Economic Advisers, concerned about domestic inflation, refused to allot additional money. During the last half of 1946, U.S. wholesale prices jumped by 24 percent, and high officials in the Truman administration agreed that spending could go no higher without dire results. Eisenhower, more than other service chiefs, worried about the gap between resources and commitments. The Navy and the Army Air Force clung to their ambitious plans and fought over the shrinking military bankroll.[34] The chief of naval operations, Admiral Chester W. Nimitz, offered no objection to the Army withdrawal, but affirmed that the Navy would remain in the western Pacific "indefinitely" and that it would need shore facilities for supplies, hospitals, and recreation. Eisenhower recommended a pullout to Robert Patterson, the secretary of war, stressing concern over the "consequences of prolonged and potentially recriminatory negotiations." He argued that surrendering the McKinley-Nichols complex rendered the Philippine bases inadequate for their assigned mission. Maintaining a naval force would avert a military vacuum and reassure the Filipinos, the Chinese, and other Far Eastern clients of continued support. The State War Navy Coordinating Committee instructed McNutt to offer Roxas a choice between a complete Army withdrawal and the maintenance of a token force. A week later, the War Department suspended Philippine construction contracts worth $42 million. Two days before Christmas 1946, Roxas accepted the token force but suggested that Army construction in the Manila area be canceled. The following month, Truman gave the order, and Army forces began to leave.[35]

Eisenhower's proposal has been called a bargaining ploy designed to weaken Roxas's resistance to the treaty, but this is not borne out by available evidence or by subsequent developments. Nothing in Roxas's papers indicates he knew of the memo until after the Army had decided to withdraw. The Army was not bluffing. By January 1948, Army forces had been reduced to under 5,000. The withdrawal did not reduce the importance of the Philippines in U.S. strategy. Eisenhower never suggested that the United States not acquire bases, only that under prevailing conditions they should not be used. The occupations of Japan and Korea reduced the need for Philippine bases and made it difficult for the Army to spare men. Withdrawal had scant support outside the Army, which had less enthusiasm for foreign bases than did either the Navy or the Army Air Force. The Navy had no intention of withdrawing, and when the secretary of the army suggested it again in 1948, both the Navy and the Air Force replied that they planned to keep Philippine bases as long as the United States remained a Pacific power.[36]

Negotiations stumbled on for another two months, during which Roxas lost an opportunity to settle an issue that would bedevil bilateral relations in the 1950s. The treaties and acts relating to independence contained conflicting interpretations of the actual ownership of the bases. Filipinos and the U.S. State Department regarded the bases as Philippine property on lease to the United States, but the War and Navy departments claimed title to the land. Roxas's lawyers wanted to settle the issue, but the Philippine president refused to prolong the talks with what he saw as an unnecessary controversy. He considered it unlikely that the United States would try to assert title to land in the Philippines. The final treaty left this issue unsettled, and only vaguely indicated the size and location of the reserved lands. The ambiguity provoked no controversy for several years, because the bases were only thinly staffed.[37]

Roxas was pleased with the final treaty. The United States had agreed to remove its troops from the Manila area, to relinquish economic rights to the bases, to grant the Philippines jurisdiction over off-base U.S. troops (except when offenses involved only Americans), and to accept civil liability for the actions of U.S. troops. The Philippines obtained more latitude in the area of criminal jurisdiction than other U.S. allies then enjoyed.

Roxas knew the value of factionalism in dealing with the United States. He presented himself as a mediator between the Truman administration and nationalist interests whose demands had to be mollified. Historians have speculated that United States officials privately threatened to cut off military aid or loans, but McNutt knew that such a move would be useless unless made openly (he wrote the coercive provisions of the trade act right into the law). Bullying Roxas would only weaken an avowedly pro-American leader against his domestic critics. Roxas assured U.S. officials that he was doing everything possible to advance their interests against stiff opposition, and McNutt believed him. Embassy cables repeatedly vouched for the president's loyalty.

Roxas also employed a tactic proven in the trade act deliberations: pitting cabinet departments against one another. In deliberations on the bases, the State Department frequently urged the
War and Navy departments to accommodate Philippine demands. Roxas seized advantages from factionalism in both governments by claiming to be the man in the middle, the man least
able to make concessions. The United States eventually had to
admit that the strategic value of Philippine bases more than com-
pensated for compromises on peripheral issues like jurisdiction.[38]

Signed by Roxas and McNutt in a public ceremony in March
1947, the treaty gave the United States the capacity to convert
the archipelago into a vast fortress, with immense central staging areas surrounded by rings of naval and fighter bases. The
United States acquired a 99-year lease on 23 base areas. The central Luzon complex (later named Clark Air Force Base) occupied a
tract larger than the District of Columbia. About half as large,
the naval installation at Subic Bay contained one of the world's
finest natural harbors. In addition, the Navy obtained rights to
most of the major ports outside of Manila Bay. Most of these
"bases" were hypothetical. Short on funds and facing no immediate threat, the United States left most of the reserved areas unoccupied and unimproved. The thinly garrisoned bases continued
to be inhabited mainly by their original occupants. The central
Luzon complex included the homeland of over 1,000 hunter-
gatherers of the Negrito tribe, and the area soon became a refuge
for Huk guerrillas. As Roxas was discovering, the bases treaty did
not translate into an unsparing U.S. commitment to Philippine
security and prosperity.[39]

To win election, Roxas had encouraged centripetal political
forces that troubled his presidency. In addition to a three-way
split in Congress—between Liberals, the Nacionalistas, and the
Democratic Alliance—that required him to solicit minority support for every bill, Roxas had to contend with divisions between
collaborators and loyalists, guerrilla factions and cacique rivals.
His Liberal party divided into warring blocs whose membership
and allegiances changed with each vote. Hoping to buy loyalty
with public disbursements, Roxas discovered to his dismay that

he could obtain no money, either locally or from the United States. He sought for two years to attain a national consensus that remained beyond his grasp. The government had "enemies on all sides," Laurel sneered. "The Osmeñistas refuse to support it. The Huks detest it. The collaborators are disappointed with it."[40]

As under Osmeña, the lack of patronage funds prevented the reimposition of patrimonial authority, whereas the government's weakness prevented it from raising funds. Mistrustful of Roxas and preoccupied with local feuds, the Philippine Congress refused to levy taxes. When the taxpayer does not trust his government, Senator Quentin Paredes explained, "you cannot expect him voluntarily to pay his taxes, much less to pay new taxes." Congress gave a blanket tax exemption to "new and necessary industries," a category that included all industries, even those which simply repackaged imported goods. The revenue bureau, meanwhile, proved incapable of collecting the few taxes in force. One study revealed that out of some 30,000 individuals and corporations who owed taxes on war profits, fewer than 300 paid.[41]

Roxas complained to Congress in June 1946 that he could raise only one-sixth of a "pared-to-the-bone budget." Two weeks after the independence ceremony in July, Roxas told the U.S. treasury secretary, John Snyder, that he would run out of operating funds in six months. McNutt warned the State Department that unless help came from outside, "employees and institutions, including the Philippine Army," would turn against the government.[42] Believing the United States would reward his cooperation in passing the trade act in June with a colossal reconstruction loan, Roxas was shocked to find even his smallest requests denied. The Export-Import Bank turned down applications for $400 million and $250 million in July. Roxas submitted a plea for a $75 million "emergency loan" through Congressman Bell, but the interdepartmental committee responsible for international lending still balked. Truman had just approved a $3.75 billion loan for Britain, and had received applications from China, Russia, Italy, and France. Treasury Department advisers pointed out that Congress would be reluctant to approve a Philippine loan so soon after passing the rehabilitation act. But the act disbursed money directly to individual claimants, not to the government. Some officials, particularly those from the Federal Reserve, felt additional borrowing would fuel domestic inflation by "increasing our deficit . . . to overcome a Philippine deficit."[43] U.S. officials discounted or ignored political barriers preventing the Roxas government from supporting itself. If the Philippines took "even preliminary steps in the direction of tax reform and the use of excess currency reserves," one Treasury Department official claimed, they could "tide themselves over." Several solutions were suggested: a central bank to free the country's currency reserve for government borrowing; emergency taxation to raise $50 million. Clayton explained that sale of army surplus property turned over by the Tydings Act could net as much as $500 million. The expectation that Roxas could marshal his government's feeble resources to collect $50 million in new taxes, or guard, much less distribute, $500 million worth of surplus goods revealed the dim understanding American officials had of the former colony's parlous state. Long association with Quezon's unchanging regime conditioned them to regard the Philippines as centralized and, in a tropical sort of way, disciplined. In 1946, these assumptions were very wrong.[44]

While McNutt lobbied in Washington for loans, Roxas attempted to bolster his leadership. First, the Philippine president tried but failed to turn popular resentment against Chinese retailers into support for his administration. In October 1946 he approved the Market Stalls Law, which confiscated the roadside *sari sari* shops of 15,000 Chinese proprietors. He ordered the Bureau of Commerce to organize Filipino retailers into provincial trading cooperatives to drive the Chinese out of business. Though popular, these policies did not rally the public behind the administration. In an increasingly familiar pattern, bankruptcy and corruption vitiated policy. The Bureau of Commerce had neither personnel nor funds with which to organize cooperatives. Bribery delayed the passage of enforcing legislation. Moreover, Roxas could not carry the anti-alien movement far without incurring the ire of the United States, whose officials reminded the president that investors disapproved of anti-alien restrictions. Even more importantly, his support for parity had cost the president his standing as an economic nationalist. According to one pundit, Roxas had "sacrificed the national dignity for an American loan."[45]

Roxas also attempted to expand patronage by enlarging public enterprises, but his plans again failed to rally support for the regime, and plunged the government into debt and corruption. Wartime confiscations augmented the government's commercial holdings, which included banks, textile mills, utilities, railroads, agricultural equipment plants, as well as processing and warehousing monopolies for corn, rice, sugar, coconut, and other commodities. Roxas expanded the public sector still further, venturing into fields—shipping, shipbuilding, and flour milling—that brought state enterprises into competition with private concerns. Independent boards supposedly ran the corporations, but were in fact an extension of the patrimonial government. Routine decisions traveled up the hierarchy to be settled by either the cabinet or the president, a procedure that maximized inefficiency and corruption. The commerce ministry promoted industrial policy with nationalist slogans that made foreign investors nervous. The head of one enterprise, under investigation for fraud, declared that "no matter how many millions of pesos may be sunk by the government into subsidizing the National Shipyards Project, it will pay incalculable dividends in . . . national consciousness and determination to exist as a free and independent nation." American businessmen cited state enterprises as the reason U.S. investors failed to respond to incentives like parity. "They're little things, like a hotel and flour mills," one said, "but they are big enough to make a businessman worry." Inefficient ventures drained the treasury, provided few jobs, and contributed to economic stagnation.[46]

The Roxas administration's failure to ignite the economy produced unrest. A year after liberation, according to McNutt, the islands had "virtually no economy." The small sums "being made in service trades catering to GIs" went to pay for imports, and as the Americans withdrew, unemployment increased. The country had almost no investment, no production, and nothing to export. Roxas had ambitious plans for reconstruction. He proposed a reconstruction lending agency, expanded air transport, communications, hydroelectric power, and "free ports" to make the Philippines a distribution and assembly center for all of Asia. His financial adviser, Miguel Cuaderno, planned a central bank to control currency and credit and to make the nation's gold reserve available for loans and deficit financing. Without revenue, however, these remained just plans. In the meantime, the absence of state-imposed restraint or avenues for legitimate enterprise encouraged corruption, which swelled dissent in Manila and the countryside. Throughout 1946, strikes led by Huk-affiliated unions paralyzed "practically every branch of industry." Hundreds of small businesses, capitalized with guerrilla pay, went bankrupt, adding their proprietors to the ranks of the unemployed.[47]

In the region north of Manila, conditions created by the weakness of central authority aroused the peasantry into armed rebellion. Without a local establishment of its own, the government vanished from areas where peasants challenged caciques. When the military, a rabble of former guerrilla units, failed to impose order, landowners hired mercenaries, "civil guards," to deal with tenants who objected to reimposition of rents. Disbanded Huk units regrouped in mid-1946 to protect themselves from this "landlord army." Fighting between civil guards and Huks induced Roxas to open a suppression campaign, but his undisciplined forces overreacted brutally against minor opposition, transforming scattered feuds into a civil war. Indiscriminate shelling drove thousands of uncommitted peasants into the Huk camp. Huk forces increased threefold in the five months after the Roxas government declared its "mailed fist" policy in September. According to its leader, Luis Taruc, the movement "was thriving on suppression."[48]

The strength of peasant groups led Roxas to try conciliation, but lacking power to enforce his policies, he only enraged landowners and fanned the rebellion. Osmeña had replaced the prewar 50-50 crop-share rule with laws allowing landlords to take only 40 percent. As unrest worsened in late 1946, Roxas went farther, granting peasants a 70 percent share and establishing an agricultural commission to hear complaints. Landlords simply defied the commission and the law and continued to take half of the harvest. Taruc, one of the seven Democratic Alliance congressmen expelled in May on vote fraud charges, remarked dryly that "a peasant who thinks he is going to get 70 percent in the central plains has another guess coming." Huk units reorganized as the *Hukbong Mapagpalaya ng Bayan* (HMB) under Taruc's leadership. They issued a modest list of demands: suspension of attacks by the army and enforcement of the government's own crop-sharing laws. "For most peasants," according to one Huk, "the struggle was in essence a fight for the consolidation" of gains already made. Moderate as these demands were, the government could not hope to meet them. Roxas could not impose reforms or end the conflict, according to one historian, "without having the armed guards of his factional supporters disarmed," an action guaranteed to alienate him "from the bulk of his supporters in the Liberal Party's higher echelons." Forced to decide between the dictates of his faction and the safety of the state, Roxas followed his faction.[49]

Despite Roxas's appeals and pessimistic newspaper reports, State Department officials refused to believe anything was seriously wrong with the Philippines. Observers in Washington and the Manila embassy expected to see the government revert to its prewar pattern, with Roxas as a new Quezon presiding over a strong central government and dispensing patronage to a contented elite. They regarded the Huks as louder and more persistent than the Sakdalistas of the 1930s, but no more threatening and, in some respects, healthy agents of reform. "With his prestige, his ability and his control of the Government," an Embassy official predicted in early 1947, "it would be easy" for Roxas to "become a second Quezon at the head of an overwhelming majority party." Richard Ely, who migrated from the Interior Department to head the State Department's Philippine Affairs Division, saw continued partisan infighting as evidence of the president's forbearance. Roxas was "an abler man than Quezon," he thought, and "much more tolerant of the opposition." Before resigning as ambassador in March 1947, McNutt predicted Roxas would serve a full eight years.[50]

Although stories of impending revolution reached American newspapers in the winter of 1946–47, State Department officials dismissed the Huk threat. The new ambassador, Emmett O'Neal, warned the secretary of state not to believe reports that the Roxas government faced a serious revolt. "No Embassy officer has heard from any Philippine or old-timer source even gossip of a concerted political revolution." The Huk movement, he said, was "essentially socio-economic not political," numbering "not more than 2,500." "I have been listening to this kind of story for some thirty years," said Ely. No real opposition could gain ground because "the people who do not like Roxas, of whom there are many, are too jealous and suspicious of each other to get an organized movement under way, and above all they lack a leader." Ely dismissed Taruc, who had "very little control over his people," and the Huks, who seemed "destined to break up into scattered outlaw bands." "Of course," he concluded, "some day the wolf may, and probably will come, but the time is not yet ripe."[51]

The State Department had less information about the Huks than did the United States Army. Army intelligence officers tried to decipher the complicated relationships between the Hukbalahap, the Communist party, political and labor organizations, and international communism. They reported that the Huks had ties to the Filipino-Chinese community and the Communist party in the United States, and that Huk leaders planned ultimately to "fight side by side with the Russians against the United States." Huk leaders, they believed, preferred legitimate political activity to violence, suggesting a political solution the Roxas government seemed unwilling to accept.[52]

Treasury officials also rejected the State Department's optimistic view of the regime's future. Snyder's advisers had warned in July 1946 that only immediate steps could avert a bankruptcy that would be costly and embarrassing for the United States. Treasury officials devised a plan to make a Philippine loan acceptable to Congress. In exchange for a $75 million loan, Roxas would agree to allow a joint Philippine-American commission to prepare a financial and development plan. Clayton worried about nationalism, but agreed with Treasury officials that Congress would like the idea, and that it would hold down future Philippine demands.[53]

State and Treasury department officials strongly disagreed over whether the commission ought to recommend borrowing against the currency reserve. The Philippines could obtain $100 to $200 million from the reserve, but it would entail establishing a central bank, and possibly imposing exchange controls or devaluing the peso. The United States would have to relinquish its power to regulate the rate of exchange, authority specifically reserved by the trade act. With the power to set exchange rates, Roxas could manipulate foreign trade and profoundly affect domestic markets and the cost of living. Clayton and George Luthringer, a former Interior Department official now with the State Department, warned that allowing the Filipinos to tamper with their currency would invite disaster. Snyder replied that the United States could enforce sound policies by disbursing the $75 million loan slowly and making disbursements contingent on compliance with the joint commission's recommendations.[54]

Comprised largely of Treasury officials, the Joint Philippine-American Finance Commission received a broad mandate to recommend fiscal, monetary, and development policies. Reporting in the spring of 1947, it optimistically appraised the prospects for economic expansion with the help of extensive state regulation. "Economically," its chairman told Truman, "the Philippines is the brightest spot in the Orient, one of the few countries in the world that is not bankrupt and dollar hungry." From the liberation to 1946, the United States spent $500 million in the local economy, and it expected to disburse $900 million more by 1950 in personal-damage payments and veterans' benefits. But though Filipinos were relatively well-off, their government was destitute. "Wealthy politicos," the chairman reported, were thwarting new taxes and "defrauding the government in large amounts." The Philippine government needed to capture more of this money by increasing corporate taxes and taxes on imports, luxuries, inheritance, and real property, as well as by enforcing existing laws. The commission rejected austerity, recommending that government services be expanded, staffs enlarged, and salaries raised.[55]

The commission advocated expanding government control of the economy, allowing it to marshal capital for national development through the use of import substitution. To conserve dollars for development projects, it recommended a pilot program of import licenses on luxuries and goods for which locally produced substitutes could be found. Merely taxing nonessential imports, it explained, would be ineffective. European experience revealed that the "imposition of direct import controls is a certain means of controlling the volume and composition of imports." Cautiously, the panel also opened the door to exchange controls by approving Cuaderno's plan for a central bank that would free the country's currency reserve for government borrowing. If implemented, the recommendations would radically enlarge the government's ability to manipulate investment and accumulate capital.[56]

The commission's development plans involved purchasing heavy capital equipment from the United States. In an appendix to the report, Thomas Hibben of the Commerce Department sketched a five-year plan calling for improvements in public infrastructure, electric power, transport, and communications. Three-quarters of the estimated $1 billion cost would go for materials and equipment, most of it from the United States. As Romulo observed, state-sponsored industrialization would not diminish need for U.S. imports, but only "alter the complexion of our imports." Instead of hair oil and canned peaches, the Philippines would import dynamos. A key component of Hibben's plan, and of Roxas's ambitions, was hydroelectric power. Throughout 1947, Westinghouse engineers surveyed the islands and prepared plans for 32 hydroelectric dams, three of which—Ambuklao, Lumot, and Maria Cristina—might be undertaken within five years. The plans included designs for industries, and chemical and fertilizer plants, to be constructed near the dams. The project cost $90 million. Under the Roxas administration's plan, drawn up by the Beyster Corporation, a Detroit engineering firm, these vast sums would come from Japanese reparations, politically the simplest of fund-raising schemes. Gathering funds through import substitution, as the joint commission suggested, involved greater political difficulties.[57]

Powerful Philippine agricultural and trading interests resisted import controls. The Manila *Chronicle*, voice of the Lopez family, richest of the sugar dynasties, labeled them a "festering source of corruption" designed to enrich "a handful of individuals who, according to all moral standards and legal requirements, should be behind bars." The Manila American Chamber of Commerce joined the protest, calling the report "a whopper." It did not share the panel's optimism regarding the government's ability to raise taxes, and it predicted that controls would "take the people's money away from them [to] finance grandiose schemes of development."[58]

The State Department reluctantly conceded the necessity of import controls. Department officials opposed barriers to trade, particularly barriers as susceptible to discriminatory use as licensing. They supported the report out of concern for the government's solvency, not out of enthusiasm for Hibben's plan. Clayton remained sure that the Philippines would soon resolve its financial problems, an attitude that provoked one subordinate to wonder if Clayton read reports from the field. Over the next three years, the department kept a close eye on Philippine tax policies, but it could not force Roxas to comply with the commission's recommendations. Withholding loans would only accelerate a fiscal crisis the United States was trying to avoid. Philippine leaders limited the Truman administration's options by refusing to raise taxes, even at the risk of destroying their own state. The United States could either watch Roxas's government self-destruct, or allow it to impose a statist, protectionist trade regime.[59]

The Joint Finance Commission's recommendations violated both the multilateralist principles the State Department was advocating in international forums and the bilateralist policies of the Philippine Trade Act. The commission acknowledged that its import control plan contradicted the intent of the International Trade Organization charter, the centerpiece of the State Department's effort to liberalize world trade. The violation compounded the transgressions of the 1946 trade act, which embarrassed U.S. negotiators at the International Trade Organization conference in December 1947. The trade act had repudiated multilateralist policies to shelter the Philippines within a bilateral relationship; the commission's recommendations contradicted the trade act to shelter the Philippines from the bilateral relationship. Import licensing was designed to protect infant Philippine industries from the damaging effects of unrestricted U.S. imports. It would hurt American consumer-goods manufacturers and trading firms. The trade act had assured peso-dollar convertibility at a rate of two to one, but the proposed central bank could evade currency restrictions by taxing or licensing exchange. Less than a year after the act's passage, the United States was abandoning safeguards for American investors and traders in order to allow Filipinos to accumulate capital and protect local industry.[60]

Roxas disliked the report, and implemented its recommendations selectively. Luxury and inheritance taxes targeted wealthy landowners, his most loyal constituency. So that the loan would be released before the end of 1947, he agreed to send a tax bill to Congress, knowing it would go no further. He adopted portions of the report that promised political dividends, seizing upon the rich patronage possibilities of import licensing. Beginning in early 1948, the government used licensing to take business from American, Chinese, and Spanish importing firms and place it in the hands of Filipinos. As an unfortunate side effect, it drove up the price of imports and the cost of living, increased unemployment, and created yet another uncontrolled economic sector, a class of Philippine importers too rich and too politically connected to tax. Roxas held up development plans in anticipation of Japanese reparations. Given the government's feeble control over the economy, the Beyster and Hibben plans were, according to one analyst, "little more than ambitious statements of Philippine aspirations."[61]

When Federal Reserve officials helped Cuaderno draft a central bank bill in early 1948, they discovered that Roxas had "very definite ideas" on how the bank should be managed. A United Nations commission observed that the proposed bank had broad powers "not yet common for central banks to possess" and "novel features" that would allow it to restrict credit to particular economic sectors, limit imports of certain commodities, and expand currency irrespective of foreign-exchange holdings. Cabinet members would serve on the monetary board, assuring that the bank would be used to satisfy the regime's clients.[62]

Roxas's broad new economic powers did nothing to fill his immediate need for funds and patronage in 1947 and 1948. Rather than adopt the commission's tax plan, the government depended on nonrenewable sources for money—like the sale of captured Japanese and surplus American property—that generated more graft than revenue. Under the rehabilitation act, the United States had turned over surplus military stores in September 1946, a hoard the Philippine government had little ability to dispose of, or even protect. Instead of the $500 million Clayton had predicted, the government realized $37 million. An investigation later revealed that cabinet officials and the president's closest aides had joined in the looting.[63]

By early 1948, the effort of appeasing the elite's various factions, courting the Americans, and fighting the Huks strained Roxas's optimism and his health. Instead of the future "in America's glistening wake" he had promised at his inauguration, he forecast a long, twilight struggle against the "lawlessness and widespread criminality" that "prevailed in practically every province and sector of the country." In March, he outlawed the HMB. Amid such dark times, the cold war afforded a small consolation. In its newly found resolve to contain communism and the Soviet Union, Roxas hoped, the United States might find the will to stop the Huks. The following month, he told an audience at Clark Air Force Base that "Communist fifth columns" were at work all over the world. The United States, he said, would soon have to "take a stand." During the speech the president grew pale, and seven hours later he succumbed to a stroke.[64]

With his passing, U.S. officials surrendered their hopes for a new Quezonian commonwealth and began to regard Philippine developments warily. The new president, Quirino, seemed even less able, and State Department officials worried that he was no match for the problems—debt, corruption, rebellion—stalking the government. Roxas was correct in guessing that only global events would prod the United States to act. Truman's officials poorly understood the imperatives that set the Philippine government on a self-destructive course, and overestimated their ability to guide Philippine policies. They relinquished control of economic instruments—currency policy, import controls—that could strengthen or bankrupt their client regime, in the mistaken belief that they could compel adherence to their recommendations. Filipinos recognized that the U.S. stake in the Philippines diminished American leverage. If anything, Roxas overestimated the lengths to which the United States would go to shore up his failing government.

In the two years of his administration, Roxas presided over his country's political independence and enhanced his government's ability to set economic policies independent of the United States. He failed, however, to control the contentiousness or the avarice of the elite. He was unable to establish the personal dominance the patrimonial state required to function smoothly. The government remained captive to its clients, who seized economic regulatory mechanisms for their own use. Quirino inherited a government just as weak and factionalized, but with even more potent instruments of economic control.

THREE

Saving the Patrimonial State

Had the United States not intervened, patrimonial democracy might have ended in the Philippines in 1951, a victim of what Benedict Anderson has called "the discrepancy between state power and cacique ambitions under conditions of popular suffrage and acute class antagonism." In March 1948, Elpidio Quirino inherited a fatally flawed state. Forced to satisfy both financial interests and the electoral machines, he had no power to address structural problems, the maldistribution of land and wealth that fueled insurrection and endangered the regime. U.S. officials saw these flaws, but like Quirino, they worked from crisis to crisis. Strategic imperatives precluded thorough reforms that might prove destabilizing. The Truman administration, according to Dean Acheson, ranked "insurance of domestic tranquillity and the provision for the common defense" ahead of "promotion of the general welfare." By rescuing the Philippine government from its own failings, the United States assured that cacique democracy and its problems would survive.[1]

To U.S. officials, Quirino appeared to be no match for the colossal problems left by his predecessor. A lawyer from the Ilocos who married into a landowning Chinese-mestizo clan, he sat in the prewar Senate but avoided service in the occupation regime, making himself a safe if undistinguished choice for the vice presidency. His stout body suffered from a raft of ailments, including an enlarged heart and edema in both legs. One kidney had stones, the other had failed completely. He lacked the statesmanlike polish of Quezon, or even of Roxas, and American officials often mistook his provinciality for simplemindedness. Meeting Walter Lippmann at a Washington party in 1947, Quirino inquired if he was "still in the writing business." Truman's advisers dismissed him as "amenable to flattery, sensitive to criticism," and "lukewarm toward the U.S." But during the 1947 bases talks, they were given a foretaste of the stubborn will that would help him weather the republic's gravest crises. The new president set about accumulating power with a guile and energy his predecessors had lacked, but the regime he inherited was too fundamentally unsound, too riven with factionalism and corruption to be saved without outside help.[2]

The Liberals' congressional majority had by 1948 divided into warring blocs, with names like Miraflor and Entente Cordiale, that held legislation hostage to the personal demands of congressmen. Senator Alyo Mabanag complained that the new president had "promised to give the minority members of Congress a share of the pork barrel funds. He has failed to comply with his promise. All of which convinces me Quirino is not a leader. He is a politician and nothing else." Disclosures of the Roxas regime's corruption—millions pilfered from surplus property stores, phony land-reform schemes, sales of visas to Chinese refugees—dogged the new administration. Quirino launched investigations and threatened to purge corrupt officials, but he encountered resistance from his own party. The Senate president, Jose Avelino, advised, "If you cannot permit abuses you must at least tolerate them. What are we in power for?"[3]

Quirino tried compromising with the regime's armed and political opposition. He apportioned patronage to minority factions and offered a cabinet post to the opposition leader, Jose P. Laurel, who had been acquitted of collaboration. He reseated expelled congressional members of the Democratic Alliance and offered amnesty to Huk units that agreed to disarm. Luis Taruc received a "hero's welcome" at Malacañan. But the compromises disintegrated. Laurel declined the offer, provoking Quirino to deny having made it. Opposition congressmen carped about their meager share of the patronage. Clashes between Huks and undisciplined troops at disarming stations erupted into full-scale fighting. In September 1948, Huk units engaged Philippine troops in gun battles near the gates of Clark Air Force Base. Taruc and other Alliance leaders returned to central Luzon to lead their troops against the government.[4]

Like his predecessors, Quirino failed to coax tax increases from Congress. Despite high prices for exports, the revenue bureau collected only 6 percent of the national income, whereas the United States (a low-tax country) collected 24 percent. Quirino refused to tax business and landed interests that supported the Liberal party. He assailed Congress with an assortment of paltry taxes, one on diplomas, another on bachelors. Congress ignored the revenue shortage and criticized the administration's "tax madness." By mid-1948, the government had exhausted its stocks of captured and surplus property and the $75 million American loan. Quirino applied for World Bank loans, and briefly considered demanding ransom for Japanese prisoners of war. The Huk rebellion became a serious drain on the treasury (consuming a quarter of the budget in 1948), but as the CIA noted, "inefficient tax collecting machinery, an inadequate tax structure," and congressional pork barrel spending were to blame for the growing deficit.[5]

Quirino could get no military or financial aid from the United States. The Truman administration remained apprehensive about the inflationary effect of foreign lending, and denied Quirino's loan requests. In June 1948, the Defense Department declined a request for $9 million in military aid. Military advisers explained that the United States had to resist Soviet imperialism at focal points, and since "the Philippines is not one of these focal points," it would not waste resources to fight Huks. The Truman Doctrine pledged the United States to support friendly regimes resisting subversion, but the National Security Council determined that Europe and Japan had first claim on scarce funds. Quirino disparaged the administration's emphasis on Europe, a continent he considered "used up, an economic liability" compared to the "virgin region" of Asia. He was even more disturbed to learn that the United States intended to cancel Japanese reparations.[6]

Loss of the anticipated reparations windfall was a serious blow. The Philippine leadership's hopes for industrial development had fixed on reparations. Truman's reparations administrator, Edwin W. Pauley, had told Filipinos in April 1946 that a large portion of Japan's industrial capacity would be moved to the Philippines. Roxas had based his plans on Pauley's statement, assuming that steel mills and even aircraft plants would be transferred from Japan. Until mid-1947, the United States had advocated removing Japanese plants; but as the cold war intensified and budgets dwindled, State and Defense officials argued that Japanese industry should be rehabilitated. "There is a huge pressure emanating from Japan and from certain circles in the United States against taking reparations from Japan," a lobbyist for the Philippine government, Julius Edelstein, reported. "These circles would like to see Japan built up to its pre-war status as a bulwark against Russia. It is the cheapest way of discharging the occupational costs of the United States." Philippine officials opposed "any attempt to build up Japan economically and militarily," but by mid-1948 they had lost hope for a reparations bailout. Elizalde, Quirino's ambassador to Washington, was characteristically glum. "All we can do," he shrugged, "is wait until the Big Powers settle first the European problem and then later decide to tackle the problems of the Pacific, where it is quite obvious that a cold war similar to that of Europe is beginning to develop."[7]

Philippine leaders feared global tensions would complicate their domestic troubles. They believed the Huks received aid from a Far Eastern Comintern said to be operating out of the Soviet Embassy in Bangkok. Military officials assured the United States embassy that Soviet submarines had been delivering supplies. In the fall of 1948, as the Berlin crisis deepened and communist armies overran Shanghai, thousands of Chinese refugees fled to Manila, unchecked by the corrupt immigration bureau. From Washington, Elizalde and Romulo warned of world war. Fearing the crisis would dry up U.S. support, Quirino launched a suppression campaign in central Luzon, telling American officials he would "clean up the Huk rebellion before the outbreak of war in Germany." Behind his resolve lay anxiety about the administration's precarious fiscal state.[8]

The president declared a policy of "total economic mobilization" in late 1948 to check communism by promoting industrial development and employment. He established an import control board, and on January 3, 1949, the central bank opened for business and lent 115 million pesos to the government. Through "total mobilization," Quirino hoped to raise revenue and dispense enough favors to unite the elite behind his leadership. Its key element was a licensing program that would decrease imports by $200 million a year. By mid-1949, the licensing board was restricting virtually all consumer goods entering the country. Industrialists like Salvador Araneta and the Elizalde brothers advocated controls as a way to escape dependency on agriculture and promote industry, but the program's chief aim was political. Licensing would allow Quirino to determine who would profit from artificial shortages and inflation, thereby increasing the administration's political leverage.[9]

The licensing program ignited disputes among businessmen in both the Philippines and the United States. Planters objected to the growing influence of manufacturers. Inflation diminished the value of agricultural export proceeds, and the sugar bloc denounced controls as a source of corruption and a hardship for ordinary consumers. Nacionalistas complained that controls were "a source of funds for [Liberal] congressmen who brazenly engaged in selling import quotas and in influence peddling at the import control office." Industrialists cloaked their motives in nationalist slogans, but their interest was in serving as both agent and gatekeeper for foreign firms entering the protected market. The Elizaldes represented Westinghouse and other manufacturers who could be induced to build plants to produce for a sheltered market. United States companies with joint-venture arrangements favored controls, as did General Electric and Allis Chalmers, who had contracts for hydroelectric development. But American manufacturers of consumer goods reacted angrily to the loss of $200 million in business. Bicycle and biscuit makers, apple growers and shippers assailed the U.S. State and Commerce departments demanding retaliation.[10]

In the United States, initially favorable official reaction to the control program had turned to concern by mid-1949. Although the program contradicted policies aimed at liberalizing trade, State Department officials considered diversification, particularly into light industry, essential to the long-term economic health of the Philippines. They hoped controls would increase employment and revenue by channeling money into industrial development. U.S. support countered objections from the sugar bloc and enabled Quirino to start the program. The State Department considered it "soundly conceived" and instructed the embassy to inform businessmen that it supported controls and would not "seek any general or specific modifications." The embassy soon reported, however, that the government was discriminating against American and Chinese importers and granting windfall profits to favored clients. The licensing program touched off a patrimonial feeding frenzy, as *rentier* tycoons and officeholders sought to swap political capital for licenses. Quirino cronies made fortunes, the largest belonging to the president's brother, Antonio, who built a business empire through access to the control board. What concerned the new U.S. ambassador, Myron Cowen, most was that the government was unable to capture any of the profits as revenue. It lost control of its regulatory instruments to its own clients. The Philippines lacked enough honest officials to run a managed currency or import controls, an embassy official warned. "I think the ambassador shares my misgivings, but he asks, 'Can we turn back?' "[11]

Import controls provided ample openings for political and economic gain. Controls consisted of a list of restricted items that changed constantly to maximize opportunities for the sale of influence and insider information. "Take the case of bond paper," Congressman Arturo Tolentino explained. "This was not under control before, but when the president included it in his latest order, the price on the open market immediately jumped up, giving undue profit to those now having stocks of this article." The State Department pressed Quirino to make fewer changes in the list and to notify traders in advance to prevent sudden price fluctuations, but for the politicians who ran the control board, fluctuations were the whole object. They had little to offer their financial patrons except licenses and advance knowledge of shortages and price changes.[12]

The 1949 presidential campaign placed Quirino under pressure to repay political patrons out of the government's dwindling fund of contracts and patronage. Import licenses—which could be dispensed directly and resold, or used to create market corners for clients in manufacturing and trade—filled the gap. Following this pattern, deficits and overt graft increased in every subsequent presidential election year. Analysts attribute Philippine corruption to local conditions: linguistic barriers, which induce voters to seek political gains as individual rewards, or Filipino values that esteem personal obligations (*utang na loob*) above notions of public trust. But in many postcolonial states, corruption served as a conservative response to uncontrolled and potentially violent democratic pressures. Third World leaders established themselves as brokers who secured stability and financial advantage for the business elite, while passing a portion of the proceeds to the electorate. Corruption helped resolve or postpone conflict, and allowed disgruntled peasants to feel connected to the political process.[13]

In newly independent regimes, such arrangements usually lasted only as long as the disposable rewards. Intrinsically shortsighted, political machines resorted to deficits and other expedients that destroyed popular and elite support and usually ended in military coups. By mid-1949, Quirino's efforts to win financial support by dispensing import licenses had undermined his popular support. The chief U.S. military adviser warned that "the wise and necessary but, nevertheless, unpopular decision to exercise import control" helped create a "hazardous situation" in which the regime's armed opponents could capitalize on public hostility.[14]

Poorly administered controls added to the State Department's list of complaints. Few of Quirino's actions aroused more anger in Washington than his proposal for a Pacific Pact in March 1949. Unable to obtain additional military aid, he attempted to force Truman's hand by establishing an Asian anticommunist alliance and inviting the United States to join. Threatened and bankrupt regimes in South Korea and Nationalist China took up the idea, as did Truman's Republican critics in Congress. To the State Department's distress, countries throughout the region assumed Quirino was acting on secret orders from Washington. Moscow and Beijing condemned the pact as a disguise for aggression. "Nobody will believe the United States had nothing to do with it," Secretary of State Acheson groaned. The proposal frustrated the secretary's efforts to keep congressional attention fixed on Europe and ply a middle course in China by avoiding additional commitments to the discredited Chiang Kai-shek. Acheson warned Romulo, the Philippines' U.N. delegate, to muzzle his president, but Quirino persisted. The June "summit" with Chiang focused press attention on the Philippine president at the height of his reelection campaign. State Department officials saw Quirino's diplomatic efforts as inept and self-glorifying, an impression reinforced by Quirino's arrival in Washington in August on what *Newsweek* called "an odyssey for dollars and votes."[15]

Acheson allowed Quirino the political benefits of a preelection state visit in return for a chance to settle disturbing issues. Meeting at Blair House, Truman and Acheson told Quirino of their concern about Philippine finances and the insurgency in central Luzon. Truman said that he wanted to offer more aid and reinforce Clark Field, but felt that unless matters improved he would be endangering troops and wasting money. Quirino replied that it was Truman's duty to support the Philippines. He laid out a list of claims, including a few never heard before. If the United States would send military aid, he smiled, the Huks would soon be eradicated. Acheson was astonished at this display of arrogance. The following day, Quirino peddled his Pacific Pact at a meeting of Asian diplomats and before Congress.[16]

Assistant Secretary of State W. Walton Butterworth marveled at Quirino's complacent assurance "that all was well in the Philippine Islands." Department officials acutely felt the urgency of the situation. A few days before Quirino's visit, the World Bank had notified Truman that high deficits and slow capital accumulation added up to an impending crisis in the Philippines. The new director of the State Department's Philippine branch, John F. Melby, saw the crisis and the Huk problem as more dangerous than his predecessors had recognized. Melby had witnessed the collapse of Chiang's government on the Asian mainland and saw in Quirino similar habits of denial and obstructionism. "Quirino does not seem to understand most problems he is facing," he observed, "nor does he appear to have much intention of doing much about those he does understand." As communist troops drove the Nationalists from the mainland in the summer of 1949, the Defense Department and the CIA reevaluated the Huk threat, concluding that the Huks received Chinese and Soviet support and aimed to overthrow the government and deny bases to the United States. The economic crisis, analysts agreed, gave the Huks a chance at success.[17]

The loss of China magnified the importance of bases in the Philippines. In May, Defense officials informed Truman that since the United States faced "the prospect of strategic impotence on the continent of Asia," military capabilities in the region depended on air and sea power in the Philippines. To abandon bases there would "penalize us one advance move while presenting to a potential enemy a move in our direction." Truman's new secretary of defense, Louis Johnson, explained that without Philippine installations, the United States could not hold Japan or Southeast Asia. Garrisons remained small, but the Thirteenth Air Force would soon move from Japan to Clark Air Force Base, where it would begin operations to support French troops in Indochina. Johnson declared that "the strategic importance of the Philippines is not open to question."[18]

Shortly after Quirino's visit, the State and Defense departments determined to rescue the Philippines as part of an effort to reverse deteriorating conditions in Southeast Asia. Revolutionary nationalism in Malaysia, Indonesia, and Indochina threatened dollar earnings and raw materials supplies of struggling economies in Europe and Japan. Policy makers feared that the loss of Southeast Asia would isolate Australia and create conditions for reversals in the Middle East. Regional specialist William Lacy argued that the region's importance "economically, politically, and strategically is so great that there can be no question of our making a fight to hold it." State Department planners decided to begin by expanding aid programs and working toward a regional alliance. The Philippines was part of the solution—as a transit point for aid and as an advocate in regional forums—but it was also part of the problem. In mid-1949, Acheson thought the Philippines looked ready to collapse. He asked Melby to plan a large-scale aid program, and in early September, Truman agreed to support it.[19]

The violent denouement of the November 1949 election accelerated the decline of Quirino's government. In October, the president had fought off a congressional move for impeachment and lashed out at his two opponents, Laurel and Avelino. The election took fraud and intimidation to a new level. Private armies battled at polling stations. An investigation showed that over a fifth of the ballots were fraudulent. Troops suppressed an election-day uprising in Laurel's home province. The election became the Huks' best recruiting device. "The unsavory character of that election did much to convince the barrio people that they could hope for nothing from the politicians," Taruc recalled. "And so they gave their support to the Huks."[20]

Treasury Secretary Snyder flew to Manila in November to assess the situation in the Philippines. The government's heavy borrowing against the exchange reserve made him uneasy. Import controls were useless without a tax on profits. Controls and deficit spending fueled inflation and capital flight. The Philippines were hemorrhaging money at a rate of $4 million a day. Three years earlier, Snyder had assured the State Department that exchange controls would never be needed. He now conceded they would. Exchange restrictions contradicted the trade act (requiring Truman's consent) and provoked complaints from American business. Even firms that liked import controls detested restrictions on exchange, which prevented repatriation of profits. Worse yet, Philippine controls were "unusually stringent." No one could hold dollars for longer than it took to exchange them. Foreign firms could repatriate only 10 percent of their profits. Acheson agreed to controls as a temporary, emergency measure if Quirino "promptly" submitted a plan for increasing revenue. Once again, Philippine bankruptcy forced the United States to repudiate its policies and grant more latitude.[21]

Exchange licensing gave Quirino's cronies an even more powerful instrument for plundering the economy. By small signs and large, the public manifested fear that controls would be mismanaged. Silver coins disappeared. A black market in dollars sprang up. Several people went to jail for illegal possession of dollars. December 1949 marked the onset of a full-fledged economic crisis. The government had no money in reserve and no power to tax. The debt reached 701 million pesos, larger than the annual budget. Acheson never received a revenue plan from Quirino, but that was the least of his worries. Intelligence reports showed that Quirino would soon be unable to meet the Army payroll, and Huk forces were gathering strength.[22]

In mid-January 1950, the political commissar of the Philippine Communist party, Jose Lava, persuaded the Huk leadership that it faced a "revolutionary situation." Reviewing the financial position of the government, he argued that increased military pressure would cause the Quirino administration to disintegrate. Disaffection with corruption and the fraudulent election would cause demoralized politicians and army units to side with the Huks. The only uncertain contingency, he found, was the possibility of massive intervention by the United States, a chance he considered remote. The United States, he figured, would not waste money on Quirino, whose corruption disqualified him as "an effective instrument of imperialist domination," and a recession predicted by Soviet economist Evgenii Varga would soon leave the United States with no money to spare.[23]

Huk units opened their final offensive in March 1950 with simultaneous attacks on 17 towns. Before the military could counterattack, the Huks struck again, overrunning several army garrisons and sacking a provincial treasury. Huk propagandists showered Manila with leaflets, one tossing his broadsides from the windows of city hall. The news shook observers from Malacañan to the Pentagon. Defense Secretary Johnson warned Truman that without "immediate constructive steps toward stability, probably requiring U.S. assistance," the Huks might seize power.[24]

Lava misjudged the readiness of the United States to save Quirino. Melby had produced a plan in late 1949 to commit $750 million to shore up the regime. He saw the problem as one of governmental weakness rather than Huk strength. Reviewing aid programs and controls, he found existing policies adequate except for their misuse by Quirino and his cronies. "Granting the fact that the Filipinos are only one generation out of the tree tops," he advised, their behavior "does not warrant the belief that any program would secure the desired objectives without some form of supervision and control." Melby saw Quirino as an obstacle that might be worked around if, in return for an aid bailout, he agreed to place key economic levers in American hands. The approach required delicacy because it involved "a partial derogation of Philippine sovereignty," but unless the United States could impose "direct, if camouflaged" supervision, the Philippines would be the next China. His superiors agreed. In January 1950, Acheson approved plans for an aid mission.[25]

Acheson concurred with Melby's emphasis on economic rather than military solutions, which accorded with his interpretation of China's lessons. He had no illusions that Quirino would step aside and allow American advisers to run the economy. The obstacle to "solution of the Philippine problem is Quirino himself," he told Truman. The China debacle taught "that if we are confronted by an inadequate vehicle it should be discarded in favor of a more propitious one." Convinced that the appearance of United States support had aided Quirino's reelection, he believed a barrage of criticism might weaken or remove him. Quirino visited Washington again in February to renew his requests for aid. He was greeted sternly and forced to accept an official economic mission. The time had come, according to one State Department official, for "a showdown."[26]

Acheson saw the Philippine problem as grave. At a Washington cocktail party, he conducted Lippmann, Martin Agronsky, and other press figures on a tour of the troubled "Western perimeter" from Berlin through Greece, Iran, and Indochina to Korea. Restoring the West's position along this line, he said, would require a long, tough battle. He ranked the Philippines as the weakest of all the perimeter's weak links. Citing a "shocking deterioration," with the president cowering in his palace and Huk units raiding the capital's outskirts, he warned of "total collapse." Quirino was the problem. In a memo to Truman, Acheson hinted darkly at "other steps" should the mission fail to weaken the president's influence.[27]

Quirino could handle himself in a showdown. He deflected the rebuke implied by the United States mission, telling the press it would be a joint panel and had been his idea. As if to prove it, he appointed a panel—the Philippine Council on United States Aid (PHILCUSA)—to prepare a long-range industrialization plan in anticipation of a large aid package. Acheson fumed at this latest deception, but Melby and the assistant secretary of state, W. Walton Butterworth, conceded that the mission would need Philippine support. Quirino chose panelists the State Department considered cooperative: Cuaderno; Pio Pedrosa, the finance minister; and presidential adviser Jose Yulo. He stepped up the anti-Huk campaign and reorganized the armed forces in line with suggestions from American advisers. The president also appeased U.S. officials by redesigning the Pacific Pact. In June, Romulo hosted a conference of delegates from Indonesia, Thailand, Ceylon, Pakistan, India, and Australia to discuss a cultural and economic union much more to Acheson's liking. Gradually, the State Department relaxed its confrontational posture and sought Philippine help in making the aid mission a success.[28]

The mission that took shape in June 1950 reflected the State Department's emphasis on fiscal reform and industrial development. Acheson chose a banker and former Treasury official, Daniel Bell, to head the mission. Johnson insisted on including a military mission headed by a former aide to MacArthur, Richard Marshall. The mission included a World Bank official, a college president, and an electric utility executive, supported by a staff from the State, Treasury, Labor, Commerce, and Agriculture departments, and the Federal Reserve. Although the Philippine economy was agricultural, specialists in finance and industry comprised most of the mission.[29]

The mission acquired a new urgency when North Korean troops attacked South Korea on June 25. Acheson interpreted the attack as "the spearhead of a drive made by the whole communist control group on the entire power position of the West." The administration moved to commit troops to Korea and to reinforce allies along the Asian rim. It augmented forces in the Philippines, accelerated aid to Indochina, and stationed naval units in the Taiwan Straits. Philippine bases supported these operations. State Department officials abandoned plans to remove Quirino, reconciling themselves to strengthening and attempting to guide his leadership. The Filipinos acted like allies. At Romulo's urging, Quirino sent 5,000 troops to Korea. Dispatched on June 27, 1950, the Bell mission became part of the larger effort to shore up the U.S. strategic position in Asia.[30]

Arriving in Manila in August, the commission discovered that the Philippines faced "nothing less than financial collapse in a period of exceptionally high income." Bell was stunned by the government's finances. "In a period of rapidly expanding national income, when the collection of taxes should involve little economic difficulty and when large revenues are essential to maintain economic stability," he found, "the government has constantly taken too small a portion of the gross national product in taxes." Landed and business classes paid almost nothing. The government could no longer borrow. It had less than two million pesos on hand and subsisted on daily tax remittances. The deficit fueled inflation, reinforcing inequities caused by mismanagement and excessive profit-taking.[31]

The 1946 trade act had succeeded in increasing export income, but had failed to distribute it equitably, diversify the economy, or increase government revenue. Privileged access to the American market allowed the Philippines to escape the "Prebisch effect," a deterioration in terms of trade that afflicted Latin American economies in the 1940s and 1950s. Although the decline of agricultural export prices relative to the price of manufactured imports may have been a cause of underdevelopment and dependency in parts of the Third World, this was not the case in the Philippines. In fact, the unit value of Philippine exports increased relative to imports in the late 1940s (and continued to do so for most of the 1950s). Low incomes did not therefore arise from the structural relationship of the Philippines to the world economy, but from internal inequities.[32]

Through ownership of land and access to the state's economic controls, the cacique elite intercepted profits from exports to the United States. Land ownership was one problem. A small and declining number of landowning Filipinos stood between the mass of tillers and the lucrative markets for which they produced.

Landowners' income grew enormously in the late 1940s, despite declining crop yields. Tenants were squeezed "between two grindstones," landlords and their increasingly infertile land.[33]

The elite squeezed urban workers by using import and exchange controls to create artificial shortages. License holders could profit from both falling import prices and rising retail prices. Manufacturers of import-restricted items, who also profited from shortages, had no incentive to increase employment or raise wages. Wages, which had risen 12 percent annually before controls, stabilized in 1948. Except for the most skilled, Filipino workers had less buying power than before the war. There were few industrial jobs to be had. The commission found only 133,000 workers in manufacturing, and most were part-time or seasonal. The gap between prices and wages in the industrial and agricultural sectors meant "exceptionally high profits" had been taken between 1945 and 1949, redistributing income to the disadvantage of tenants and laborers.[34]

The commission adopted a conservative approach to chronic problems it observed during seven weeks in the Philippines, advising higher levels of aid to support policies already adopted. Concerned primarily with the country's fiscal state, Bell returned to Washington with a report that dealt with tax collection and military aid. Acheson dismissed it as "too much of a banker's report" without "enough discussion of the development angle." With help from the panel's other members, State Department officials took the report through four revisions, deleting Marshall's section on military aid and adding nine "technical memoranda," some contributed by Philippine officials. Following a line taken by the Interior Department during the war, the panel chose to reduce agriculture's importance instead of addressing its "age-old" problems directly. In the report's single page on tenancy, it recommended enforcing the 70-30 crop-share law, expanding rural credit, and encouraging "enlightened" management of large estates. The government could only ameliorate conditions for peasants, the members advised, by creating new work opportunities in industry.[35]

The report that arrived on Truman's desk on September 2 recommended dispensing $250 million in loans and grants to support a five-year development program. In exchange, the Philippine government would agree to raise taxes and submit to supervision and control. The program would diversify the economy, encourage industry, and improve conditions for workers and peasants. Truman approved the report, and told Acheson to "see if we can't arrange to save the Philippine Republic." He turned the plan over to the Economic Cooperation Administration (ECA), which had dispensed Marshall Plan aid in Europe, and assigned its head, John Foster, to negotiate a deal with Quirino.[36]

Foster found wide disagreement among State and Treasury officials over how far the Filipinos should be allowed to go to protect industry and raise revenue. The embassy's economic adviser, Eugene Clay, urged Foster to abolish import and exchange controls. Bell warned that without controls, capital flight would recur, and he advised that supervision could prevent favoritism and corruption. Controls, he felt, should be supplemented and eventually replaced by measures that would hold back imports while earning revenue. Bell suggested a tax on exchange (which violated the 1946 trade act) or import duties (which violated both the trade act and the General Agreement on Tariffs and Trade). State, Treasury, and Commerce officials found both options distasteful. The simple solution, a Federal Reserve governor pointed out, "would be to have taxes and more taxes." Other officials agreed, but pointed out that Quirino would never do it. On Snyder's recommendation, Foster decided to continue controls and permit a 25 percent tax on exchange, in effect devaluing the peso and abandoning yet another of the restraints imposed by the 1946 trade act.[37]

Released on October 28, 1950, the Bell report received mixed reviews in Manila. The Philippine leadership concurred in the emphasis on industrial development. Economic Coordinator Salvador Araneta called the report "a priceless contribution." "Exactly what we need," agreed the president of the Junior Chamber of Commerce. Quirino's aides claimed credit. During the mission's stay in Manila, Philippine officials had presented the commission with a five-year development plan involving large-scale capital investments in power development, road building, industries, and social programs. The Bell report's section on industry borrowed heavily from these recommendations. Quirino's aides found "practically complete agreement" between the Bell report and their industrialization plans. They later bragged that their recommendations "were substantially adopted by the Bell Mission."[38] Quirino disliked the report's emphasis on U.S. control. Romulo told Acheson the report would have been "perfect" except for the part about supervision, which "played directly into unfriendly hands." Acheson replied that he could not explain how such a mistake had been made, but he regretted the embarrassment. Quirino mobilized his staff to find out how the ECA disbursed aid in Europe and to devise "an arrangement which would not infringe upon our sovereignty." He conceded that the United States should help with planning, but once programs had been agreed upon, "it will be the ministerial duty of the United States representatives to deliver the money to us." Meeting with Foster on November 7, he probed the issue of "supervision and control," giving the names of several hydroelectric projects and inquiring whether the United States would object to their continuance. Foster assured him that aid did not "involve United States direction, control or supervision but only advice and consultation." The president relaxed. He found Foster "sympathetic and in a mood to help us, contrary to our fears."[39]

Philippine officials were "pleasantly surprised" to discover how few sacrifices Foster demanded. "To every proposal of the President," an adviser remarked, "he seemed to have one more favorable to us." Foster agreed to supply $250 million in aid in return for laws enacting an agricultural minimum wage, a 25 percent tax on exchange, corporate and income tax levies totalling 56 million pesos, and "a bold resolution expressing the policy of Congress" to enact the reforms recommended in the Bell report. Quirino agreed. The tax proposal met the usual resistance in Congress. Some members felt it best to wait. "Whether the American people like it or not," one legislator observed, "American aid is coming here because of the worsening world condition." American businesses joined the opposition. They objected to the 25 percent exchange tax and higher corporate tax rates. Caltex and Shell oil companies threatened to close shop. These objections could not outweigh the advantages of a $250 million aid bonanza. On March 28, 1951, Quirino signed legislation enacting the new corporate and exchange taxes and a minimum wage, and the ECA office began taking grant applications a week later.[40]

The Truman administration recognized that by rescuing the Quirino government it prolonged the rule of leaders who might again imperil the Philippines. Amid anxieties caused by the fall of China, the attack on Korea, and the deterioration of colonial rule in Southeast Asia, it seemed the only course. "We should resign ourselves to dealing with Quirino," an embassy official sighed. "It is unlikely that any of his opponents would be any more dependable." Senator Abraham Ribicoff suggested that an aid program for the Philippines might do more harm than good, since "the incompetents might be thrown out" in a prolonged crisis. Bell and the deputy undersecretary of state, Dean Rusk, replied that the United States could not take the risk. State Department officials believed less hazardous strategies might transform the Philippine leadership. They thought teams of American advisers could check corruption, and that with U.S. support, efficient and cooperative officials would rise to prominence. But American money, military assistance, and supervision reinforced cacique rule. By helping to defeat the Huks, guaranteeing external security, and promoting industrialization, the United States protected the oligarchy and helped it modernize.[41]

The Huk rebellion reached high tide in mid-1950 and abruptly subsided. On August 26, several thousand Huk troops raided 11 towns across central Luzon, seized a provincial capital, and overwhelmed an army depot, capturing 86,000 pesos and 140,000 rounds of ammunition. The head of the U.S. military advisory group judged the situation "definitely out of hand." Gambling on the Quirino government's deterioration, Huk leaders planned to establish a revolutionary government and launch raids on Manila. The raids never occurred. On October 18, 1950, acting on information from a Huk informant, the newly appointed secretary of national defense, Ramon Magsaysay, arrested 105 Communist party officials, the entire politburo, and thereby decapitated the movement. It took over a year to suppress the Huks in central Luzon, but after 1950 the movement posed no threat to the government.[42] The rebellion's reversal of fortune has been variously explained. At least part of the blame goes to the Huk leadership, which in early 1950 chose to intensify the conflict in a bid to overthrow the government. Many field commanders disapproved, considering their units unprepared and preferring political accommodation to complete overthrow. The strategy divided the movement and may have provoked Taciano Rizal to betray the politburo to Magsaysay. As Benedict Kerkvliet has shown, the Huk rank and file had modest expectations, demanding enforcement of existing crop-share laws and an end to depredations by the Army and civil guards. Magsaysay suppressed the movement by attempting to satisfy those demands.[43]

Soon after taking charge of national defense in August 1950, Magsaysay established direct control over army units through daily, unannounced inspections. He used United States aid ($13 million in 1951) to improve the morale, rations, and personal comforts of soldiers, removing incentives to looting. He diminished the role of large-unit sweeps, which had characterized the administration's "mailed fist" policy, and restricted the army to defense and interdiction operations. By occupying towns, imposing curfews, and setting up roadblocks, the army interrupted the Huks' supply and communications. Isolated, hungry bands soon began to surrender. When Magsaysay disbanded the civil guards, many Huks decided they had fought long enough. "Once the landlords and the government showed they would stop abusing us," one Huk explained, "we were ready to put aside our guns too."[44]

Magsaysay persuaded the Huks that he would look after their welfare. By diverting a large portion of the military budget to public-works programs, he built roads and dug wells in barrios throughout central Luzon. The army drained the Candaba swamp and apportioned reclaimed plots to landless peasants. Magsaysay also took steps to assure avenues for legitimate political action. He protected peasant unions and set up grievance boards. The army and the U.S. military advisory group supervised the 1951 mid-term election, in which the opposition Nacionalistas obtained a congressional majority. By the end of 1951, Huks could point to evidence that the government had been forced to respect peasant demands. Many Huks returned to their barrios claiming they had won.[45]

Military advisers directed and supported many of Magsaysay's policies, but the United States failed to adopt his low-lethality approach to counterinsurgency. The Huks' defeat is still regarded as a success for United States "psywar" and antiguerrilla tactics. Strategists applied Philippine "lessons" in Vietnam, and continued to construe parallels to brushfire wars in the 1980s. Counting only works available to the public, the military and its support organizations have produced almost two dozen studies of the winning tactics employed in the anti-Huk campaign. These studies dwell on tactics devised by American advisers: psychological warfare (the forte of CIA agent Edward G. Lansdale), and the army's few large-unit maneuvers. They neglect Magsaysay's strategy, which emphasized limiting military operations to a few discreet roles. U.S. officials, like the authors of these studies, often failed to see how their own actions fit into larger patterns of Filipino behavior, and how their policies could be turned to Filipino ends. In economic policy, too, advisers failed to recognize how little their supervision affected patrimonial dealmaking. Rather than undermining cacique power, oversight by the United States in many ways reinforced it.[46]

Growth in the Philippine economy in late 1951 and 1952 contributed to the decline of the rebellion and Filipinos' increasing confidence in their government. Much of this growth was due to the Korean War, which increased demand for Philippine products, particularly copra (used in explosives). Philippine export earnings increased by 30 percent a year in 1950 and 1951. The war revived Japanese industry, and Philippine trade with Japan doubled in 1951. The Central Bank arrested capital flight, and exchange reserves peaked at $391 million in May 1951. Inflation subsided, and Filipinos enjoyed a small increase in income. Growth allowed landowners to grant wage increases while continuing to intercept the bulk of the export proceeds. Encouraged by government incentives and American investment, many landowners invested in manufacturing. Aid policies supported this shift.[47] American supervision enhanced public confidence while allowing Filipinos to direct the economy. Filipinos "from all walks of life," according to one reporter, "are not only willing to have Americans supervise the disbursement of American aid, . . . they demand it." "Somehow," the *Chronicle* observed, "the people, government officials and plain citizens alike, have come to pin a great deal of their hopes for future economic security on the ECA." Aid officials earned some of their popularity by giving Filipinos the power to veto projects supported by the United States. The approval process gave Philippine politicians from both parties access to American largesse. PHILCUSA, expanded to include Nacionalistas, served as gatekeeper for projects that originated in cabinet departments. After approval, the ECA disbursed funds to the government, not directly to targeted corporations. The procedure created multiple opportunities for political leverage and corruption, as a U.S. congressional investigation discovered in 1953. Araneta and other economic nationalists steered aid money into manufacturing enterprises belonging to themselves or their cronies.[48]

United States support reassured investors and opened opportunities for joint ventures. The ECA extended investment guarantees to cover American firms in the Philippines, the only country outside of Europe to enjoy such protection. Pharmaceutical firms responded first. Sharp and Dohme, Pfizer, Eli Lilly, and Squibb all arranged joint ventures with Filipino partners. Reynolds Metals, Ford, Goodyear, Union Carbide, and Colgate Palmolive followed. Studebaker became the first joint-venture car maker in the Philippines, with a Manila plant turning out three Larks a day in 1952. The signing of a mutual defense pact between the Philippines and the United States in 1951 further boosted investors' confidence, as it did Quirino's. At the signing, he observed that the new agreement "gives us a feeling of security and will permit the unhampered development of our country."[49]

American firms naturally sought Filipino partners with access to patronage and influence. "Local people can help you, especially with your contacts and your dealings with government," one American businessman advised. Cacique politicians obliged. "If there's anything I enjoy doing," explained Andres Soriano, partner in Coca-Cola's franchise, "it's planning big industries. I get a kick out of it." Joint ventures provided "a new formula for producing wealth which does not require either labor or capital," according to Manila's mayor, Arsenio Lacson; "all you have to do is belong to the Liberal Party, have a little imagination, and either occupy a high position or have a relative holding a high government office."[50]

Because entrepreneurial success required access to state financial instruments, the landed elite became the manufacturing elite. In most developing countries, adoption of protectionist controls stimulated growth of a national bourgeoisie with interests opposed to those of the landed class. But in the Philippines, landowning families used their political clout to attract joint-venture partners and finance new enterprises. Prominent dynasties—like the Aranetas, Tuasons, Elizaldes, and Sorianos—whose fortunes had once derived exclusively from sugar, now dominated manufacturing, which grew at an annual rate of 12 percent. These families continued to dominate politics as well, but as their diverse holdings increased, they acquired a conflicted set of interests.[51]

Control of industry by landlord-capitalists had unique implications for the development of the Philippines and its relations with the United States. Cacique entrepreneurs stressed control over growth, often resisting policies for industrial development. Their contradictory interests required that the United States accede to a complicated trade formula that allowed Philippine sugar free entry to the American market while protecting Philippine industries from U.S. exports. Filipinos became demanding, querulous partners in an increasingly testy relationship.

The dispute over a peace treaty with Japan showed U.S. officials how difficult it would be to satisfy this elite. Not all of the Asian allies readily accepted the need to revitalize Japan as an anticommunist bastion. Australia, New Zealand, and the Philippines opposed rearmament and feared Japan's industrial potential. The United States extended security guarantees in 1951 to soothe these anxieties and encourage its allies to accept a Japanese peace treaty. Filipinos accepted the treaty, but it was not enough. They wanted reparations, but not in a form acceptable to the Truman administration. U.S. officials offered reparations in the form of services, which they hoped—and Filipinos feared—would encourage trade links with Japan.[52]

Filipino entrepreneurs dreaded competition from Japanese industry and joint ventures. They imagined a scenario in which Japan's wartime cronies would establish industries to compete with American joint ventures. The resulting product competition would drive down prices, push out U.S. capital, and bind the Philippines to "the industrial economy of Japan, tighter and more inflexible than it has ever been in . . . her trade with the United States." The Filipinos rebuffed efforts to promote links to Japan. They restricted trade and travel. They continued to demand $8 billion in reparations "in cash, or its equivalent in consumer or production goods, especially the latter," and refused to ratify the peace treaty, keeping the Philippines technically at war with Japan for most of the 1950s. It was not the last time the caciques' jealous control of their manufacturing sector would clash with United States interests.[53]

The Philippine government suffered from deep-seated, structural inequities, yet the United States responded to the crisis of the 1940s with a series of partial solutions that restored stability and reduced inflation while reinforcing corruption and maldistribution of wealth, assuring itself that "remedial political and economic measures" would be adopted later. The regime's bankruptcy compelled U.S. officials to concede substantial economic control; Quirino's misuse of power led to more concessions, until Truman's advisers could "see nothing but downward spiral ahead." Removing Quirino in 1950 was rejected as too risky. Facing communist challenges in Korea, Formosa, and throughout Southeast Asia, the United States could not afford to destabilize an ally that "could be the key to Soviet control of the Far East." Quirino did not co-opt the United States. Acheson still planned to remove him in the next election. The United States retained tremendous powers, but it was unwilling to assume the costs, risks, and political burdens of exercising them.[54]

Acheson, Melby, and Rusk believed that renewed commitment to the Philippines made them more able to control Philippine policies and prevent crises. Filipinos knew that the opposite was true: Asia's growing tensions allowed them to demand more. The larger its commitment, the less leverage the United States would have. The State Department underestimated the extent to which Filipinos could demystify U.S. authority and employ it for their own purposes. U.S. policies strengthened not only Quirino's regime, but the entire patrimonial structure, allowing caciques to transform themselves into crony capitalists.

FOUR

Magsaysay and the Illusion of Influence

United States officials felt confident of their ability to coax cooperation from the Philippine government. With the full panoply of military advisers, CIA assets, economic controls, propaganda, and aid programs in place, they believed they could encourage helpful local officials and prod recalcitrant ones along a course to stability. Few recent studies of the Philippines or the Third World suggest the situation might have been different. Students have accepted U.S. officials' estimates of their influence on dependent states, finding class and ideological explanations for the collaboration of postcolonial leaders. Dependency theorists describe how the shared interests of elites in core and periphery states facilitate transnational cooperation. Revisionists incorporate the same idea in studies of U.S. dominance in the Third World. Yet even where its hegemony was as visible as it was in the Philippines, the United States enjoyed less influence than its policymakers supposed.[1]

In describing opposition to U.S. influence in the Third World, historians have focused on its obvious forms: nonalignment, revolutionary nationalism, armed struggle. It is easy to underestimate the extent to which client states also hindered U.S. policy, precisely because such resistance was subtle or hidden. Where gross power inequities are involved, James C. Scott observes, people seldom risk overt confrontation. They penetrate authority by multiple acts of insubordination, "noncompliance, foot dragging, deception." Such tactics widen the gap between perceptions and realities. Faced with nationalist and communist challenges in Korea, Taiwan, and Southeast Asia, and hamstrung by limited re-

sources, United States officials needed friends. When they replaced Quirino with their own candidate, they thought they
could sweep aside the last obstacles to cooperation, but they obtained little more than the illusion of influence.[2]

The former manager of a bus line, Ramon Magsaysay took the
oath of office as third president of the Republic of the Philippines
in January 1954. In a gesture taken from President Andrew Jack-
son, he threw open the doors of Malacañan to thousands of Manilans, who roamed the marble halls, blinked at the chandeliers,
and marveled at the trappings of their government's highest office. Magsaysay had taken his campaign to the countryside,
stumping from barrio to barrio under banners declaring "Magsaysay Is My Guy." American newspapermen, diplomats, and,
later, historians interpreted his ascent as a demonstration of the
power of the United States to control the workings of the Philippine political system. "In many ways," *Time* magazine reported,
"the Magsaysay victory was a U.S. victory." The new president
was "America's Boy," manufactured, packaged, and delivered by
diplomatic and military officials and the CIA's master manipulator, Edward G. Lansdale.[3]

State Department officials believed they had found a way to
bypass the corrupt elite that menaced the stability of the country. They regarded Magsaysay as a genuine reformer, a common
man with few ties to landlords, *rentier* industrialists, and cronies
who ran Quirino's administration. They believed he had achieved
high office—secretary of national defense, then president—because of United States support. "The United States government
has successfully expended some money and much time," the undersecretary of state, James E. Webb, told Truman, "to situate
Magsaysay both politically and militarily in a decisive position."[4]

Despite Magsaysay's open, even flamboyant pro-Americanism,
leaders of the Nacionalista party rejected the American reporters'
claim that Magsaysay was an American creation. Senator Claro
M. Recto dismissed the "propaganda" that claimed "a certain
Colonel Lansdale was behind the scenes pulling the strings of
four million Filipino voters as if they were just so many mari-
onettes." "If one single person could justify the claim of having

made a maximum political investment," he argued, it was Jose Laurel, who had sacrificed his own presidential ambitions to put Magsaysay at the head of the Nacionalista ticket. Laurel admired Magsaysay's ability to manipulate Americans, using their fear of communism to obtain aid and concessions. He considered this skill characteristically Filipino. Since colonial times, Laurel observed, "the Filipinos have known how to resist and repudiate the importunities of the most arrogant of American 'proconsuls.' "5

In Tagalog, *magsaysay* means "to tell a story," and the new president was a storied figure. Knowing the value of image, he allowed people to see in him the qualities they wanted to see. Politicians, peasants, military advisers, and diplomats all considered themselves joined to him by loyalty and shared commitment. Quirino and his archenemy Laurel both referred to him as "a son." Peasants in central Luzon considered him "one of us," and U.S. military advisers prized his pro-Americanism. Magsaysay occasionally cultivated myths about himself, embroidering the story of his lowly origins, hinting at plots on his life by shadowy opponents; but by remaining largely silent, he permitted observers to create their own myths. American reporters invented an imaginary Magsaysay of humble beginnings (a "carpenter's son" in *Time*, a "farm boy" in *Reader's Digest*) who was fiercely anticommunist, a tireless reformer, loyal to the United States, suspicious of Philippine politicians. Robert Aura Smith of *The New York Times* observed that "he was in no sense a professional *politico*. He had no organization behind him, no family interest or obligations, no debts to pay."6

With his election in 1953, Magsaysay became the central character in one of Washington's most durable legends. As retold at hearings and briefings, the legend identified him as a political outsider who had captured power with help from the Central Intelligence Agency. According to one agent, "The CIA's operation that made Ramon Magsaysay president of the Philippines in 1953 established a pattern of paramilitary, psychological, and political action mistakenly imagined to be workable anywhere, anytime." As late as 1964, President Lyndon B. Johnson's assistant secretary of state for Far Eastern affairs, Roger Hilsman, was looking for "a Vietnamese Magsaysay" to rescue the Saigon government.7

The legend's vagueness contributed to its durability. American officials who aided Magsaysay's rise knew him as an able leader, better than the alternatives, but less than ideal. Few of them stayed on to dispute the legend. After the 1953 victory, the ambassador and the chief military adviser retired. Lansdale went to Saigon to try to create a government from scratch. The remaining officials had little incentive to challenge the accepted wisdom. Later, State Department and CIA officials tried to repeat the Philippine success, according to Larry E. Cable, "without recognizing or articulating the essential personal attributes which rendered the original Magsaysay effective in a unique environment. As a result, they were all too ready to mistake virtually any local strongman for a suitable candidate."[8]

Historians adopted and expanded on the legend, using the Magsaysay-Lansdale relationship to represent neocolonial domination by the United States. But Magsaysay's papers and his aides' recollections reveal that he was neither free of debt, as Smith claimed, nor as indebted to the United States as some contend.[9] Like his predecessors, Roxas and Quirino, Magsaysay entered office beholden to the interests that put him there. Working within the patrimonial political system, he built a base capable of ensuring his election to the presidency. U.S. officials ranked among his favored clients, but so did sugar planters, industrialists, and regional political warlords. U.S. officials overestimated his loyalty to the United States and his commitment to reform. They hoped he would push reforms, negotiate a new bases treaty, and cooperate with initiatives in Southeast Asia. But in the course of his rise, Magsaysay allied himself with Philippine economic and political interests, who also demanded a price.

Magsaysay built his career on transnational patronage ties. His father, a Chinese mestizo, taught woodworking at an American-run trade school in Iba, Zambales, and invested his earnings in several farms and a trucking company. The son flunked out of the University of the Philippines, then worked as shop superintendent for a bus line and, like Quirino, married into a landed mestizo family. He entered politics as *lider* of a local faction, organizing support for party bosses in return for a share of the spoils. His connections and access to trucks and buses made him useful to U.S. forces as they retreated to Bataan. In 1942,

MacArthur made him a captain in the guerrillas, a promotion that made his career. When American forces returned in 1945, his status as a "recognized" guerrilla leader conferred substantial political benefits.[10] Magsaysay studied successful politicians and imitated their use of patronage. Like Quirino's first secretary of defense, Ruperto Kangleon, and other politicians with guerrilla credentials, Magsaysay parlayed his control of unit rosters and veterans' benefits into a political base. His roster grew from 1,100 in early 1945 to 10,441 two years later. It gave him discretion over who would receive "back pay" and veterans' benefits. The list included Magsaysay's mistress, Rosario Nicanor, who held the rank of lieutenant. Each "guerrilla" signed a loyalty pledge. Magsaysay's war service provided other benefits as well. MacArthur appointed him provisional governor of Zambales in 1945. A year later, he won a congressional seat after campaigning in his uniform.[11]

In Congress, Magsaysay became the acolyte of the political bosses who dominated his region. He allied himself with the speaker of the House and political chieftain of west central Luzon, Eugenio Perez. Perez had used his office to amass a huge personal fortune, shrugging off indictments along the way. Magsaysay called him *manong*, "uncle." Perez gave the congressman chairmanship of the Committee on National Defense, a post Magsaysay used to build a reputation as an advocate for veterans. It was on a visit to Washington in March 1950 to lobby for veterans' benefits that Magsaysay met Lansdale.[12]

Lansdale made it his business to advance Magsaysay's career, but by the time the two became friends, Magsaysay was already a leading figure in his own right. A former advertising man who had served as Roxas's military aide, Lansdale joined the CIA in 1949, and was due to leave for Manila in a few months. Magsaysay impressed him. "I decided he should be the guy," he remembered, "to lead the anti-Huk campaign." Lansdale claimed that he recruited Magsaysay and used official pressure to persuade Quirino to appoint him as secretary of national defense. In fact, Filipino patrons placed him in the cabinet. According to Magsaysay and Quirino, Perez suggested the appointment to the president in early 1950. Quirino offered the job several times before

Magsaysay accepted. He was the obvious choice. As Quirino observed, his background resembled that of his predecessor, Kangleon, and he headed the relevant committee. Lansdale arrived in the Philippines in October 1950, a week after Magsaysay took office. "I already knew we shared things in common," he recalled. He liked the new defense secretary and invited him to move into his quarters at the compound of the military advisory group (JUS-MAG) near Camp Murphy.[13]

The two men formed an association based on mutual career-building. Lansdale helped Magsaysay obtain national prominence and U.S. aid, and Magsaysay's rising fortunes built Lansdale's reputation as a master manipulator. By his own admission, Lansdale contributed few of the ideas that went into the anti-Huk campaign. His greatest influence was on Magsaysay's image. American newspapers hungered for evidence that the United States stood for democracy in Asia and not for the bankrupt, authoritarian regimes of aging despots like Chiang and Syngman Rhee. They wanted a dynamic, democratic chieftain to pit against Ho Chi Minh and Mao Tse-tung for the leadership of young Asia. Lansdale gave them one. He cultivated Manila's U.S. press corps and fed them stories of the lanky, plain-spoken, cabin-born man who was beating the communists at their own game. Lansdale's superiors in the CIA credited him with "inventing" Magsaysay.[14]

Alliance with American military advisers served Magsaysay's ambitions. The advisory group wanted to enlarge the defense secretary's power and patronage base in order to win the war against the Huks. After Major General Leland Hobbs took command of JUSMAG in July 1949, he urged Quirino to integrate the Philippine Constabulary with the army, declare a state of emergency in central Luzon, and establish a "Devil's Island" to which "convicted dissidents may be shipped." The ambassador, Myron Cowen, disagreed, fearing that a larger, more aggressive army would provoke more dissidence. Cowen opposed emergency measures that could invite abuse. The conflict peaked in September 1950 in a dispute over the suspension of habeas corpus. Hobbs considered emergency powers like holding suspects without charge and summary trials necessary. Cowen felt such powers and accompanying mistreatment would stiffen resistance. Each side pressed its views on Quirino. Promising loyalty, Magsaysay prevailed on the president to side with Hobbs. "Sensing his earnestness," Quirino gave Magsaysay the authority he wanted.[15] Magsaysay's strategy for fighting the Huks complemented his strategy for advancement. Under the guise of "psychological" warfare and improving the Army's public image, he used U.S. aid to copy many of Quirino's most popular social programs. The most famous Magsaysay program, the Economic Development Corporation (EDCOR), resettled several thousand Huks and retired army soldiers on farms in Mindanao. By Lansdale's account, an American adviser took the plan from an ancient Roman practice, but in fact, EDCOR was nearly identical to the Quirino administration's Land Settlement and Development Corporation, which had been establishing colony farms in Mindanao since 1939. Magsaysay repackaged it and added a publicity campaign. He took public works and patronage away from Quirino's minions, and built roads, schools, and community centers under the umbrella of the army's "civic action" program, which Lansdale saw as a way to "use soldiers as cheap labor in public works projects." The army drained the vast Candaba swamp and apportioned reclaimed land to grateful settlers. With money from the Chinese community, it installed artesian "liberty wells" in peasant barrios.[16]

These programs aimed chiefly to enhance Magsaysay's reputation. They addressed the agrarian problem only superficially. EDCOR resettled just five thousand tenants in ten years. Neither wells nor drainage attacked the sources of peasant unrest, which arose from overpopulation, modernization, and the breakdown of a traditional system of obligations between landlord and tenant. They did improve cooperation between peasants and the army in areas formerly controlled by the Huks, and to a greater extent they added to Magsaysay's popularity. As late as 1955, central Luzon tenants told pollsters that they mistrusted the army but had "confidence that the president would personally intercede for them if their rights were violated."[17]

Magsaysay's new stature attracted political and commercial opportunities. Wealthy men sought his help and rewarded him for it. Soriano, the richest man in the Philippines, engineered Magsaysay's appointment to the chairmanship of Philippine Air

Lines, one of the country's largest corporations. Quirino asked Magsaysay to administer the 1951 off-year elections. The army guarded the polls, and Magsaysay took the credit for polling that was relatively graft- and violence-free.[18] In return for Quirino's support, Magsaysay publicly praised the president's leadership and offered proof of his fealty. After captured Huk documents revealed an assassination plot in late 1950, Magsaysay volunteered to sleep across the doorstep of Quirino's bedroom. Quirino later recalled declining Magsaysay's offer to assassinate two politicians, Justiano Montano and Lorenzo Tañada, who had criticized the president. He appreciated Magsaysay's devotion. "He'll never betray me," he told his brother Tony. "I have proven his loyalty. No one has ever offered to commit a murder for me."[19]

According to his biographer, "Magsaysay had the widest discretion, subject to the least auditing," of any top official. He had a large discretionary fund furnished by JUSMAG and Manila businessmen, who raised two million pesos. Ironclad support from the press and influential politicians gave him unchallenged authority over his department. He enlarged his influence in Congress by favoring legislators with gifts of patronage, transportation, protection, and guns. "You take care of the Huks," he assured one major, "and I'll take care of the politicians."[20]

Discretionary funds and patronage did not free Magsaysay of the strain of meeting the conflicting demands of supporters in business, the administration, and the United States government. He kept a pace that exhausted aides. He flew into rages, threatening and even striking subordinates, when a cabinet minister or anyone with "more prestige" provoked him. Aides learned to "take these explosions and be good shock absorbers." He suffered hypertensive headaches, which debilitated him for part of every afternoon. Seldom did he take refuge in leisure. He enjoyed opportunities his office gave him to grant favors and personally dispense justice, often sitting with peasants for hours to arbitrate a dispute. He preferred to handle problems personally and individually, rather than as part of a general policy.[21]

Lansdale and other advisers prized Magsaysay's cooperation in reforming the army and defeating the Huks. They praised his "courage, coupled with a genuine faith and admiration in the

United States," believing his efforts directly challenged entrenched interests. "He was stepping on toes, ruffling egos and hurting the pocketbooks of some powerful people," Lansdale boasted. But military officials overestimated both his courage and the genuineness of his loyalty to the United States. Magsaysay did not challenge his country's political system; he profited from it. He used his connection with the United States to enlarge his patronage base and further his career. He returned the favor by helping his JUSMAG friends, but he also traded favors with Philippine politicians who helped him. He differed from other traditional politicians only in the extent of his obligation to JUSMAG.[22]

The U.S. advisers mistook the defense secretary's loyalty to Hobbs and Lansdale for faith in the United States. Magsaysay cultivated relationships with individuals, not institutions. He felt indebted to Hobbs and Lansdale (he remained lifelong friends with both), but not to Cowen or other U.S. officials. Nonetheless, JUSMAG's impressions became accepted lore. To Washington officials, Magsaysay represented an unconventional, pro-American, self-sacrificing leadership unlike anything they had seen before.

As their investment in Magsaysay's success grew, officials paid less attention to the defense secretary's ties to indigenous interests. Those with a career stake in Magsaysay—Lansdale, Hobbs, a succession of ambassadors—proclaimed his undiluted loyalty. A few State Department officials with experience in Philippine affairs remembered how they had been misled by earlier leaders, like Quirino. Old State Department hands, however, enjoyed little job security in the early 1950s, and their doubts did not carry much weight.[23]

Despite the Quirino regime's increasing stability and impressive progress against the Huks in 1951 and 1952, United States officials were determined to replace Quirino and his cronies with more vigorous leadership. The Philippine administration, a "small group of individuals representing the wealthy propertied class," according to the National Security Council, lacked "courage and initiative to take bold, vigorous measures to wipe out corruption." State Department and Economic Cooperation Administration officials regarded Quirino as an obstacle to land reform and other measures they considered essential to elimination of unrest. "If we are stuck with Quirino" after the November 1953 elections, Cowen warned, "we shall have to redouble our efforts" and "control to the maximum degree every centavo of aid." Although Quirino supported the United States through his representatives at the United Nations and regional forums, his reputation for corruption undermined his usefulness as a regional leader at a time when U.S. officials wanted the Philippines to take a more prominent position.[24]

The United States needed energetic allies in Southeast Asia. In August 1952, the National Security Council optimistically cataloged the ingredients of the free world's preponderant power. The United States and its allies controlled the "vast bulk of the world's economic resources" and military might, power enough to retard the growth of Soviet military strength and separate the Soviet Union from its allies. Nonetheless, the NSC warned, the free world had weaknesses. In Asia, nationalism left a residue of animosity toward the West, and slow growth prevented governments from satisfying their people and establishing stable regimes. The NSC regretted that the United States was "obligated for one reason or another, to work with unpopular and undemocratic governments." Although no one considered the Philippines right for the part, the United States needed just one progressive, democratic country to serve as a model.[25]

Deterioration of the French military position in Indochina made it imperative to find allies. In early 1951, Viet Minh forces overran French garrisons along the Chinese border and began to consolidate their control of the countryside. Although French troops and Bao Dai's National Army occupied towns along the Tonkin Gulf, Viet Minh attacks made their hold precarious. United States aid—$775 million by 1952—became critical to French defense. Secretary of State Acheson and the head of the policy planning staff, Paul Nitze, worried that France would withdraw. They resolved to buttress French will with aid that might reach "a billion a year," but they anticipated resistance in Congress. A regional alliance, incorporating the Philippines, Thailand, and possibly Indonesia, would clear away congressional opposition while reassuring the French and Bao Dai.[26]

The United States placed high stakes on the outcome of the

conflict in Southeast Asia. The "loss of any single country" in the region, according to the National Security Council, "would probably lead to relatively swift submission to or an alignment with communism by the remaining countries of the group." India and most of the countries of the Middle East, except Pakistan and Turkey, would follow suit, imperiling Europe. If the United States lost Southeast Asia, according to the State Department's Soviet specialist, Charles Bohlen, it "lost the cold war."[27]

Under Quirino, the Philippines had little to offer a regional alliance. Although it contributed a battalion to U.N. forces in Korea, the bulk of its army was preoccupied with the Huks. Pentagon officials dreaded a collective security organization that included the Philippines, which they felt would become a way to wheedle military aid from the United States. The Filipinos did have a few minor advantages, and with adjustments might acquire more. For one, they were brown. The whites-only pact with Australia and New Zealand (ANZUS) aroused suspicion in South and Southeast Asia, where journalists and officials saw it as an instrument for reasserting racial hegemony. Since ANZUS's inception, the State Department had advocated including the Philippines to dispel the race issue. But to be a model ally, the Philippines needed model leadership. Secretary of Defense Magsaysay set an example of public service, and U.S. officials believed that as president he could serve in a similar role for the region.[28]

Truman selected Admiral Raymond Spruance in January 1952 to be the U.S ambassador to the Philippines, the agent for reforming and later replacing the Quirino regime. The victor of the Battle of Leyte Gulf enjoyed a reputation for sternness, and as ambassador Spruance turned this side of his character toward Quirino. Philippine officials learned, according to an embassy official, that here was a man in the tradition of colonial governors Cameron Forbes and Leonard Wood, "who required the Filipinos to live up to their promises—to toe the mark—to put their house in order and deserve the help and assistance they expected." A Manila journalist called him "an incredibly efficient piece of machinery in human form."[29]

Spruance concluded that progress in the Philippines required Quirino's removal. "All we can do here," he wrote his daughter, is to "hope to get enough honest Filipinos in the Government to correct conditions. . . . We cannot get the laws enforced against the wealthy minority who are now in control." He took an uncooperative and critical stance in order to undermine the Liberal regime before the 1953 elections. He refused to help Quirino with preparations for an international trade fair and another Pacific Pact conference, or to lend support to appeals for increased veterans' benefits and the revision of the trade act recommended by the Bell mission.[30] Stonewalling Quirino proved costly. By postponing the renegotiation of the military bases agreement, Spruance unknowingly sacrificed the best chance the United States would have in the 1950s to obtain favorable terms from a politically vulnerable administration. His release of the Hardie report stalled progress on land reform for two years. An American specialist on land reform, Robert Hardie described the plight of share tenants and recommended expropriating and subdividing estates. Quirino and Perez attacked the report as an attempt to undermine the administration. Hardie hoped his plan could be completed by July 1955, but amid the furor it never got a hearing.[31]

Toward the end of 1952, Spruance began to prepare for Quirino's defeat in the 1953 campaign. He made repeated calls for a clean election, implying that Quirino could only win by cheating. Magsaysay told the ambassador that these statements filled Quirino with "bitter resentment." Spruance considered Magsaysay the "only figure with qualities desirable from a U.S. standpoint." He and his counselor, William Lacy, played a small but melodramatic part in negotiating Magsaysay's defection from the Liberal party, with the admiral concealing the agreement in his bedroom safe.[32]

The newly inaugurated Eisenhower administration retained Spruance in office and attached even greater importance to his mission. Eisenhower's National Security Council reaffirmed the Truman administration's policies regarding the need for new, vigorous leadership in the Philippines. In a thorough review of security policy in 1953, the council reemphasized the critical strategic importance of Southeast Asia, underscored the perilous position of Indochina, and stressed the need for a regional pact.

State and Defense officials in the new administration reevaluated
the potential military contribution that "national forces" like the
Philippine Army could make to defense of the region against a
Chinese assault. Like its predecessor, the Eisenhower administration sought the kind of cooperative, energetic leadership it believed Magsaysay could provide. Spruance and Lansdale persisted
in their efforts to place Magsaysay in Malacañan.[33]
The United States flagrantly intervened in the 1953 election.
The list of CIA dirty tricks, by one account, included money
laundering, arson, and blackmail, but ironically, these depredations fail to convey the scope of interference. The election was
about the United States. All candidates recognized that the electorate would judge them on the primary qualification for the
presidency: the ability to extract the most money from the United States with the fewest strings. The press divided its coverage
between the campaign and American opinion of the campaign.
Stray comments of American columnists played under scream-
ing headlines, and no visiting American escaped interrogation.
Isaac Stern, arriving in Manila on a concert tour, disappointed reporters by declaring his neutrality. Candidates complained that
the United States did not intervene enough. Liberals demanded
a clear statement of preference (or nonpreference) from the embassy. Nacionalistas wanted the United States to administer the
polling. Unable to escape, U.S. officials tried to assume the guise
of referees, but their bias was too obvious and their agents too eager.[34]
Both parties attempted to secure American support by nomi-
nating Magsaysay. In the months before the conventions in early
1953, leaders reshuffled the memberships of the two major parties. Fluid coalitions of regional factions, the parties had few dis-
agreements on policy. They functioned, according to a newspaper columnist, "as mere machines, and not as repositories of
ideals. Defections are tolerated, and very often, rewarded." ("Political promises are made and broken," Quirino advised one defecting congressman. "Think of your own future.") Of the two,
the Nacionalistas had been the party more critical of the United
States. Its leaders, Laurel and Recto, had been imprisoned for collaboration and allegedly bore a grudge. But being "propertied

men, careful, conservative and timid, as a whole," they recognized Magsaysay's value and negotiated his defection 13 months before he quit the administration in February 1953. Nacionalista leaders acknowledged that they had chosen Magsaysay for his United States support. "I know pretty well how I stand in the eyes of the American people," Laurel explained, "but if Magsaysay wins, I think America will go out of her way to help us because he is a friend of America, a great friend. To the American people, Magsaysay is the physical embodiment of Democracy's courageous stand against Communism in the Far East." He assured Nacionalistas that the candidate would remain loyal. "Don't worry," he told a congressman, "Magsaysay will be like my son, and he will follow our suggestions—Senator Rodriguez, Recto, and myself."[35]

The Liberals, too, wanted Magsaysay on their ticket, but Quirino stood in the way. A large portion of the Liberal leadership favored dumping the incumbent. Aware of these designs, Quirino criticized his defense secretary, precipitating Magsaysay's resignation and defection to the Nacionalistas. Anti-Quirino Liberals turned to Romulo, who enjoyed even stronger American backing than did Magsaysay. At the Liberal convention in May, Romulo nearly seized the nomination with help from the influential sugar-planters bloc, but Quirino's men used their control of the podium to thwart him. Romulo and supporters formed a third party, the Democrata.[36]

Candidates made the preferences of the U.S. government the campaign issue. Shortly after declaring his candidacy, Magsaysay told a gathering on Leyte that U.S. aid would be cut off if Quirino were reelected. The president called the charge "preposterous," a revelation of his opponent's poor understanding of American policy. Quirino tried to maintain that he, not his opponent, had Washington's favor, then to portray himself as a Filipino David against the American Goliath, an ironic twist that made for easy lampooning. "Sycophants to General MacArthur, orderlies of Mr. McNutt, apologists for Mr. Cowen, minions of Mr. Acheson," Recto crowed, the Liberals "must now pose as the guardians of our sovereignty from the 'meddling' of, of all people, the reserved and silent Admiral Spruance." Insofar as other issues intruded during the campaign, they remained accessories to the principal issue, U.S. aid. Quirino's corruption and failing health, Magsaysay charged, would lead the United States to suspend aid. Romulo argued that Magsaysay's "political immaturity" would prevent him from securing a fair share for the Philippines. Quirino stood on his record of success in obtaining American money. The president's support flagged, and Romulo, sensing the trend of events, opted for merger with Magsaysay. By July 2, five months before election day, the Nacionalista vice-presidential nominee, Carlos Garcia, told reporters that the Liberals were finished.[37]

Quirino was dying. He spent most of the campaign in the Johns Hopkins University Hospital, undergoing treatment. Newspapers daily speculated on his chances for survival, and Romulo for a time expected to inherit the Liberal machinery. Returning to Manila on September 7, the bandaged president hobbled from the plane to discover his party in disarray and nearly every organized group aligned with the Nacionalistas.[38]

Magsaysay anticipated a Nacionalista victory, but felt sure that unless he won decisively, Quirino would try to steal the election. Rather than assemble a coalition merely to win, Magsaysay attempted to enlist the support of every powerful constituency. To avoid offending backers, he promised not to raise taxes (even though State Department policy encouraged increased taxation) and played down land reform (which the United States advocated). Although he built his campaign around his relations with the United States, he allied with Quirino supporters whom embassy officials regarded as corrupt and obstructionist. He astonished Spruance by enlisting the help of Quirino's notoriously corrupt brother, who had parlayed his contacts into a commercial empire and participated in all the scandals of the late 1940s. Spruance and Lacy grew uneasy with Magsaysay's choice of company, but agreed on the need for an overwhelming margin of victory.[39]

Magsaysay cut deals with all the traditionally dominant constituencies: sugar and coconut planters, industrialists, the Catholic Church, as well as economically powerful but politically weak groups like American and Chinese businessmen. As his campaign gathered momentum, it attracted constituents anxious to protect their concessions and privileges. The prospect that the

Nacionalistas could secure a favorable revision of the trade act attracted support from huge state-supported business combines like the Soriano group, as well as younger entrepreneurs represented by the Jaycees, Lions, Elks, and other such organizations.[40] Agricultural interests, particularly sugar and coconut planters, defected from the Liberals. Sugar planters and processors traditionally warred over the legally mandated share each would receive of the export profits. By changing the share a few points, the administration could punish either bloc by millions of pesos, and Liberals had always been able to count on support from the sugar interests. Renegotiation of the trade act, with the prospect of enlarging or reducing the total profit, threw open this zero-sum game. Quirino kept the processors loyal by naming Yulo as his vice-presidential candidate, but the planters had more money, newspapers, and votes. Planters had another incentive for defecting to the winning side. Many had overdue loans from the government-owned Philippine National Bank. The victor could bankrupt hundreds of planters by calling the loans. Coconut producers with an eye on the approaching trade act revision lent support to Magsaysay. The strong Nacionalista turnout in the sugar and coconut regions, read in Washington as evidence of Magsaysay's appeal to rural folk, probably resulted more from the influence of the planters.[41]

The Catholic Church, which had spiritual authority over 95 percent of Filipinos, weighed in behind Magsaysay. The hierarchy and a lay organization, Catholic Action, had previously asked Quirino to include religious instruction in the schools. Counting on the Church's customary silence on political matters, he had refused, and even appointed a Freemason as education minister, decisions he had reason to regret during the campaign. Priests preached Magsaysay from the pulpit and joined Nacionalista registration drives. Manila's archbishop issued a pastoral letter endorsing Magsaysay in all but name. "Unless evil men are excluded from office and good men placed in office," he admonished, "justice will not be done." Spruance regarded the letter as "constructive." Quirino protested to the Nuncio, but until the Philippines obtained its own cardinal in 1959, the Philippine Church answered to Rome through Francis Cardinal Spellman of New

York, who thought Magsaysay symbolized "the national courage through wisdom and Christian kindliness."[42]

Chinese businessmen, fed up with police inspections and outraged by arrests on rebellion charges of elderly Chinese merchants, contributed money to the Magsaysay campaign. Some overoptimistically hoped a change of administration would "herald in a millennium of Filipino-Chinese relations." Community leaders recognized that Nacionalista rule would be no gentler, but felt that Quirino's policy of rounding up Chinese businessmen to be imprisoned and squeezed for contributions deserved retaliation. Unable to vote, the Chinese spoke loudly at campaign time through contributions. In 1953, their donations dwarfed those of the American community. Chinese businessmen in Manila alone donated 1,700,000 pesos (one peso = 50¢) and, according to one official, would have donated 5 million pesos had the Nacionalistas tried to collect.[43]

By all accounts, money from American businessmen also found its way into Magsaysay's coffers, although amounts and donors remain unknown. Accepting funds from foreign donors violated Philippine law, and Quirino threatened to block remittances through the Central Bank. Magsaysay denied knowingly receiving funds from Americans, but admitted that some might have slipped through. Recto later charged that Magsaysay had a $1 million bankroll, but during the election Nacionalista leaders complained about the paucity of contributions. Lansdale was the conduit for $250,000 from American corporations, small change in the world of Philippine campaign finance. These funds, however, carried the Nacionalistas through the early cash-poor days of the campaign.[44]

In line with instructions to avoid interfering, the CIA funneled money not to the candidate or party but to "independent" antifraud civic organizations. To mobilize soft money from the United States and to assist Magsaysay under the guise of encouraging free elections, JUSMAG helped to organize the National Movement for Free Elections. Headed by two of Magsaysay's aides, Jaime Ferrer and Jaime San Juan, the movement obtained money from civic organizations in the United States like the Lions and the Jaycees, CIA front organizations (the Catherwood Foundation, CARE, and the Committee for a Free Asia), and the Coca-Cola Company. Soriano owned the world's third-largest Coca-Cola franchise and supported Magsaysay, but he preferred not to make a direct donation. The movement organized a national network of pollwatchers to prevent Quirino loyalists from stealing the election.[45]

U.S. officials disliked many of Magsaysay's political allies, particularly the Nacionalista party's leadership. Laurel and Recto were "perfectly capable of using Magsaysay for all he is worth and then discarding him when he had served his purpose," according to a State Department official. Lansdale's team would have preferred an independent candidacy. According to his assistant, Charles Bohannon, the Nacionalista affiliation was "really a terrible thing." With American backing, Magsaysay "did not need the support of any party or politicians at all." State Department officials concurred, believing Magsaysay's popularity made political alliances unnecessary. The candidate persisted in soliciting support from regional warlords. Poll figures show he knew what he was doing. The Nacionalista "old guard" and sugar bloc senators defecting from the Liberal party delivered most of his votes. Laurel and his son, Jose, Jr., Recto, and Eulogio Rodriguez carried Magsaysay in the populous Tagalog-speaking provinces of southern Luzon. Planter bloc senators Fernando Lopez and Thomas Cabili delivered the Visayas and Mindanao.[46]

Magsaysay's most important backers opposed U.S.-sponsored reforms. Throughout his term as ambassador, Spruance pushed for the reform plan dictated by the Foster-Quirino agreement of 1951, which he considered essential to long-term stability. It included increasing taxes, a minimum wage for agricultural workers, and protection for labor organizations. The Hardie report of 1952 laid out a program of land reform. The Quirino administration satisfied the terms of the Foster-Quirino agreement with an initial frenzy of legislation, but the program remained largely unimplemented. Congressmen made repeated attempts to repeal the legislation that had gone through. In 1952, Magsaysay's allies had organized a campaign that gutted the minimum-wage law. One of Magsaysay's key backers, Salvador Araneta, advocated repeal. Planters also opposed Hardie's land-reform plan.[47] Magsaysay's business supporters, especially American businessmen, objected to tax increases the State Department considered essential. Quirino raised taxes after the Bell report, but then allowed rates to subside to previous levels. Filipinos remained among the world's least-taxed peoples. To satisfy supporters in business, the Nacionalista party adopted a no-new-taxes platform. Business groups like the Jaycees also opposed American initiatives to strengthen unions.[48]

Magsaysay's Filipino supporters disagreed over economic policy. The Bell mission had recommended revising the 1946 trade act. Quirino asked for negotiations in 1953, but the Eisenhower administration delayed talks to deprive him of a success. Revision would be the first item on the agenda of the new administration. Business interests, especially consumer-goods manufacturers, favored tariff protection for industry, but sugar and coconut producers feared that American exporters would retaliate against the sugar quota. If American goods were excluded, even "such comparatively insignificant elements as the Virginia leaf tobacco exporters and the rattan furniture manufacturers could give [us] a great deal of trouble," the Philippine Sugar Association's lobbyist in Washington warned. Feuds between planters, processors, and industrialists had paralyzed the Quirino administration. Magsaysay's coalition brought the same groups, with all their divisiveness, under new leadership.[49]

U.S. officials remained certain that Magsaysay was a new type of leader who would be useful for reforming the Philippines and providing leadership in Asia. He represented "a clean break with the reactionary and corrupt politicians characteristic of both parties," the CIA reported. Belatedly, the State Department became concerned that overt involvement in the election would provoke a backlash. In July, the National Security Council warned that "any attempt to influence the elections would be bound to become public knowledge and would be prejudicial to our own best interests." It applauded Spruance's "formal, neutral, and correct attitude toward Magsaysay the candidate." All American personnel, even Lansdale, were told to stay out of politics. To remove him from the maelstrom, Secretary of State John Foster Dulles recalled Spruance at the height of the campaign. The ambassador, JUSMAG, and Eisenhower administration officials continued to call for free elections in statements interpreted as critical of the administration. The State Department ignored Elizalde's protest against official pronouncements alleging that "the election will not be free." The embassy's assurances and support for the National Movement for Free Elections quashed the "meddling" issue as far as the Filipino press was concerned.[50]

Lansdale continued to work for a Magsaysay landslide. Finding restrictions on partisanship confining, he ignored them. "How in hell can a guy fight for a free election without getting close to a candidate?" he wondered. If asked, he would "deny to all and sundry that we are doing any more than what orders say." Romulo accused him of planting anti-Quirino stories in American newspapers, and Quirino exposed him as a CIA agent. JUSMAG expelled him from its compound, and the chief adviser told reporters Lansdale would probably leave the country. Regarding his cover as a nuisance, Lansdale reestablished himself at Clark Air Force Base under the guise of assistant to the historian. "How is the agent of American imperialism?" reporters would josh when they saw him at Magsaysay's headquarters. Recognizing that in this election, American opinion counted more than Filipino opinion, he fed stories to the Luce publications, the Manila correspondent for *The New York Times*, Tillman Durdin, and columnists like Stewart Alsop. Manila papers reprinted the stories, interpreting them as evidence of the American preference. Washington took them as proof of Lansdale's success. Elizalde complained Lansdale was "brazenly giving the impression that he was behind the build-up for Mr. Magsaysay in the American press." Even American business leaders, like the general manager of National City Bank, complained that Lansdale was "less than completely subtle in his activities," which were, in any event, unnecessary. Magsaysay had a sufficient margin to assure victory.[51]

In the final weeks of the campaign, Lansdale, the embassy, and Magsaysay loyalists mounted an intimidation campaign against

Liberals who might be plotting fraud. Rumor mills, newspapers, and embassy cable traffic began to carry stories of preparations for a coup to avenge a stolen election. The stories so artfully blended truth and fiction that their authors hardly knew what to believe. Lansdale insisted to his superiors that the rumors were "real." The revolt would include "the cream of combat commanders" of the Philippine army along with seventeen thousand civilian commandos armed in advance by Magsaysay. But in an interview in 1981, Bohannon, Lansdale's adviser, remembered it as "purely a propaganda ploy . . . part of the psycho war we were engaged in against the Administration." Magsaysay privately discounted the rumors but made plans for his family to be taken to Subic Bay when the shooting started. Quirino recognized that the climate of fear hurt his campaign and made repeated but ineffective assurances that the polling would be fair. State Department officials worried that violence would stain Magsaysay's reputation as a democratic leader and diminish his usefulness as a spokesman in Asia. Lacy arranged for the aircraft carrier *Wasp* with a destroyer escort to place Manila under its guns two days before the election. He told his skeptical superiors that the port call would make a point subtly, but an American-owned newspaper announced the real purpose of the visit, and Quirino issued another tirade against foreign meddling.[52]

The Eisenhower administration had every reason to be satisfied with the outcome on November 11. Magsaysay won by a two-to-one margin. The election left 9 dead, 12 wounded, and several score missing. Troops had to be rushed to Pasay City and parts of Cavite. Yet American newspapers declared election day "relatively" nonviolent. A visiting congressional study mission found a "high degree of orderliness that may well serve as a model for other Asian countries." Dulles told Spruance that the election gave the United States an "opportunity to bring to the forefront in the Western Pacific non-Western leadership which is respected and competent and which can help invigorate and unify non-communist Asian forces in Indochina, Indonesia, and perhaps Formosa and Korea." Romulo and Magsaysay would make "a splendid team for this purpose." Two weeks after the election, Vice President Richard M. Nixon arrived to size up Magsaysay's qualifications for Asian leadership. Noting his "magnetic appeal" and "genuine regard for the people's welfare," he advised the president-elect to take six to nine months to set his house in order. Magsaysay should not tour Southeast Asia, Nixon told Spruance, but Asian leaders should be brought to Manila to get a look at Magsaysay. Above all, he "must not allow Magsaysay to fail, and United States agencies must ask for and be given such funds and assistance as needed to accomplish success with something spectacular at an early date."[53]

The United States had invested a substantial effort in Magsaysay's success, but still it had not won an unfailing ally. The new president's alliances to groups with conflicting interests and demands naturally diminished his loyalty to the United States. Moreover, the patrimonial leadership style officials had once admired handicapped him in his new role as reform president and international statesman. Eisenhower's advisers wanted Magsaysay to mount a "vigorous attack" on Philippine social and economic problems and become a "symbol in the war against communism." Dulles and Admiral Arthur Radford, chairman of the Joint Chiefs of Staff, wanted to negotiate a new military bases treaty. None of these hopes was fulfilled. Within months of the inauguration, Magsaysay's coalition had fragmented and a growing nationalist movement threatened relations with the United States. Neil Sheehan writes that "from the American imperial perspective, the Philippines of 1954 was the best of surrogates." But in April of that year, the National Security Council saw Magsaysay's government as unfit for the role Dulles had envisioned. "Radical ultra-nationalism" and the failure of land reform severely limited Magsaysay's usefulness as a symbol of pro-Western nationalism. The NSC laid part of the blame on Magsaysay.[54]

Magsaysay made his commitment to reform contingent on U.S. aid. He built an agenda and political strategy around the expectation that Washington would back him. At his inauguration, he told reporters to expect an aid honeymoon. The United States, he said, would "fix up" the Philippines and use it to showcase the benefits of aligning with the West. Believing he had the money and patronage to command loyalty, he chose his cabinet from among the same collection of joint-venture capitalists, sugar barons, and career bureaucrats who had served Quirino. Few in his administration had an interest in reform, and those who did advocated only policies that involved no sacrifice. Magsaysay failed to translate his concern for the peasantry into a program. Although his inaugural address predicted a Philippines of "small, independent, contented" farmers, it contained only vague proposals for agricultural reform. He and the new agriculture secretary, Araneta, designed a land-reform program in January, but it depended on the United States to pay for expropriation of large estates. Magsaysay discarded land reform when the anticipated flood of aid turned into a trickle.[55]

Aid dropped by almost half in Magsaysay's first year. Eisenhower had campaigned as a budget-cutter, and fiscal conservatives in his administration thwarted attempts to boost aid to the Philippines. Aid levels crept upward after 1956, but too slowly to keep pace with 15 percent annual increases in Philippine government expenditures. Needing to satisfy his clients with increased public spending, Magsaysay resorted to borrowing. The deficit ballooned, triggering inflation, destabilizing the peso, and frightening investors. Magsaysay appealed to Spruance and Dulles, reminding them he had been elected because he "could get more aid than any others from the United States." Dulles sympathized, but came to resent this "tendency on the part of the Filipinos to be on the 'gimme' side."[56]

Magsaysay's patrimonial leadership encouraged factionalism. The Nacionalista-Democrata coalition outnumbered its opponents overwhelmingly in both House and Senate. But rather than marshaling these majorities behind a policy agenda, Magsaysay rewarded his patrons—Laurel, Recto, and Rodriguez—by granting them a free hand in Congress. The old guard alienated Democratas and reformist congressmen friendly to Magsaysay. The coalition disintegrated amid squabbles over patronage and spoils. Halfway through his first year, the president had difficulty extracting even routine legislation from Congress.[57]

Because he had less interest in institutionalizing reform than in solving problems by direct action, congressional deadlock bothered Magsaysay less than it did officials at the embassy.

Magsaysay preferred to exercise leadership by personal dispensation. Shortly after assuming the presidency, he negotiated a series of landlord-tenant disputes in central Luzon. His encouragement induced many landlords to cooperate voluntarily with peasant groups in establishing mediation procedures. He expanded rural improvement programs with his discretionary funds. None of these actions changed law or policy. Embassy officials who formerly praised Magsaysay's energetic attention to peasant problems complained about his rusticating. The new administration had accomplished "relatively little in its first seven months," according to one diplomat, "in part because of the President's predilection for travelling about the country and solving local problems himself." While Magsaysay toured the provinces, Congress joined Araneta and others in the administration to repeal the rural minimum wage and gut laws protecting tenants and laborers. Far from being the reformist government Dulles wanted, the Magsaysay administration reversed the progress made on tenancy legislation in 1951 and 1952. "For all his great leadership qualities," Dulles complained, "President Magsaysay has not proven himself a very shrewd or able politician."[58]

As the following chapter will show, the Magsaysay administration frustrated Dulles's attempts to obtain a new bases treaty. The Eisenhower administration wanted to expand Clark Air Force Base and the naval base at Subic Bay to accommodate the growing military traffic between the United States and Southeast Asia. With Magsaysay in office, Radford and other Pentagon officials figured negotiations would be a snap. Overconfident, Spruance adopted an unnecessarily truculent position in the opening days of the bases talks and provoked the foreign minister, Garcia, who broke off negotiations. Recto and other nationalists among the old guard rushed to Garcia's defense, attacking the bases in Congress and the press. A series of ugly incidents between GIs and Filipinos kept the issue alive and fueled popular resentment. Radford and Dulles disliked Magsaysay's fainthearted defense of American policies, but admitted that he had in Recto "a very clever and ruthless opponent."[59]

Officials in Washington imagined more conflict between Magsaysay and the nationalists than existed. The Philippine presi-

dent included Recto and other nationalists in his inner circle of
advisers, especially on foreign affairs. "RM himself acknowledged
on more than one occasion," according to an aide, "that it helped
his position vis-à-vis the Americans to have a powerful segment
within his administration aggressively demanding more extreme
reforms in [United States-Philippine] relations than he could
openly come out for." The U.S. chargé in Manila warned in April
1956 that Magsaysay intended to hold up the bases agreement
"until we do something to meet some of their demands on us."
Dulles and Radford, however, continued to regard the nationalist attack on the bases as the tactic of "cheap politicians" baiting Magsaysay before the 1957 elections. They postponed negotiations, expecting a second Magsaysay landslide to push aside obstacles to the new treaty.[60]

The National Security Council declared in January 1954 that
"Magsaysay's personal qualifications justify the hope that he
may develop as a leader of the anti-Communist forces in East and
Southeast Asia," but Magsaysay never assumed that role. Dulles
pressed him to appoint Romulo as foreign minister. He believed
that Romulo, a Pulitzer prize–winning journalist and renowned
orator, would introduce a bold, anticommunist voice to regional
politics. Magsaysay, however, had other plans for Romulo; he
sent him to Washington as his personal representative to lobby
for aid and revision of the Philippine Trade Act. Until late 1956,
Recto exerted a strong influence on foreign affairs, advising the
president and steering the administration away from active support for U.S. policies in Asia. Recto feared that the United States
might provoke China and endanger Philippine security. On his
advice, the Magsaysay administration, over U.S. objections, refused to extend diplomatic recognition to South Vietnam. Magsaysay agreed to host the Southeast Asian Treaty conference, but
allowed Garcia and Recto to establish the Philippine position.
Garcia succeeded in softening the language of Dulles's treaty
draft, deleting references to "communist aggression" and adding
a clause recognizing the right to self-determination. Magsaysay
turned up briefly at the opening session dressed in a sharkskin
suit and two-tone shoes, then closeted himself with Pentagon officials to talk about aid. By 1957, the National Security Council

admitted that Magsaysay had contributed little to U.S. influence in the region. "On balance," it found, "Philippine influence tends to be felt in those countries already allied with the U.S., whereas it is slight in countries committed to 'neutralism.' "[61]
U.S. officials seldom expressed disappointment by criticizing Magsaysay. They blamed themselves for not offering more support or sending more aid earlier in the administration. The illusion was complete. Believing they had created Magsaysay, they considered his failings their own.

In March 1957, the presidential plane, the *Mt. Pinatubo*, crashed after a campaign stopover in Cebu. Magsaysay left behind no lasting reforms. He had not become an Asian leader, nor had he given the United States the bases treaty it wanted. Yet officialdom from Dulles and Radford down to CIA agents in the field mourned the loss as a critical blow to U.S. policy in Southeast Asia. They continued to believe, right up until his death, that Magsaysay might live up to his legend. After the tragedy, they clung to the legend. The United States Information Agency worked to "keep alive the memory of Magsaysay as both a Philippine and an Asian leader." In June 1957, Eisenhower announced a postage stamp bearing Magsaysay's likeness under the inscription "Champion of Liberty."[62]

Magsaysay attempted to establish himself as a broker between his American and Philippine clients, but after his first thousand days, he found himself caught between increasing demands of indigenous interests and the shrinking largesse of the United States. Realizing that his political fortunes lay with his Filipino supporters, he sided with them in disputes that became numerous and intractable. As the following chapter will show, he did not shrink from holding U.S. objectives—like the bases treaty—hostage to political and economic demands of his Philippine allies. Despite repeated betrayals, U.S. officials felt their only course lay in strengthening Magsaysay against nationalist politicians they imagined to be his opponents. In doing so, they merely passed money and assistance to the nationalists through the man both sides considered an agent.

Magsaysay's story demonstrates the variety of strategies client states could employ to create autonomy. Deception played a key role. U.S. officials sensed the rising fortunes of international communism and their own military and economic limits, making them eager, even desperate, to believe they had found an anticommunist champion. Magsaysay played the part, according to an aide, because "it was in this role that he was known in the United States, and he valued the esteem and friendship of the United States not only for the tangible benefits this could bring to the Philippines, but also for the political advantage that it offered him." He used customary bargaining ploys: playing on his regime's weakness, pitting bureaucracies against one another, and asserting that he alone could keep nationalism in check.[63]

Cliental strategies imply tradeoffs for policy. Mark Gasiorowski has demonstrated that U.S. support in Iran strengthened the government, separating it from domestic constituencies and resulting, after sufficient provocation, in the overthrow of a powerful ally. Magsaysay was a different type of client. He sought aid on behalf of his constituents, not to enlarge his personal power. As a result, his government remained popular, but useless for many of the duties a client like the Shah could perform. Magsaysay lacked the power to follow aggressive domestic and international policies the United States demanded. He also encouraged the growth of an economic nationalist constituency that felt threatened by military and trade links to the United States.

FIVE

Nationalism and the Bases

Magsaysay's seeming collaboration concealed a widening divergence of Philippine and United States interests. As Philippine industry grew and the United States deepened its commitment to defend Southeast Asia, each country placed more demands on the other; areas of agreement became smaller, criticism sharper and more frequent. Magsaysay's first year marked the beginning of modern Philippine nationalism, a critique of bilateral relations that animated political discourse until 1991. The timing and ferocity of the nationalist outburst owed much to the actions of Eisenhower's new administration, which confirmed Filipinos' darkest fears about the intentions of the United States. Overestimating Magsaysay's autonomy, State and Defense department officials failed to heed warnings of the elite's dissatisfaction.

Nationalist movements everywhere presented a critical challenge to Eisenhower's administration. Between 1945 and 1960, 40 countries, containing vast resources and over a quarter of the world's population, achieved independence. Eisenhower felt that the United States needed to prevent these countries from isolating themselves economically and aligning with the Soviet Union. The president and his subordinates believed that if former colonial powers would yield the levers of colonial control to cooperative local elites, nationalism might stabilize postcolonial states and orient them economically and strategically toward the West. The Philippines, they felt, demonstrated how this could be done.[1]

Nowhere did the administration have a better chance of handling nationalism than in the Philippines. Eisenhower spent four years there in the 1930s and understood the country's politics better than many of his subordinates did. His global policies, however, left little room for sensitivity. He intended to regain the initiative in the cold war and to do it cheaply. In mid-1953, he led a thorough review of policy assumptions, which produced National Security Council paper no. 162/2 and a policy known as the "New Look," stressing cost reduction and bold ventures to stem the communist advance. Employing covert action, surrogate troops, and nuclear intimidation, the administration planned to sustain an aggressive posture while reducing conventional forces and spending. Allied countries would bear a larger share of cold war risks and burdens with fewer rewards.[2]

The United States needed the Philippines to bring the New Look to Southeast Asia. NSC 162/2 declared the region vital to the security of the free world, and Eisenhower's advisers wanted to seize the initiative from the Viet Minh and respond aggressively if Chinese troops invaded Indochina. To recast the United States as a benefactor of progressive nationalism, State Department officials wanted Magsaysay to furnish an example. He could help organize a Southeast Asian alliance and push through a treaty expanding naval and air bases. The administration had little to give Magsaysay in return. The New Look called for reductions in aid, concentrating it on areas facing immediate threats.[3]

Eisenhower's handling of nationalism had profound implications for Philippine economic development. As in many postcolonial countries, nationalists in the Philippines advocated industrialization. But whereas in Brazil and other countries support for import controls and protectionist measures came from a growing urban bourgeoisie, in the Philippines nationalism was an instrument the politically dominant landed elite used to extend control over dynamic sectors of the economy. The elite's two objectives were to obtain control of economic levers still in the hands of the United States government and to exclude the Philippine-Chinese middle class from new enterprises. Nationalism was an explosive mixture of elite ambition and racial animosity.

* * *

Declining assistance levels discredited Magsaysay and set the stage for the rise of nationalism. Expecting the United States to reward his electoral victory, Magsaysay planned to consolidate his support with U.S. aid money. But aid dropped sharply in 1954. With the Philippines stabilized, the United States turned its attention to other Southeast Asian hotspots. Dulles, the secretary of state, lobbied for aid to the Philippines, but fiscal conservatives in the administration and Congress compelled the State Department to concentrate on Indochina and other threatened countries. Magsaysay resorted to deficit spending, which fueled inflation and destabilized the economy. Nacionalista leaders criticized U.S. ingratitude and partiality toward less-cooperative countries and fanned the resentment of landlord-politicians who depended on loans and grants from the United States.

State Department officials wanted to enlarge the aid program to boost Magsaysay as an ally and reformer. Spruance argued in December 1953 that U.S. leadership in the Far East depended "to an important degree on the success of the Magsaysay administration." "We must demonstrate that friendship toward the United States earns friendship from the United States." Dulles thought Magsaysay could serve as a model. His "personal qualifications," Dulles told the National Security Council, "justify the hope that he may develop as a leader of the anti-communist forces in East and Southeast Asia." He instructed embassies to encourage ties between the Philippines and other Asian governments and planned for Magsaysay to tour Southeast Asian capitals and host a pan-Asian conference on trade and defense. Department officials agreed that "a successful attack on Philippine problems" would enhance Magsaysay's prestige, and favored a substantial increase in aid for industrial and rural development.[4]

Dulles had only modest ambitions for a Philippine aid and reform program, but even those were too much for budget-cutters in Congress and the administration. Two years earlier, Spruance and Acheson had supported Hardie's ambitious program to purchase and divide large estates. In 1954, with the Huks quiescent, Dulles favored land reform as a way to strengthen Magsaysay politically. An inexpensive program would suffice. He wanted Magsaysay to enforce land-tenure laws and expand rural credit, irrigation, and wells for drinking water. Dulles had little money to spare for even a modest program. Aid under the Foster-Quirino agreement peaked in 1952, and budgets for 1954 and 1955 contained smaller sums for rural improvement. Budget-minded conservatives in the administration and the 83rd Congress had targeted foreign aid for drastic cuts.[5]

Eisenhower entered office committed to reducing overseas aid. Concerned about the growth of the federal budget, he filled his cabinet with fiscal conservatives like George Humphrey, the treasury secretary, and Budget Director Joseph Dodge. He advocated liberalizing trade as an alternative to development assistance, and in 1953 "trade not aid" became the slogan of his drive for extension of the Reciprocal Trade Act. The policy enjoyed broad support within the administration. A presidential commission on foreign economic policy headed by Clarence Randall ratified the reduced-tariffs, reduced-aid formula in its report in January 1954. Although some key officials—notably Dulles and aid administrator Harold Stassen—supported increasing aid, Humphrey had enough support in the administration and Congress to thwart or drastically curtail any increases.[6]

Foreign aid had few enthusiasts in Congress. Attempting to save domestic programs from budget cuts, members began to regard overseas spending as an extravagance. During hearings in the spring of 1953, Senator Everett Dirksen attacked aid policies in the Far East, singling out the Philippines. He criticized the Economic Cooperation Administration for tolerating the program's poor bookkeeping and projects that "nobody seems to know anything about." "If these projects, which aggregate $1,500,000, are so vital to Philippine industry," he inquired, "should they not be financed by the few wealthy bankers and industrialists likely to be benefitted rather than by the U.S. taxpayers?" Congress shaved $3 million off economic and technical assistance to the Philippines for 1954, leaving the smallest annual outlay since 1950.[7]

Magsaysay had anticipated an aid honeymoon. "We've got to fix up the Philippines," he told reporters, so "we can invite people over here from Indonesia and places like that and say 'see what our American friends have helped us to do.' " According to his biographer, he wanted to exercise power by "bending to his will" the many intermediaries, cabinet officials, local and national politicians, "by exploiting their self interest and dependence on him as claimants." He planned large capital outlays to build roads, a program that enjoyed support from peasants and caciques alike.[8] Magsaysay's land-reform initiative, the first in Philippine history, relied on U.S. aid. The new agriculture secretary, Araneta, planned to introduce legislation in early 1954 to break up large estates. Scion of a Negros sugar dynasty, Araneta had sold some of his landholdings in the late 1940s to invest in manufacturing. He saw land reform as an opportunity for other landowners to diversify, and to assure cacique control of the rapidly growing industrial sector. He told sugar planters that they must be "made to realize that we are living in a new age, that it is time for them to switch their investments from land to industries and banking." Araneta's plan called for the government to supply cash inducements for landlords making the change. He expected the United States to support the program, but early in 1954 cutbacks and a personnel shakeup at the United States aid mission signaled that no new aid was forthcoming. First Hardie and then the aid administrator, Roland Renne, departed for Washington. The new administrator looked warily on projects involving large outlays. Magsaysay and Araneta shelved land reform and concentrated instead on retail nationalization.[9]

Foreign-aid advocates in the Eisenhower administration gained ground after 1954, but the change came too late for Magsaysay. Dulles and Stassen, the aid administrator, persuaded Eisenhower to ask Congress for a modest $200 million program for Asia. Congress approved but cut it by half in 1955, then eliminated it the following year. Magsaysay increased spending at an annual rate of 15 percent, running a deficit to support road-building, the military, and pork-barrel projects. Between 1953 and 1956, while the Philippine military budget remained at about $75 million a year, military assistance dropped from $40 million to $10 million. Rather than increase taxes, Magsaysay borrowed from the Central Bank, triggering inflation, destabilizing the peso, and widening the gap between rich and poor. He laid over 2,500 kilometers of new roads, but with the population increasing and farm incomes declining, tenants found it difficult to remain on the land, and by the thousands followed the new roads to cities to search for work.[10]

Magsaysay failed to satisfy the elite's hunger for loans and patronage. Liberal senators and members of the administration attacked Magsaysay and the United States for not providing more aid. Pointing to the sums allotted to Vietnam and Korea, editorialists criticized American "ingratitude" and urged Magsaysay to take a tough line. The president implored the State Department for money. He reminded the ambassador that he, Magsaysay, had been elected because he "could get more aid than any others from the United States." He refused to visit Washington in response to Eisenhower's invitation without a promise of aid, and warned that "Americans do not understand the Asian mind when they fail to realize the importance of gifts."[11]

Reduction of aid did not itself cause the upsurge of nationalism during the Magsaysay years, but it heightened anti-American sentiment, particularly among cacique capitalists, the chief beneficiaries of U.S. loans and grants. Underwritten by American money and sheltered by agreements, Philippine industry was less vulnerable to market forces than to changes in bilateral relations. To manufacturers, aid reductions indicated a shift in American attitudes: at best, a tendency to take the Philippines for granted; at worst, hostility toward industrialization.

The Philippine manufacturing sector had grown at a rate of 15 percent a year during the Quirino administration. As in other developing countries, industrial promotion policies created a class of entrepreneurs whose livelihood depended on market protection and money from the state. Joint-venture capitalists like Hilarion Henares and Gil Puyat resembled Latin American entrepreneurs, concentrating solely on manufacturing and defining political interests that set them apart from landowners. They, however, were few. Landlord-capitalists dominated Philippine manufacturing, and by 1954, landowning families, emboldened by assured profits and low risks, were moving into industry in ever greater numbers. Since success required connections, caciques with ties to the regime were among the first to change. In Latin America, the industrial bourgeoisie acquired political power slowly and after many setbacks. In the Philippines five years after import and exchange control began, a large portion of the elite had turned to industry.[12]

Diverse holdings gave this class a peculiar and conflicted set of political objectives. As landowners and exporters they chafed under protectionist policies that raised prices and diverted dollar earnings to industry, but as industrialists they profited from the same policies. Moreover, caciques differed in the extent and direction of their diversification. The Elizalde and Soriano clans invested chiefly in industry but kept a hacienda or two. The Lopez family, which owned the *Manila Chronicle*, did the opposite, purchasing a few factories to complement its primary interest in sugar. Araneta drew half his earnings from manufacturing and half from sugar. Though most moved assets from land to industry, those with falling political fortunes went the other way. Overlapping interests prevented the social conflicts that followed industrialization in Latin America. Instead of a distinct national bourgeoisie rising to challenge the feudal class, industrial and landowning interests mingled in each member of the Philippine elite.[13]

Although landlord-capitalists dominated the Magsaysay regime, their diverse portfolios caused them to define interests as they always had, particularistically, and prevented them from uniting behind a policy on trade, land reform, or industrial promotion. They did, however, share many of the same apprehensions about the control of industry. In the first year of the Magsaysay administration, the landed elite saw two threats to its supremacy in manufacturing: the Chinese middle class, and the U.S. military bases outside of Manila.

As the Huk rebellion subsided between 1951 and 1953, Filipinos' age-old mistrust of Chinese merchants reemerged in a movement to Filipinize industry and the retail trade. As in some other parts of Southeast Asia, nationalism in the Philippines began in the twentieth century as a reaction to Chinese merchants rather than to European colonizers. In the last years of U.S. rule, Chinese businessmen dominated economic sectors like retailing

(55 percent Chinese-owned), lumber (85 percent), and marketing of commodities, especially rice. They made up a large portion of the shopkeeping middle class. When Filipinos—landowners and peasants alike—borrowed money, took goods to market, or bought articles, small or large, they dealt with the Chinese. Chinese economic power aroused more animosity than did the colonial government's merely political domination. After independence, the Philippine Congress legislated against Chinese access to mineral and natural resources and entry into professions, but a combination of U.S. and Chinese pressure and government weakness prevented the Roxas and Quirino administrations from acting against Chinese control of retail trade.[14]

Most Philippine-Chinese families had lived for generations in the Philippines, but remained aliens owing to naturalization laws that defined nationality by race. Philippine courts retroactively denaturalized ethnically Chinese citizens born under the American regime, and ruled that mixed-race children of Chinese fathers could not claim citizenship. The term "Filipino" designated a racial and class distinction, applying to the mestizo elite and the largely poor Malay majority, but not to the technically alien shopkeeping class. The Philippine retail nationalization movement, an alliance of anti-Chinese business leagues and old guard Nacionalista politicians, united the upper and lower classes against the middle.[15]

Nationalization fed on fears that the Chinese would use their retailing dominance to gain control of industry and land. After years of experience in retail and internal commerce, Chinese families were poised to move capital and talent into manufacturing. Chinese firms already dominated the textile industry, and in the early 1950s ventured into the production of flour and steel. As manufacturers, Filipinos feared Chinese competition, and as landowners, they worried that the Chinese would use wealth as Filipinos always had, to buy land, and through land, power.[16]

Land remained the key to political power. The hacienda functioned as the basic unit of organization, mobilizing votes by dispensing favors and seasonal employment. Since Filipinos' entrepreneurial advantage lay in their political clout, which assured access to the state's financial instrumentalities, the hacienda retained a preeminent, honored place in even the most diversified portfolio. "Your land is like your most beautiful dress, the one that gives you good luck," Congresswoman Hortensia Starke, proprietress of vast sugar lands on Negros, explained. "If someone takes it away from you, he only wants to destabilize you, to undress you." By law, foreigners could not own land, not even a house plot, but caciques knew law was no protection against wealth. With enough money and a Filipino relative, anyone could acquire a hacienda, and Chinese industrialists made no secret of their ambitions to do so. To Filipinos, continued alien control of retail, "the keystone upon which our distributive system rests," would lead ineluctably to loss of land and to economic and political "slavery." The 1953 Nacionalista landslide brought to power legislators determined to act against this threat. "Nationalism is on the march," declared Congressman Domocao Alonto; "beware those who would venture to oppose it."[17]

Magsaysay entered office resolved to nationalize the retail trade. Leading figures in the nationalization movement held key positions in the cabinet and Congress. Magsaysay's "thinly veiled dislike of the Chinese" was revealed, according to an embassy official, when he denied foreign exchange to Chinese firms. In January 1954, Congress took up 47 anti-Chinese bills, most targeting the retail sector. Filipino businessmen clamored for government action against their Chinese competitors. Newspaper comment reached a high pitch in March, when the government of the Republic of China hinted at retaliation. Embassy officials watched the nationalistic frenzy warily and steered clear of it. Although they disapproved of anti-Chinese laws, they recognized that it was not their fight and concentrated instead on preparations for the bases talks.[18]

Philippine nationalism and U.S. strategic policy collided in March 1954, when the Eisenhower administration's fiscal conservatism and strategic needs combined with the heightened apprehensions of cacique capitalists, who saw the large U.S. military bases outside of Manila as another threat to their control of land and manufacturing. To meet communist challenges in the region, Pentagon officials wanted to expand installations in the Philippines, but budgetary constraints prevented them from buying the necessary land. In attempting to work around this barrier, officials stumbled into the nationalists' line of fire. Filipinos suddenly saw the foreign military presence as an economic threat similar to the one posed by the Chinese.

For Filipino manufacturers, the bases had always been a disorderly intruder in their sheltered economy. The issuance of military scrip during the 1949–50 fiscal crisis revealed the bases' economic power. Issued by the Defense Department in early 1950, the certificates replaced the peso as the unit of currency in Olongapo and Angeles and began turning up in Manila, wreaking havoc with the Central Bank's effort to control the money supply. Filipino manufacturers keenly felt the bases' economic muscle. Makers of everything from paint to automobiles worried less about local competitors than about black-market goods from Clark and Subic. The magnitude of the PX trade is difficult to determine, but it undoubtedly grew along with the size of the garrison. A 1977 investigation found that even with a 100 to 200 percent markup, black-market goods could compete with domestic equivalents. Filipinos also worried about foreign control of such large tracts of land and everything it implied—mineral rights, wealth, and power.[19]

Under the 1947 treaty, the United States controlled vast territories Filipinos called the "baselands." The largest, Clark Air Force Base, occupied 250 square miles, equivalent to Manhattan, Brooklyn, the Bronx, and Staten Island combined. Thirteen unused bases, on deep-water bays and inlets, comprised almost 500 square miles of commercially valuable land. The United States owned title to substantial and costly parcels purchased before the Second World War, including tracts in commercial and residential areas of Manila worth millions. Beneath the baselands lay unexplored mineral wealth, manganese, nickel, and, some claimed, gold.[20]

The baselands contained whole barrios, two Negrito tribes, and a city. At the northern tip of Subic Bay, the 60,000 citizens of Olongapo lived in a municipality entirely within the base. A Navy lieutenant commander, one junior grade lieutenant, and a Marine administered the city under a set of regulations known as the Yellow Book. Philippine residents paid over $700,000 annually for city improvements. Admiral Radford, chairman of the Joint Chiefs of Staff, called it "one of the happiest little towns in the Philippines." Despite security problems, the Navy liked having the city inside the base, where it could control prostitution and gambling, supervise off-duty sailors, and keep a handy supply of low-cost labor. Clark Air Force Base, which also had an on-base population, kept its Filipino employees in compounds surrounded by barbed wire and guards. Newspaper editors considered the bases poor copy, and few Filipinos knew about conditions there.[21]

The bases aroused few objections until 1954. The 1947 treaty accommodated Filipinos' economic concerns by guaranteeing subsoil rights and restricting the business activities of servicemen. During most of the Quirino administration, the United States exercised only nominal control. The perimeters of Clark and Subic remained unmarked and unguarded, and the other bases remained unoccupied. After 1950, the bases became more important to aid and military operations in the Far East. The force doubled, from fewer than 5,000 in 1950 to 10,520 the following year. Over the next few years, the number of U.S. civilian employees increased by half, from 400 in 1951 to 639 in 1958, and the number of Filipino employees increased from 9,000 to 13,000. The bases became a stopover for personnel en route to Southeast Asia and Taiwan, with 33,000 passing through Clark in 1954. Traffic and personnel increased as the bases assumed a variety of missions—supply, training, and nuclear dispersal—missions that required the United States to enforce its control of the baselands.[22]

The New Look increased demands on Far Eastern bases, particularly those in the Philippines. Defense officials regarded Philippine installations as critical to the effort to sustain French forces in Indochina. Believing a French capitulation would doom Southeast Asia, the Truman administration assumed an increasing share of the war's financial burden, contributing a half billion dollars, nearly half the total cost, in 1953. As Viet Minh forces closed around French positions along the Tonkin Gulf, Clark Air Force Base became an essential transshipment point for trucks, tanks, ammunition, and food. Planes arrived with American markings and left with French. France's decision to fortify Dien Bien Phu, an outpost that could be supplied only from the air, increased the importance of Philippine bases. Clark became the last stop for French troops airlifted into battle, and the first stop for wounded evacuees returning to France and North Africa.[23]

When the siege of Dien Bien Phu began, administration officials considered three plans for U.S. intervention, all involving strikes from Clark. On March 25, 1954, Radford proposed Operation Vulture, a nuclear strike against Viet Minh positions around Dien Bien Phu. With the short flying time, Air Force Chief of Staff General Nathan Twining later explained, "you could take all day to drop a bomb. Make sure you put it in the right place. No opposition. And clean those Commies out of there." The French counterproposed a series of conventional strikes by twenty B-29s from Clark. The Joint Chiefs drafted plans for 300 Philippine-based fighter bombers to attack the Viet Minh stronghold at Tuan Giao near the Chinese border. Eisenhower rejected all the plans as risky, militarily and politically. The proposals nonetheless revealed the bases' importance to operational planning during the months in which officials initiated talks with the Magsaysay administration.[24]

Philippine bases figured into U.S. plans to contain China and deter nuclear attack. Dulles, Radford, and other Eisenhower advisers anticipated a Chinese invasion of Indochina, and determined to respond with "immediate, positive, armed force" against China. Dulles planned to use Chinese Nationalist troops supported by American air and sea power to seize the island of Hainan. Close to staging areas in the Philippines, Hainan's geography would allow the United States to take full advantage of its naval superiority. The Seventh Fleet depended on Philippine bases to supply its operations in the South China Sea, and the Hainan option placed new demands on bases and training facilities.[25]

As part of the New Look, the Defense Department began drafting plans in early 1953 to deploy nuclear weapons to foreign bases. On June 8, 1953, Eisenhower ordered nuclear forces to Guam, the first of a series of deployments that by 1955 would place overseas a third of the U.S. stock of hydrogen weapons and almost half of the atomic bombs. By dispersing the nuclear stockpile, Radford hoped to decrease its vulnerability to Soviet attack and position bombs closer to trouble spots. To Radford, the New Look placed "maximum reliance on nuclear weapons from the outset." During his tenure as chairman of the Joint Chiefs, he recommended nuclear attacks on Asian targets three times. Near war zones in China and Southeast Asia, the huge Philippine bases were essential to nuclear deployment, and Radford planned to modernize them for their new role.[26]

Preparing Philippine bases to meet the demands of the New Look required facilities and land. The Air Force wanted to lengthen airstrips to accommodate the jet-propelled B-36 bomber. The Navy needed permission to fill five acres of Manila Bay to lengthen the strip at Sangley Point. Pentagon officials wanted bombing ranges and areas for training and maneuvers close to the potential battle theaters in China and Vietnam. To contact ships in the South China Sea, the Navy wanted to place transmitters in the Zambales Mountains above Subic. The Air Force needed dispersal and recovery airstrips away from its main facilities to protect planes from nuclear attack. Filling these needs would require substantial tracts of privately held land.[27]

State Department officials believed they could get what they needed from the new Magsaysay administration, and shortly after Eisenhower took office, he directed the State and Defense departments to prepare to negotiate a new military bases treaty. An ad hoc committee of officials from the State, Justice, and Defense departments and the Bureau of the Budget met throughout 1953 to devise strategy for negotiations to follow Magsaysay's election. Members hoped to obtain a treaty that would enlarge Clark and Subic. In return, the United States would relinquish smaller bases. The committee expected less resistance from the pro-American Magsaysay than from the 83rd Congress, which complained in 1953 of the expense of keeping 200 overseas installations.[28]

The president's committee wanted to avoid asking Congress for money. Members felt they could not "approach Congress with a request for funds to purchase land while at the same time we are giving away surplus land holdings of material value." In addition to the 118,940 acres to be added to Clark and Subic, the State Department wanted 260 acres in downtown Manila for consular and information facilities. Philippine negotiators would probably require the United States to purchase the land at full price and then grant only a lease. Panel members agreed that unused bases provided a solution. Since the Defense Department owned some of the vacant baselands outright, having purchased them during the colonial period, the United States could offer deeds to unused land in return for the property needed.[29]

State and Defense officials disagreed on how to approach the Philippine government. Philip Bonsal, in charge of Philippine affairs, wanted to make Magsaysay a gift of unused tracts and ask him to furnish the new baselands in the interest of mutual defense. Middle-ranking military officers agreed, but Radford and Defense Secretary Charles Wilson thought the United States would be in a stronger position if it brought titles to the negotiating table. Spruance strongly favored this approach. A few State officials questioned the deeds, arguing that the 1947 treaty superseded the Defense Department's title. Wilson took the question to Attorney General Herbert Brownell, who replied that the United States could claim title on the basis of both deeds and the Tydings-McDuffie Act of 1934, which allowed the United States to "retain" bases after independence. The Defense Department could claim ownership of all the lands reserved under the 1947 treaty.[30]

State Department officials foresaw the damage the Brownell opinion could cause and tried to suppress it. The embassy counselor, James Bell, argued that issuing a legal claim would invite a legalistic response, and Brownell's opinion would provoke charges of imperialism. A messy public debate would damage Magsaysay. Spruance replied that negotiations would be "fruitless unless the United States entered armed with definite tangible assets." He would make Philippine acceptance of American title "the necessary first step." The matter went to the president, and in a Christmas Eve telephone call, Eisenhower told Dulles his "experience out there" told him the United States ought to make a present to Magsaysay of all unused military bases. "The

American forces out there have always taken a high-handed attitude with respect to the ownership of property." Forcing the title issue would be "kicking [Magsaysay] in the teeth." Radford and Assistant Secretary of State Walter Robertson urged the president to let Spruance negotiate in his own way, and Eisenhower relented. He had better instincts than his subordinates but was unwilling to impose his views over the objections of his administration. Spruance decided to present the Brownell memorandum to Garcia, the vice president and foreign minister, on February 11, before the first round of talks.[31]

For Magsaysay, the bases negotiations appeared to present no problem. His advisers intended to use the negotiations to clarify the Philippines' position in global strategy and to learn whether the United States intended to defend the Philippines in the event of general war. Expecting that the Americans wanted to acquire bases or expand existing ones, they considered the process "purely mechanical." They would seek an exchange of one leased area for each new lease, and assumed title was not at issue, since the 1947 treaty superseded previous titles. They pondered the possibility that the United States might want to purchase title to some of the baselands, a request they would not entertain. "The Philippine government," the chief of the military planning group advised, "should not sell real estate." They had no clue that Spruance would claim to hold title to existing bases.[32]

Amid the furor over retail nationalization, newspapers paid little attention to the opening of the bases talks in late February, but on March 16 the Brownell memorandum stole the headlines. State Department officials had expected it to incense some Filipinos, but the storm of rage that followed the document's appearance caught them off guard. Filipinos saw it as revealing a hidden agenda for the economic enslavement of the country. In response, a small but important section of the Nacionalista old guard, along with a major newspaper, the *Chronicle*, redirected anti-Chinese invective at the United States and turned the bases into symbols of foreign encroachment. Employing the rhetoric of retail nationalization, Nacionalista politicians denounced the decision as a bid to establish extraterritorial enclaves. Official and public outcry, an embassy official reported, "bordered on the hysterical." Philippine negotiators broke off talks. Senator Lorenzo Tañada accused Spruance of trying to establish "little Hong Kongs." The United States intended, according to Ramon Mitra, "to gobble us completely." In a phrase often used against the Chinese, Congressman Jose Laurel, Jr., accused Spruance of forcing Filipinos "to become strangers in their own land."[33]

Garcia asked Senator Claro Recto to draft a rebuttal, and Recto drafted the rejoinder Bell feared. Author of the constitution and renowned as a legal scholar, the senator from Batangas regarded United States power with suspicion, but before 1954, his attacks on the United States had been qualified and apologetic. As his biographer notes, the Brownell memorandum "caused him to open a wide front in a campaign that would expose the colonial practices of the United States." His reply suggested that the United States wanted to use the baselands for commercial exploitation. He attacked the United States for seeking "an obnoxious extraterritoriality, impairing the status of the Republic." The Philippines had granted bases "as a matter of expediency, not to serve and foster any other interest of the United States." The *Chronicle* amplified his rhetoric, charging Brownell with "territorial hijacking" and hinting at "a secret agreement by which the Philippine government has sold the people down the river."[34]

For the elite, Recto's polemic touched a raw nerve. Sensitive to the precariousness of their economic position, landowners and industrialists believed the United States might use its military bases to achieve control of the country's economy and resources. Subsequent developments confirmed their fears. On March 25, Agence France Presse reported that the United States planned to use the Brownell memorandum in the coming trade negotiations. The story proved false, but Washington's denials only added to its credibility. Later that year, Air Force officials erected barricades to prevent Filipino miners from extracting manganese from a site inside Clark Air Force Base. Editorialists concluded that the Air Force had stolen the miners' claim and intended to take the manganese for itself. Magsaysay rushed to Clark and had the barricades removed, but the damage was done. From that point, landowners and businessmen regarded the bases as a menace, the thin end of a wedge that could separate them from the land and resources they controlled.[35]

Recto's nationalism targeted an elite audience. As the *Chronicle*'s political commentator, I. P. Soliongco, explained, it "attracted the faith and loyalty of a class of Filipinos, who because of their economic station, cannot be dismissed as if they were peasants." Recto appealed to the landlord-capitalists, whose livelihood depended on import controls and other nationalist measures. He argued that the United States would use military power to open Philippine markets, a claim made credible by the black market in goods imported through the bases. Manufacturers saw Clark and Subic as treaty ports, little Hong Kongs. U.S. aid and land-reform initiatives, Recto claimed, aimed to cripple industry and keep the Philippines dependent on farm exports. He linked industrialization, nationalism, and Filipinization in an agenda: "Exploitation of our natural resources by Filipino capital; development and strengthening of Filipino capitalism, not foreign capitalism; increase of the national income, but not allowing it to go mostly for the benefit of non-Filipinos."[36]

Recto placed economic concerns ahead of issues of sovereignty and foreign affairs. He advocated national dignity and a neutralist foreign policy, but as his positions on the Southeast Asian Treaty and the 1955 trade agreement revealed, he readily sacrificed those goals to the primary aim of advancing Philippine economic interests. The movement's economic focus led U.S. officials to underestimate its durability. Alert for signs of creeping neutralism but seeing none, Dulles dismissed nationalism as a tactic of "cheap politicians" baiting Magsaysay before the 1955 midterm elections. Although the Philippine president included leading nationalists like Recto and Tañada in his inner circle of advisers, especially on foreign affairs, State Department officials imagined a power struggle between Magsaysay and the Nacionalista leadership. Following a presidential statement backing the nationalists, Senator Arturo Tolentino quipped, "This is going to be even harder for those Washington 'sources' to understand. Mr. Magsaysay is not acting like he's supposed to." Dulles and Radford criticized Magsaysay for his fainthearted defense of their policies, but they saw nationalism as a passing fad. They postponed talks and attempted to appease the nationalists.[37]

United States officials learned that avoiding nationalist outbursts meant structuring policy to suit the landlord-capitalist elite. The elite had less interest in creating new wealth than in preserving control over the manufacturing sector. Filipinos preferred to postpone development or provoke a recession rather than allow aliens to benefit from economic growth. Legislators admitted that retail nationalization would open a void in the economy that Filipino entrepreneurs might not fill, that Filipinization would mean inflation and unemployment. They welcomed these sacrifices as the price of economic freedom. When passed in 1955, retail nationalization caused Chinese investors to withdraw most of the country's development capital and provoked a recession that put 1.2 million Filipinos out of work.[38]

Economic nationalism meant continued protection for Filipino manufacturers, a policy that led to the growth of monopoly industries that profited from shortages and low output. The Magsaysay administration had ample instruments to nurture new industries. Import and exchange controls designed to ease the effects of the 1950 fiscal crisis encouraged industry, as did tax breaks, the overvalued peso, and government spending. Magsaysay's planners spoke of jobs and development, but instead of targeting industries with employment and earnings potential, they dispensed favors to the regime's clients. The cumulative effect of numerous patrimonial decisions directed capital from landed families and the state into highly profitable consumer-goods industries with little potential for growth or employment. Firms that assembled, mixed, or repackaged American brands for sale in the protected market predominated. Such "industries" fueled inflation, created few jobs, and left the economy as dependent on imports as before. During the Magsaysay years, industrial income increased, industrial wages declined, and manufacturing created fewer jobs per peso invested than any other sector. The firms created no capital base—machine shops, tool-and-die factories, skilled technicians—on which industry could build, a situation one economist calls "industrialization without development." Manufacturing could not grow without capital infusions from landholders and foreign lenders, and the industrial sector became a burden on the economy instead of a propelling force.[39]

The objective of nationalist foreign policy was to prevent the United States from interfering with policies that retarded devel-

opment. Manipulation of the economy in the name of Filipinization secured credit, tax breaks, and competition-free markets for
favored Filipino entrepreneurs. Politically protected capitalists
enjoyed large profits and low risks in enterprises geared for inefficiency and underproduction. Before 1954, U.S. policies inadvertently advanced this system by promoting import and exchange
controls, but the United States regarded these measures as temporary and had urged the government to take steps leading to decontrol. After the Brownell memorandum, it became "essential,"
the National Security Council warned, "to avoid actions which
would tend to substantiate charges of improper interference." To
keep its bases, the United States would have to respect Filipino
nationalism, a course that meant abetting underdevelopment.⁴⁰

Despite the furor over the bases, Magsaysay remained eager to
accommodate U.S. strategic interests when tangible rewards and
few political risks were involved. Dulles's proposal in early 1954
for a Southeast Asian treaty provided one such opportunity. Philippine leaders had advocated a Pacific version of the North Atlantic Treaty since 1949, and Magsaysay saw little problem in re-
newing the proposal. By supporting collective defense, he could
reassure the State Department and Congress of the loyalty of the
Philippines, and raise his stature as an opponent of communism
in the weeks before trade talks opened.

The National Security Council stressed regional alliances in
its original formulation of the New Look, but the reasoning behind collective security in Southeast Asia changed as the conflict
in Vietnam intensified. In February and March 1954, the Joint
Chiefs declared Formosa and the Philippines vital to the United
States, to be held even at the risk of general war. Rather than a
costly NATO-type defense, the Joint Chiefs planned to supply
training, landing craft, and jets to the Filipino and Nationalist
Chinese armies, and to coordinate defense under a loose regional
arrangement. As Eisenhower contemplated air strikes to relieve
the French garrison at Dien Bien Phu, Dulles declared that the
Viet Minh challenge "should be met by united action." Unable
to construct a regional pact before the Geneva talks in late April,
he determined to use a Southeast Asian treaty to regain the ini-

tiative after the French defeat and the partitioning of Indochina. As diplomats and military advisers, including Lansdale, fashioned a state out of the chaotic factionalism of South Vietnam, Dulles persuaded Magsaysay to host a conference. A treaty could remove the racist overtones of the ANZUS agreement and overcome Britain's resentment at having been excluded from earlier defense treaties. It could also add to Magsaysay's prestige as an Asian leader.[41]

Philippine officials had begun to consider such prestige dangerous. During the campaign, Magsaysay had said he wanted to join the United States in a regional defense organization, and his foreign-affairs advisers, including Recto, endorsed joint defense planning. As the implications of the New Look became clear, however, a close alliance looked less attractive. The administration's consensus broke in February and March when Dulles, in three strongly worded speeches, outlined a new Asian strategy that raised the stakes of military cooperation. Philippine diplomats understood the new strategy to mean that local conflicts, including the one in Indochina, might provoke the United States to initiate a general, probably nuclear, war with China. Troops would be withdrawn from the Far East, Dulles indicated, so the United States could reserve its mobile striking force for targets of its own choosing. Brinkmanship terrified Magsaysay's advisers, who felt that the United States was endangering the Philippines while minimizing its own risks. The Philippine ambassador to the United Nations, Salvador P. Lopez, advised that "the 'new look' . . . clearly requires that we take a long second look at our mutual defense arrangements with the United States."[42]

Although Philippine officials favored collective defense chiefly as a way to obtain economic benefits from the United States, they were apprehensive about how the United States might behave in a military crisis. France's defeat at Dien Bien Phu, despite "maximum aid, short of fighting men," from the United States, "radically changed the power picture in Asia," according to Laurel, and raised doubts about the ability and willingness of the United States to defend its allies. Garcia represented the Philippines at the Geneva Conference and viewed the outcome as "a major tragedy in world diplomacy," and possibly "the signal for more speedy war preparations." Filipinos feared that in a confrontation with China, American forces would again abandon the Philippines. The United States had committed itself to defend the Philippines in a 1951 treaty, but Filipinos remained suspicious of this promise, which was more ambiguous than the "instant retaliation" pledge given to European allies. In July, shortly after agreeing to host a conference on Southeast Asian defense, Magsaysay remarked that he would only approve a NATO-type treaty, committing each nation to defend the others. Recto criticized the faltering U.S. commitment to Philippine defense. Without a pledge of immediate retaliation, he argued, the Philippines should repudiate ties to the United States and adopt an Indonesia-style neutrality, "making no enemies where we can make no friends." In August, Philippine officials demanded military aid, a retaliation pledge, and trade concessions from the United States in return for accepting the treaty. The New Look and Dien Bien Phu raised the stakes, and thus the price for Philippine cooperation.[43]

Magsaysay had ulterior reasons for wanting to associate himself with the Southeast Asian treaty. Philippine leaders worried less about defense talks than about negotiations to revise the Philippine Trade Act, which opened in Washington the following week. The Southeast Asian conference required a delicate balancing of military and economic security concerns. To enhance his country's prestige in the United States, Magsaysay needed a successful conference, but he needed to avoid provoking China or encouraging a reckless American strategy.[44]

Philippine negotiators wanted to earn American gratitude by helping produce a successful treaty, but foresaw two possible outcomes, either of which might produce the desired result. In their preferred version, SEATO would resemble NATO, committing each nation to aid the others and involving a large American force in place. Failing that, Magsaysay would accept an agreement merely ratifying the Mutual Defense Treaty and creating no new obligations or enemies. Dulles's draft treaty, sent to the participants in August, proposed a loose, ANZUS-type organization pledging each member to react according to its constitutional processes against "Communist aggression" directed at any signatory or at Cambodia, Laos, or South Vietnam. Philippine officials supplied copies to reporters, who published the secret draft. Peking radio denounced it as "preparation for war," and *Pravda* printed similar charges. Magsaysay proposed his own draft, also leaked, containing an instant-retaliation pledge, including Formosa, and creating a 100,000-man standing army. Every country except Pakistan rejected it. Frustrated, the Philippine team, headed by Garcia, decided to accept the weaker treaty while seeking an instant-retaliation pledge and "huge" military aid from the United States.[45]

The conference opened amid panic in the Philippines. On September 3, 1954, Communist Chinese artillery shelled the Nationalist-held islands of Quemoy and Matsu. Rumor spread through Luzon and the southern islands that Chinese troops had landed and Manila had been bombed. It touched off runs on rice markets and banks. Hundreds of parents arrived at Manila universities to collect their children. Philippine politicians worried that the United States intended to provoke a war with China that could reach Philippine shores. Recto warned Garcia not to "talk big or provoke the stronger nations." To rid the pact of some of its aggressive overtones, Romulo suggested a "Pacific Charter," acknowledging the right of national self-determination and pledging members to resist imperialism. Recto agreed to accept the Dulles draft if Romulo's charter were included. Magsaysay concurred.[46]

When Dulles arrived in Manila on September 3, he appeased Filipino critics with a lavish promise of swift retaliation against any aggressor, but disappointed military leaders by refusing more aid. Magsaysay claimed the "automatic reaction" pledge as a victory, but continued to regard a weak SEATO structure as provocative. The Philippines joined Thailand and Australia in insisting on a NATO-type treaty, while Garcia instructed his negotiators to avoid talk that might arouse China. He emphasized that the conference's objectives were nonmilitary, to ensure sovereign equality of states and "improve their social well being and economic livelihood." He demanded passage of the charter, shirked commitments to Indochina, and rejected the clause in the Dulles draft defining the aggressor as communist.[47]

The government in exile shortly after Quezon's death. From left, front: Jaime Hernandez, finance secretary; Osmeña; Resident Commissioner Romulo. Back: Mariano Erana, justice secretary; Arturo Rotor, secretary to the president; Manuel Nieto, secretary of agriculture; Ismael Mathay, budget commissioner; Alejandro Melchor, undersecretary of defense. Courtesy of the Library of Congress.

MacArthur announces his return to the Filipino people while Osmeña drinks from a canteen. Courtesy of the Library of Congress.

Liberated Manila. The reconquest destroyed 90 percent of the city.
Courtesy of the American Historical Collection, Manila.

Under pressure from MacArthur, Osmeña reconvened the Commonwealth Congress in a Manila schoolhouse in June 1945. Several senators had to be released from prison to attend. Also on the dias are Roxas (left) and Jose Zulueta. Courtesy of the Library of Congress.

Congressman C. Jasper Bell sponsored the 1946 trade act that opened American markets to Philippine sugar and gave American businessmen special rights in the Philippines. Courtesy of the Library of Congress.

The last high commissioner, Paul V. McNutt. Courtesy of the Library of Congress.

Manuel Roxas visiting Clark Air Force Base in April 1948. Base commander General Eubanks is at right. Courtesy of the American Historical Collection, Manila.

Quirino in 1949. "If you cannot permit abuses," his advisers counseled, "you must at least tolerate them." Courtesy of the Library of Congress.

Ambassador Myron Cowen represented the United States at the height of the Huk rebellion. Quirino is at left. Courtesy of the American Historical Collection, Manila.

Ramon Magsaysay, "America's Boy," used his ties to American officials to enlarge his power. Courtesy of the Library of Congress.

Cargo arrives at the port of Manila for transshipment to Indochina, Thailand, Pakistan, and Taiwan via Clark Air Force Base. Thousands of tons of supplies and 33,000 passengers passed through the base annually. In 1953, the year this photo was taken, the base P-X sold over $6 million in goods. Courtesy of the U.S. Air Force.

Carlos P. Romulo, Pulitzer Prize winner, Brigadier General in the U.S. Army, President of the United Nations, ambassador, foreign secretary; he was the Philippines' most effective diplomat. Courtesy of the Library of Congress.

America's allies. From left, Felixberto Serrano, Prime Minister Mohammad Ayub Khan of Pakistan, President Carlos Garcia, Chief Justice Ricardo Paras. Courtesy of the American Historical Collection, Manila.

Garcia greets Eisenhower on his arrival in Manila, June 15, 1960. Courtesy of the Library of Congress.

Other delegates joined the Philippines in softening the draft's belligerent tone. Dulles complained that none of the nations had any "desire or intention to hold the balance of Indochina." He initially resented the Pacific Charter, which upset the colonial powers, but to appease Asian delegates he obtained the grudging consent of France and Britain. Once the charter had been accepted, Garcia could compromise on other demands and help the United States obtain a consensus. In the final sessions, the Philippines broke with Thailand and Australia and accepted the ANZUS formulation. Garcia agreed to include Cambodia, Laos, and Vietnam in the treaty area under a separate protocol, and to separate the charter from the treaty. Signed on September 8, the treaty obligated each signatory to respond to aggression "in accordance with its constitutional processes," participate on a military planning council, and increase its capacity to resist, all obligations the Philippines had already accepted under the Mutual Defense Treaty. Painlessly, the Philippines obtained an instant-retaliation pledge and confirmed its standing as an anticommunist ally without incurring any additional burdens.[48]

The treaty gave Laurel valuable leverage in negotiating with the State Department and Congress for a new trade agreement. Laurel recognized that his party's fortunes rode on his ability to obtain a trade agreement that met the diverse needs of the Philippine elite. Much was at stake. Two-thirds of the Philippines' exports, valued at $400 million, went to the United States. Copra and sugar, half the country's dollar earnings, sold in the American market at artificially high prices, an arrangement that allowed American consumers to subsidize Philippine sugar barons at a rate of $40 million a year. Under the 1946 act, a schedule of increasing tariffs would start to eliminate this trade in 1955. Planters wanted Laurel to obtain a longer period of free trade for Philippine exports, whereas industrialists wanted him to eliminate free trade for U.S. imports. Sixty-nine percent of the goods entering Philippine ports came from the United States. Manufacturers wanted tariff walls in addition to import controls already restricting the flow of American goods. Magsaysay's advisers thought tariffs could help produce "a radical shift" from a chiefly agricultural economy "to one which emphasizes industrial development for the home market." The president wanted to eliminate the provision in the 1946 act that limited his ability to devalue the peso. Laurel's team included Central Bank president Miguel Cuaderno, furniture manufacturer Gil Puyat, Lorenzo Sumulong and other sugar-bloc Liberals, and a large contingent of old-guard Nacionalistas. To satisfy this group, the United States would need to make concessions that amounted, according to one State Department official, to an indirect subsidy. "In plain terms, the Philippine Delegation wants dollar aid."[49]

State Department officials wanted to strengthen Magsaysay. Fearing trade talks would touch off another nationalistic tantrum, they enjoined their negotiators to be both generous and sensitive. The genial New Hampshire publisher who headed the U.S. panel, James Langley, noticed his superiors' anxiety and concluded that he had been chosen as a fall guy. Upon meeting Laurel, Cuaderno, and Puyat, he judged the Filipinos to be demanding but forthright, people he could work with. The Filipinos' staunch support in the cold war, he felt, merited a "grand gesture." His superiors agreed. Robertson, the assistant secretary of state, instructed Langley to offer the most generous concessions Congress would accept. Robertson's deputy for economic affairs, Charles F. Baldwin, suggested that Congress might welcome liberal trade concessions as an inexpensive way to bolster the Filipinos' will to resist communism. Department officials believed tariff autonomy could allow Magsaysay to increase his revenue without relying on aid, and that in the long run, industrialism might provide employment for the rapidly growing Philippine population. Keeping in close touch with the House Ways and Means Committee, Langley sought an agreement to satisfy the demands of Philippine industrialists and commodity exporters without antagonizing American business groups.[50]

Laurel intended to stretch American generosity to its limit. He recognized that his country's strategic value gave him license to push Langley. In opening the talks on September 20, he observed that the Philippines was "an important link in your own security system." The United States could not "permit the Philippines to weaken internally without weakening her own security." The Philippine team found it could be "reasonably stern in its demands." The United States would not risk losing the Philippines, one panelist remarked, "just because of certain trade disadvantages or the sacrifice of a few millions."[51] Laurel used nationalism for leverage. He focused on parity, the clause in the 1946 act according U.S. citizens equal investment rights in resource exploitation, public utilities, and some businesses. Recto called it "our trump card," a provision for which Americans would pay a high price. But neither Recto nor any of the members of the Philippine mission had any intention of eliminating parity, which allowed the Magsaysay government to discriminate against Chinese businessmen without alarming American investors. Langley recognized the protests aimed "primarily to improve their bargaining position." Cuaderno and other Philippine negotiators spent a large part of their time in Washington encouraging executives from Firestone, U.S. Rubber, and Lehman Brothers to invest in Philippine manufacturing. Abrogating parity would dry up investment, an outcome neither country wanted. After exhausting the issue's utility, Laurel proposed a formula that actually expanded parity to cover "any form of business enterprise" and allowed Filipino investors identical privileges in the United States.[52]

The final agreement satisfied nearly all of the diverse Philippine economic interests. Some have seen the Laurel-Langley agreement as a continuation of the 1946 trade act, but Laurel and other Philippine leaders recognized that it gave them substantially greater freedom to industrialize while continuing to receive privileged access to U.S. markets. The chief provision allowed the Philippines to impose high tariffs (half of full duty) on imports from the United States, whereas Philippine goods only incurred 5 percent of full duty. Tariff rates for both countries would increase on a schedule, but Philippine tariffs would rise faster, reaching 75 percent in 1962 and 90 percent in 1965. By contrast, Philippine goods would incur only 40 percent of duty in 1965. The chief effect was to assure Philippine exporters of continued profits. The United States also surrendered the restrictions on Philippine economic autonomy in the 1946 act. The Philippines acquired freedom to devalue the peso and to impose export taxes. Laurel reported that the United States accepted "almost all of the

Philippine proposals" and that the mission got everything "both from the standpoint of material and commercial advantage as well as from the equally paramount standpoint of national honor and sovereignty." The State Department, too, was pleased. A generous trade treaty, Robertson hoped, would soothe nationalists and limit demands for aid.[53]

The stature of the Philippines as a cold-war ally helped push the agreement through a reluctant Congress. The new Democratic Congress resisted tariff reductions, and Eisenhower had narrowly won the Reciprocal Trade Act in March after heroic lobbying. Philippine lobbyists braced for a fight over their bill, introduced May 5. Corporations and trade associations like RCA and the National Foreign Trade Council pushed for passage. Vice President Nixon and other administration officials twisted arms. Congressmen, however, had grown resistant to trade-not-aid appeals. American sugar producers, farm exporters, and manufacturers of textiles, paint, and other consumer exports opposed the agreement and had backing from Southerners who controlled key committees in both houses. Magsaysay's reputation and a well-timed concession helped neutralize this opposition. Promising to repeal a cigarette import ban, Magsaysay swung Southern committee members behind the bill. In floor speeches leading up to passage in late July, members of both houses conceded that the bill lopsidedly favored the Philippines, but that "America has no better friend in Asia and President Magsaysay needs this new trade agreement to carry out the plans of his administration." They applauded Romulo's defense of U.S. policy at the Asian-African conference at Bandung in April. They regarded passage as a reward for Philippine support, a sign of trust in the Filipinos' economic sense.[54]

With SEATO and the trade agreement, the National Security Council enjoyed a short-lived optimism in late 1955. The worsening Philippine economy and increasing nationalist criticism eroded that optimism in the following year. Filipinos continued to be outraged by U.S. control of Olongapo and incidents between miners and military police at Clark. They criticized the United States for giving economic aid to neutral nations. Dulles felt badgered by the "many detailed causes of friction relating principally to trade and commercial and monetary matters." The Philippine economy deteriorated. By May 1956, partly owing to the success of anti-Chinese economic measures, 12 percent of the labor force was jobless. Agricultural incomes declined, and growth in GNP barely kept pace with the rising population. Deficit spending fueled inflation, and the government's supply of foreign exchange dwindled.[55]

Under Laurel-Langley, the Philippine government could have increased revenues and kept industries protected while abandoning the corruption- and favoritism-ridden import and exchange control system. It did neither. The Philippine Congress retained import and exchange controls and erected tariff walls as a redundant protection for already sheltered industries. Tariffs imposed on restricted goods earned little revenue. According to one political economist, the Philippines had "developed exchange and import controls into a complex and responsive policy instrument" that gave political authorities wide discretionary powers over the economy. Because controls allowed government officials to make or break individual firms, they not only enhanced the value of public office, they (along with Filipinization) were the instruments by which powerful landed politicians regulated the creation of wealth.[56]

Embassy officials finally began to regard Philippine economic problems as rooted in intractable social and cultural impediments. Ideally, new industries would absorb surplus rural population migrating into cities, but manufacturers of shoes, soap, and matches protected by the Laurel-Langley agreement employed few workers and had little interest in expanding. The chargé, Horace Smith, complained that Filipinos blocked development "for fear of 'exploitation' particularly by non-Filipinos." They refused to invest in new enterprises "unless the rate of return and the minimization of risk are obviously more favorable than traditional investments" like land or trade. Amid pessimism about the economic future of the Philippines, embassy officials began reminding Philippine leaders of the bases' economic benefits. "Clark Field provides the only promise of a decent job for many citizens of landlord-ridden, poverty stricken Pampanga province," one diplomat observed. "Subic Bay is the only absorber of excess population in the remote and underdeveloped provinces of Zambales and Bataan. Without Sangley Point the city of Cavite would be a ghost town."⁵⁷

Postponing negotiations only made a bases treaty more difficult to achieve. In early 1956, Magsaysay told Dulles that bases talks could not begin unless the United States renounced the Brownell memorandum. On July 4, Nixon visited Manila and withdrew the title claim, and the following month a new bases negotiator, Karl Bendetsen, formerly undersecretary of the Army, arrived with presidential instructions to "bend over backwards" to meet Philippine demands. After two days, the embassy reported that more than "a simple land settlement problem" was holding up a settlement. Philippine negotiators insisted on extending "the reality of Philippine sovereignty" over the bases, including Philippine laws covering taxation, customs, immigration, water, mineral, and timber resources, and criminal offenses. The last stipulation proved the most stubborn. Both State and Defense department officials believed a compromise on criminal jurisdiction would incite other countries to seek revisions, touching off a global round of renegotiations. Rather than yield to "transitory Philippine attitudes," Bendetsen, Dulles, and Radford agreed to postpone talks again, this time until after the 1957 Philippine elections.⁵⁸

Without a bases treaty, the U.S. Navy and Air Force resorted to informal arrangements with the Philippine Army, providing funds to lengthen airfields on Philippine bases that could be pressed into service in a crisis. State Department officials considered this a better arrangement and "cheaper in the long run," but the military branches insisted that the growing strategic importance of the Philippines required the United States to have its own installations there. The United States used informal, covert arrangements to enlist Filipinos into cold-war service. As Joseph Smith, a CIA agent, explained, beginning in 1954, "a large number of activities were being run from Manila to try to use Filipinos as our alter egos to spread democracy throughout the SEATO security area." The Philippines supplied reservists, nurses, and technicians to U.S. aid missions in Thailand, Malaysia, Burma, and Vietnam.⁵⁹

Through secret arrangements, Magsaysay could help the United States and augment his patronage base without incurring the political risks of overt collaboration. Although private organizations, like the Jaycees, sponsored the programs, Magsaysay directed the operation himself through the army and his private security detail. He explained to Romulo that the programs gave his supporters dollar earnings, jobs, and training. Napoleon Valeriano, Magsaysay's bodyguard, and a group of officers known as Freedom Company trained a palace guard for Vietnamese president Ngo Dinh Diem, helped the CIA organize anticommunist front groups, and schooled Vietnamese troops and officers in Huk-tested antiguerrilla tactics. Magsaysay's attorney, Jaime Orendain, went to Saigon in July 1954 to help Diem draft a constitution, and stayed to join Oscar Arrellano, head of the Philippine Jaycees, in organizing Operation Brotherhood, a huge relief effort for Vietnamese refugees fleeing the North. Free clinics staffed by 105 Filipino doctors and nurses treated 400,000 patients before the migration ended in July 1955. Although Filipino operatives continued to be used throughout the Vietnam War, the CIA eventually concluded that they had limited usefulness. "They simply had been associated with the Americans too long," Smith explained. "A Chinese told me in Singapore one time, 'They have brown faces but they wear the same Hawaiian sports shirts the Americans do.' "[60]

With Magsaysay's death in March 1957, the structure of informal domestic and international arrangements, according to Smith, "came rather quickly apart." The president had been in Cebu, lining up the support of local political dynasties for what he anticipated to be a difficult election fight against Senator Claro Recto. On March 17, news of the president's death reached the vacationing vice president, Carlos Garcia, an old-guard Nacionalista with close ties to Laurel and Recto. "Neither Garcia nor any other outstanding national figure appears to be capable of leading a positive reform program or acting as a bulwark of a forthright pro-American foreign policy," the assistant secretary for intelligence reported to Dulles. None of the possible leaders was in Magsaysay's position "to withstand the appeals of chauvinistic nationalism." After three years of dealing with a government that boasted of its pro-Americanism, the Eisenhower administration had achieved few of its long-term goals and was compelled to strike short-term arrangements to protect its principal interests.[61]

Despite the appearance of collaboration that Magsaysay maintained, the interests of the United States and the Philippine elite became increasingly difficult to reconcile between 1953 and 1957. As caciques fixed their ambitions on manufacturing, they became more demanding and more suspicious of the United States. They insisted on unrestricted control over the economy, tariff concessions, more aid, and firmer defense guarantees at a time when the United States sought to redirect aid to countries in immediate danger. Nonetheless, accommodations remained possible. The United States could make concessions in the areas of trade and economic autonomy, and Filipinos could display loyalty to U.S. strategic aims by participating in SEATO and informal security arrangements. Bilateral relations became a bargain in which each side obtained its primary short-term interest while sacrificing secondary goals.

Eisenhower's development program has been criticized for its narrow, anticommunist aims and inadequate recognition of the social roots of economic problems. To assess the administration's performance on development, however, is to make an unwarranted assumption that either the United States sought development and failed, or Filipinos tried to develop and were thwarted. Neither was true. Development failed because all parties pursued other, more important objectives. Filipinos sought economic control at the expense of economic growth, whereas the United States sought to keep its military bases. U.S. officials considered growth essential to retaining the bases in the long run, but when forced to choose between the bases and development, they chose the bases.[62]

Dependency and world systems theories provide a more comprehensive explanation for the failure of development. They argue that expanding core economies faithfully reproduce their own class divisions on the periphery, creating a class identity among elites that facilitates their joint exploitation of Third

World labor and resources. Students of United States–Philippine relations employ a similar analysis in describing the behavior of the American-educated Filipino elite. But this explanation overlooks the importance of security issues and nationalism. In the Philippines, the United States defined its interests in primarily strategic and geopolitical terms. Secure bases and collective security agreements mattered more to the makers of U.S. policy than did economic growth, land reform, or American business interests. Although Filipinos defined their aims in economic terms, they did so in ways their American classmates from Yale and Michigan would neither understand nor applaud. Philippine nationalism defined a movement that jealously protected the nation's industry and resources from those who might challenge entrenched power. The elite and the United States had a symbiotic but mutually suspicious relationship. Rather than identifying with United States interests, the Philippine elite eyed U.S. policy warily, alert for violations of their power to apportion economic benefits among the country's classes, races, and dominant families.[63]

Collaboration involved more complex motives and bargaining—and more recriminations—than dependency or world systems studies suggest. The United States used trade and aid to mollify Philippine leaders, who accommodated U.S. strategic interests when it involved few sacrifices, carried compensating benefits, or could be arranged secretly. Filipinos disagreed over the strategy that would employ their strategic value to best advantage. Supporters of Magsaysay argued that Americans responded better to cooperation and appeals to their sense of obligation, whereas Recto advocated a tougher approach, demanding aid and trade concessions as the price for alliance. The first strategy depended on the trust and admiration Magsaysay enjoyed in Washington, and Garcia knew he could never match his predecessor's skill at manipulating American guilt. But even in Magsaysay's final years, his approach had fallen from favor, as smaller amounts of aid failed to cover larger deficits. With the president's death, Philippine leaders became more openly aggressive in their demands.

SIX

Filipino First

Philippine diplomats took a sterner, more confrontational line in dealing with the United States after 1957. Many educated Filipinos saw United States and Philippine interests drifting apart, as Eisenhower's military and economic policies exposed them to more risks with fewer compensations. Philippine treaty violations, complaints about the bases, and demands for aid frustrated Eisenhower's advisers, who feared official ineptitude would accelerate trends toward economic stagnation and neutralism. Philippine leaders never seriously considered severing ties to the United States. Garcia adopted a "get-tough" policy as a tactical maneuver to obtain more of what the Philippines had sought for the previous decade: more aid, more security, more power to manage the economy.

Magsaysay's death at the beginning of an election year threw the country into disarray. His successor had neither the charisma nor the political backing to hold the coalition that had won in 1953. An experienced but undistinguished old-guard Nacionalista, Garcia had little support outside his home province, the small southern island of Bohol. But he possessed a determination that surprised his opponents. In two months, he won the leadership of the ruling Nacionalista party. He purged younger party members who had entered national politics with Magsaysay in 1953, causing them to form a new party under Manuel Manahan. Other Nacionalistas joined Recto's Nationalist-Citizen's party. Garcia won the loyalty of the bulk of the ruling party with government dispensations, patronage, and dollar allocations that drove the government—already burdened with Magsaysay's deficits—close to bankruptcy. The Liberal party, too, suffered from a candidate surplus. After a divisive convention, Jose Yulo, leader of the sugar planters' bloc, seized the nomination, but not before the runner-up, Tony Quirino, walked out with his followers to form a splinter party. In November, seven candidates vied for the presidency. The CIA reported that none had the political strength or independence to withstand growing tendencies toward neutralism and corruption.[1]

The outcome left the government weak and opposition divided. With help from an election-day hurricane in Manahan's Luzon stronghold, Garcia emerged with a 41 percent plurality. Manahan and Yulo each took a quarter of the vote, leaving neither in a position to lead the opposition. For the United States, the election had two bright spots. Recto took a meager 8 percent of the vote, a demonstration, embassy officials hoped, of the narrow appeal of nationalism and neutralism. With the support of the Church, Diosdado Macapagal defeated Jose Laurel, Jr., in the vice-presidential race. As congressman, Macapagal had pushed for resumption of base negotiations and closer ties to the United States. Ambassador Charles Bohlen entertained a brief hope that he would be named foreign minister, as Philippine vice presidents usually were, but Garcia appointed a loyal career diplomat, Felixberto Serrano. Split between Macapagal, Yulo, and Manahan, the opposition lacked focus. Garcia assumed control over a financially strapped government after an election in which a majority of Filipinos voted for someone else. State Department analysts predicted stability would "deteriorate over the next four years."[2]

Garcia struggled with the need to strengthen his government and reward followers amid budgetary and balance-of-payments crises. He announced plans to increase the budget by 25 percent, but Congress refused to enact taxes to cover new spending. Bohlen warned that the United States would offer little aid and suggested that the government curtail spending and try to attract foreign investment, but his suggestions won no applause in Manila.[3]

Filipinos shared their government's displeasure over the scantiness of aid. Magsaysay had complained that aid had declined relative to the budget. After his death, the State Department cut aid in absolute terms. International Cooperation Administration programs, which had supplied $25 million annually from 1955 to 1957, fell to $19 million in 1958. Officials predicted deeper cutbacks in 1959 and 1960 as a recession hit the United States and Eisenhower's interests shifted to Laos, Indonesia, and India. Philippine columnists and politicians drew comparisons between American generosity toward less-reliable nations and stinginess toward the Philippines. Embassy officials believed this criticism would redound against the bases and the aid program. "Nowhere more than in the bases issue," they warned, "has the Filipino feeling of lack of equal stature and their subordinate role been more manifest." Investigating the foreign-aid program in 1959, a commission headed by Theodore Draper cautioned that the consequence of such perceptions "will be to make our aid a growing source of envy and recriminations among recipient nations."[4]

Amid budget crisis and growing anti-American sentiment, Garcia's supporters and opponents advocated a tougher line. The president visited Washington in June 1958 hoping to obtain $500 million in grant aid, but he returned with only $125 million in loans. Planners in the State Department and Budget Bureau had revised the concept by which they granted aid, deemphasizing one-country programs that produced for protected markets in favor of export-oriented regional development. The largest project on Garcia's list, a steel works at Iligan, contradicted these plans, since Japan produced steel. Despite lack of aid, Garcia stuck to his plans, and by the end of the year the government had borrowed heavily from New York banks. Recto urged the president to follow Indonesia's lead and flirt with the Soviet Union to extract more aid from the United States. Serrano argued that the Philippines should demand aid as a settlement on prior claims and as "rent" on bases.[5]

Garcia decided to use the bases as leverage. Serrano resurrected the Omnibus Claims, an assortment of uncollected debts dating to the 1930s that had been used as a bargaining chip by every administration since independence. Previous presidents had brought up one or more of the claims during aid negotiations, but Serrano compiled a list totaling $972 million. Impending base negotiations made the State Department take the claims seriously, and the secretary of state, Christian Herter, helped Philippine officials lay their case before Congress. On August 4, 1959, he presented Romulo a check for $24 million to cover Philippine losses from the 1934 dollar devaluation. He promised to ask Congress for $73 million in additional war-damage compensation and to consider a few other claims. Serrano continued to press, and Manila columnists applauded his toughness.[6]

The aid battle was the opening of a sterner policy that extended to bases and treatment of foreign business. Filipinos felt vulnerable in 1958. The government again approached insolvency, while a few hundred miles away Communist and Nationalist Chinese forces renewed a conflict that appeared likely to end in world war. The Manila Observatory announced Sputnik 2's passage over the capital as newspapers described the damage a hydrogen bomb could wreak on the Philippines. Manufacturing came under pressure from agricultural interests who wanted to curtail the privileges afforded by protectionism. Nationalist politicians and newspapers fanned these fears. Garcia's administration rejected Recto's appeal for a neutral foreign policy, abrogation of the bases treaty, and an end to grant aid, but embraced nationalist slogans, according to an embassy official, "as a screen for . . . domestic failures and as a weapon in its relations with the United States."[7]

Discussions on the military bases continued through most of Garcia's tenure. The United States found it could strike bargains on property and security and assuage Filipino fears about their country's role in a general war, but issues pitting sovereignty against the functioning of the bases defied resolution. Little is known of the negotiations between November 1958 and October 1959 that produced the Bohlen-Serrano agreement. Rejecting Pentagon suggestions to appeal directly to the Philippine people, the State Department opted for quiet, one-on-one talks between Bohlen and the foreign secretary. The United States asked for a press blackout, and files on the negotiations remain classified. Two facts emerge from the available documents: the United States considered the talks the most important item on its Philippine agenda; and Bohlen achieved only partial success.[8]

The Eisenhower administration made the settlement of questions relating to the bases its principal objective in the Philippines in 1958. "The problem of military bases is one of basic importance to U.S.-Philippine relations," the National Security Council warned. "Failure to resolve outstanding issues on a basis acceptable to both parties could in turn affect the entire range of U.S. government interests." The Pacific command saw the talks as do-or-die. Should they "fail once again to achieve mutual satisfaction, the United States may not find it as easy to slip back into an existing and satisfactory status quo," the commander of Pacific forces predicted. "In the next go-round the stakes are higher. The United States cannot afford another recess."[9]

The Joint Chiefs attached greater importance to the bases in the late 1950s than they had earlier in the cold war. In explaining their requirements, they emphasized the importance of the Philippines in virtually every contingency. Some areas—Vietnam for example—were important only in limited war. Not so the Philippines. The Joint Chiefs considered bases there a "basic feature of U.S. strategy" for general war, part of the defensive line running from Japan to the Kra Isthmus. They were a crucial staging area for mobile "rapid response" forces that would be used in a limited conflict. Proximity to "Communist China, Japan, Taiwan, Indonesia, and the countries of the South East Asia mainland" made the Philippines "essential within this concept." The bases provided training areas and logistical facilities to support operations throughout the SEATO area. They were "an essential part of a world-wide base system designed to deter Communism." The Joint Chiefs warned that "any reduction in this base system creates a point of weakness which invites Communist aggression."[10]

The base system was in trouble. The United States found it increasingly difficult to hold onto bases in Spain, Libya, Saudi Arabia, and other countries. In 1957, Eisenhower dispatched a former assistant secretary of defense, Frank Nash, to survey the global system, and was disturbed by the "spreading commitments of the U.S. both in the Atlantic and the Pacific areas" that Nash found. The National Security Council grew accustomed to the president's lectures on the difficulties inherent in maintaining overseas outposts. The president warned them to prepare for the day when they would "have to make choices about our commitments." For the Defense Department, that day had not arrived. The Navy rejected Eisenhower's suggestion that it close Sangley Point, finding the small, highly visible base on Manila Bay an "essential element of the U.S. base complex." Military officials argued that diplomacy could obtain what they needed.[11]

After the failure of Karl Bendetsen's mission to renegotiate the bases treaty in 1956, the Pacific command and the State Department tried to ameliorate Philippine grievances. They arranged with Magsaysay to create a council to arbitrate disputes with local residents and station Philippine liaison officers at base headquarters. Commanders hired Filipino guards, chauffeurs, and truck drivers to reduce incidents between servicemen and Filipinos. They drew boundaries for Olongapo and turned municipal facilities over to Filipinos. They flew the Philippine flag. This made it easier for Garcia to reopen talks in late 1958, but did not address the key differences.[12]

In initiating talks, the Eisenhower administration sought to remove irritants they believed threatened the bases' continued existence. With the death of Magsaysay, the Joint Chiefs gave up the idea of adding large tracts to the bases and decided to provide military aid to construct joint-use facilities under the control of the Philippine Army. Unlike the Bendetsen talks, negotiations focused on Philippine grievances—criminal jurisdiction, the duration of the treaty, the status of Olongapo—to enlist Philippine cooperation in protecting installations and to reverse the trend of opinion against the bases.[13]

Of all the issues, criminal jurisdiction was the most serious. Violent confrontations between servicemen and Filipinos were common. Guards frequently mistook miners or Negrito tribesmen for saboteurs, and a Philippine official alleged in July 1958 that 20 civilians had been killed by base guards over the previous decade. The military often preferred to protect its troops from Philippine justice. In April 1958, a sailor stabbed a Filipina in an Olongapo bar. Following its practice, the Navy spirited the culprit out of the country. Filipinos were not alone in objecting to such incidents. In a famous case, the Army attempted to evade trial by a Japanese court of William Girard, a soldier accused of killing a Japanese woman. The Supreme Court, in a move that won praise in Asia, ruled against the Army, and turned Girard over to the Japanese. In May 1959, midway through the Bohlen-Serrano talks, 3,000 Chinese rioters sacked the embassy in Taipei after the acquittal by court martial of an American soldier accused of shooting a Chinese student. Philippine newspapers paid close attention to such incidents.[14]

For Filipinos, the jurisdiction issue had emotional implications that compounded the sense of insult other Asians felt. The unwillingness of the United States to recognize Philippine authority seemed to many Filipinos a judgment on their political maturity. This galled members of the elite, graduates of Harvard and Yale law schools, who took pride in their judicial system and the "rule of law." The issue insulted their honor in the same way their fathers' honor had been trampled by the Army-Navy Club's exclusion of Filipinos in the 1920s. "Our legal system is the same as yours, our bill of rights and the guarantees of the rights of an accused in the courts are identical to yours, and our judges have been well trained in the due process of law," Arturo Tolentino told the New York Bar Association. "There is no reason to doubt their capacity to do justice to American soldiers violating Philippine law, unless you want to admit now that your experiment in democracy in the Philippines has been a failure." Philippine courts were mild in judgments and rigid in procedure, but these features failed to reassure military authorities.[15]

Commanders felt they needed to use force against intruders. Scavenging, sometimes by organized gangs, threatened base operations and provoked shooting incidents. In August 1958, on the first day of the second Taiwan Straits crisis, scavengers stole the radar approach control antenna at Clark Air Force Base, temporarily closing the airfield. A month later, pilferers removed buckles on guywires supporting communications antennae, causing three to collapse. Intruders killed five Filipino security guards during 1958; other guards were assaulted or fired at. Surrendering legal jurisdiction would inevitably involve turning over for trial American soldiers acting under orders to defend base property. The Pentagon dreaded the Congressional attention that would follow such an occurrence. In 1957, after the Girard incident, Eisenhower narrowly prevented the House from mandating exclusive American jurisdiction over soldiers assigned overseas. "There seemed to be an almost hysterical fear, particularly in Congress," Bohlen observed, "of letting Americans be tried by systems of justice not in conformity with ours."[16] Filipinos demanded more jurisdiction than the United States had conceded to any host country. Under NATO status of forces agreements, the United States publicly acknowledged local jurisdiction over its troops while obtaining a secret, gentlemen's agreement that errant soldiers would be turned over quietly to base commanders for punishment. In 1957, the United States struck a similar bargain with Japan, but required other Asian countries explicitly to waive prosecution of servicemen on base or under orders. Filipinos were probably correct in assuming that racial prejudice accounted for the difference, but rather than demanding equal treatment, they sought the NATO terms without the gentlemen's agreement. They wanted to punish Americans who flouted the law. Many felt American racial assumptions made strict enforcement necessary. As one columnist observed, "The American soldier in say, England, has or assumes an attitude toward the English and their laws quite different from the attitude of an American soldier in the Philippines toward the Filipinos and their laws." Barely a week into the talks, the two sides reached an impasse. No rephrasing could mask the fact that Bohlen wanted to make sure Filipinos would not prosecute servicemen, whereas Serrano wanted to make sure they would.[17]

Serrano wanted to use the talks to press security issues raised by Sputnik and the latest Taiwan Straits crisis. In early 1958, after the Soviets launched the first satellite, Deputy Secretary of Defense Donald Quarles aroused a storm in Manila by announcing that the United States would seek Far Eastern sites for medium-range missiles. Recto and the nationalist press asserted that the United States was trying to divert atomic attacks to the Philippines. Bohlen denied that the United States sought sites, but Serrano asked assurance that no missiles would be deployed on the bases. Later that year, after the People's Republic of China resumed shelling Nationalist-held offshore islands, the Garcia government decided it needed some independent capacity to defend itself. Serrano reported that American actions in the straits increased the danger of a war with China that would spill over onto Philippine shores. Days before the bases talks opened, Serrano presented Defense Secretary Neil McElroy with a request for military aid that included big-ticket items like ships, jet fighters, and tanks. McElroy replied that he had no money to spare and that the United States would defend the Philippines. The Defense Department had encouraged the Philippine Army to improve its capabilities in order to be able to contribute troops to defend the SEATO area, but Serrano envisioned a more ambitious program than the United States would support. The National Security Council expected "that our handling of this request for increased military assistance will have an important effect on the successful outcome of the [bases] negotiations," and agreed to supply more jets and howitzers and to consider delivering seven tanks and a destroyer escort ship.[18]

After a series of false starts, negotiators found that they could make progress only by avoiding the principal issue. Setting criminal jurisdiction aside, Bohlen and Serrano agreed on boundaries for the bases and terms for returning Olongapo. The United States agreed to shorten the 99-year lease to 25 years, not to station ballistic missiles, to turn over unused bases, and to consult before launching combat operations. The Philippines allowed the United States to enlarge Subic Bay and Sangley Point and gave it access to three joint-use training areas. Signed October 12, 1959, the Bohlen-Serrano agreement provided a moment of goodwill. It "established a revitalized basis of Philippine-American friendship," according to Serrano, and indicated that "firmness in the pursuit of our national interest . . . is the only way of assuring American respect."[19]

Scarcely a month after the agreement, guards at Clark Air Force Base shot a suspected looter, resurrecting the linked issues of base security and jurisdiction. Base commanders opened negotiations with their Philippine counterparts and reached an agreement under which the Philippine Constabulary would patrol the base perimeter. Thorny problems remained, the National Security Council reported, "particularly with regard to new arrangements covering criminal jurisdiction over offenses committed by

U.S. servicemen." Soon after Bohlen's replacement, John D. Hickerson, arrived in Manila in 1960, negotiations resumed. Talks continued, with temporary suspensions, until the conclusion of the Blair-Mendez agreement in 1965.[20] Negotiations became institutionalized, keeping American attention fixed on ways to soothe nationalist resentment rather than on the state of the Philippine economy or the difficulties of American business.

Writers have portrayed Garcia's "Filipino First" policy as a moment of nationalist action in which Philippine leaders, suddenly alive to the dangers posed by foreign investment, tried briefly to resist before succumbing to pressure from the United States. Some argue that the Philippines became a haven for investment owing to the State Department's efforts to assure that American companies operated without restrictions. But the Filipino First movement merely made explicit a policy of penalties and incentives Philippine administrations had used for over a decade to manage industrialization and investment. American investors did not consider the Philippines a haven. The few who started businesses found profits could be made, but only by those willing to play by Philippine rules. The State Department offered no help. Preoccupied with its own, chiefly strategic interests, the United States sought to avoid conflict over economic questions and urged businessmen to get along by going along. Industrialization and foreign investment proceeded on a plan of Philippine design.

The Filipino First movement began on August 28, 1958, with National Economic Council resolution 204, which committed the government to assuring "substantial participation of Filipinos in commerce and industry." Garcia's economic advisers emphasized that "allocation of foreign exchange to enterprises is now the most effective instrument by which the resolution can be achieved." The Central Bank had used foreign-exchange allocations to control industry and foreign investment for a decade, beginning with imposition of controls in 1949. Magsaysay's administration had enlarged its role in managing the industrial sector and refined its techniques for controlling business. Magsaysay concealed these manipulations behind an official policy that welcomed U.S. investment into an ostensibly open free-market system. The Filipino First movement placed industrial policy at the center of Garcia's nationalist agenda and cloaked it in words designed to intimidate domestic and foreign critics. This resurgence of nationalism emerged from an industrial policy that had become increasingly difficult to defend.[21]

Like elites in other postcolonial nations, Philippine leaders wanted their country to industrialize. They believed the Philippines would not be completely independent politically until the country no longer depended on imported manufactures and foreign commodity markets. They saw expanding domestic manufacturing as the shortest route to material betterment, the solution to pressing economic and social problems. Large landowners recognized that the rural social structure would deteriorate unless the surplus population could find urban jobs. Although sugar interests had opposed protectionist policies in 1949, their resistance diminished as sugar clans—notably the Araneta, Tuason, Elizalde, and Soriano families—established manufacturing ventures. By 1955, only import trading firms, mostly foreign-owned, stood to lose from expansion of manufacturing. But although industrial development had no vocal critics, it did not enjoy unconditional support from even its staunchest boosters.[22]

The Magsaysay and Garcia administrations supported industrial development only if new ventures were Filipino-controlled. After coming to power, Nacionalista leaders strove to reduce Philippine-Chinese economic power, even at the price of unemployment and stagnation. Pointing to Venezuela and Puerto Rico, where profitable foreign-owned plants multiplied amid poverty, they argued that investment and trade conferred no benefit unless "Filipinos and not foreigners are in control of the economy." "What is the value to the Filipino people of increased national production," Senator Edmondo Cea asked, "if its benefits do not go to them?"[23]

Economic nationalists like Cea defined control loosely. Chinese capital did find its way into industrial ventures, often with help from nationalist politicians. The Philippine leaders' objective was to prevent industrial wealth from becoming a political threat to landed families. Often it was sufficient for a Chinese investor to cut in a Filipino *padrino*. "Nationalists do go in for graft, but it is no use arguing that they are not true nationalists," a writer observed. "They believe in nationalism—and in lining their pockets." As Recto explained, "Patriotism is a means of livelihood and growing rich."[24]

For good reason, Philippine economic managers assumed that without government intervention, Philippine-Chinese businessmen would seize control of manufacturing. As investors, Filipinos were risk-averse, concentrating capital in safe ventures like land and trade. Anti-Chinese laws in the 1930s and 1940s forced the Chinese out of trade and landowning and into retail and processing, endowing them with both liquidity and managerial skills. The Retail Nationalization Act of 1954 pushed Chinese capital out of yet another stagnant sector. Unless restrained by still more government intervention, Chinese money and talent would migrate into the rapidly growing manufacturing sector.[25]

Magsaysay's government employed a panoply of instruments to shield manufacturing from Chinese encroachment. State industrial combines already excluded Chinese investment (in fact, all private investment) from many industries. Magsaysay curtailed the state sector, partly in response to American urging, but also because the newly formed Central Bank provided more precise instruments for regulating business and reducing Chinese participation. The Central Bank employed import controls, tax incentives, and exchange allocations to determine size and profitability of whole industries and individual firms.[26]

Generous incentives steered capital into manufacturing. Magsaysay's administration granted select manufacturers a preferred status, entitling them to tax breaks and exchange allocations. Incentives had a strong effect on foreign investment, directing nearly all incoming American capital into manufacturing, rather than mining and utilities where it had previously concentrated. The administration made local equity participation a prerequisite for preferred status, causing U.S. firms to reorganize as joint ventures. American and Filipino businessmen recognized the preferred designation as a requisite for business success.[27]

Exchange controls gave the government its most useful instru-

ment for controlling business. Controls allowed the government
to dictate what goods were produced, how many were produced,
and, most important, who did the producing. "Exchange control
equals economy control," a U.S. congressional committee observed in 1956. "Through its government bank, a government
can control the entire economy of the country, and the central
bank becomes the bottleneck through which all trade and financial transactions must funnel at the bank's, i.e. the government's,
pleasure and terms." By selectively dispensing dollar allocations
through the Central Bank, Philippine policymakers could regulate the productivity of any firm that depended on imported materials. The size of a firm's allocation of exchange determined
how large the operation would be initially and how rapidly it
could expand. Although controls targeted Chinese-owned business, they restricted all transactions. The U.S. Commerce Department warned investors in 1956 not to be deceived by pronouncements welcoming capital into a seemingly open, compet-
itive system.[28]

Upon taking office, Magsaysay cut allocations to Chinese
businesses and strengthened the Central Bank by passing the No
Dollar Import Law, which prohibited the importation (through
barter or other means) of any good for which a dollar allocation
had not been issued. Since nearly every Filipino manufacturer depended on imported materials, the Central Bank could direct
business operations, and even consumer tastes. It compelled au-
tomakers to produce jeeps rather than cars, and diesel- rather
than gasoline-fueled vehicles. The bank's president, Cuaderno,
required three American tiremakers to convert to locally produced rubber. Exchange allocations gave Philippine officials a
powerful, responsive instrument for Filipinizing industry and distributing windfalls to favored importers.[29]

American business found controls increasingly oppressive. U.S.
overseas investment reached all-time peaks in 1956 and 1957,
but capital flowed into the Philippines no faster than usual.
"This is not the kind of climate that attracts dollars," *Fortune*
magazine observed. "Exchange controls are being used to discriminate in favor of Philippine businessmen as against foreigners." The State Department offered little help. Throughout the

Magsaysay administration, the United States supported controls and opposed devaluation, chiefly for political reasons. After a researcher from Cornell University, Frank Golay, wrote an article advocating devaluation, the embassy's economic secretary observed that his arguments had merit "only from the balance of payments point of view." Devaluation would shift income from importers, who supported Magsaysay, to sugar exporters, who, in the imagination of State Department officials, opposed the president and the social program sponsored by the United States. That devaluation "would work against the aims of the Magsaysay administration and hence against U.S. interests goes without saying." The Eisenhower administration supported controls and discouraged businessmen from challenging the Central Bank.[30]

Corporations tried to resist Philippine control, with little success. In 1956, Henderson-Trippe, an American trading concern, sued the Central Bank over its dollar allocation. Embassy officials worried that the suit, the first ever against the Central Bank, would provoke anti-American reaction, and urged the firm to drop it. Cuaderno argued the case before the Supreme Court and won. Pepsi-Cola had more success with pressuring the government through labor unions. Cuaderno granted Pepsi a small initial allocation, but instead of limiting output, the company established a large plant in early 1956 and began bottling at a rate that used all its imported syrup in a few months. In June the firm announced it had no more syrup and suspended operations until it received another dollar allocation. Pepsi workers marched on Malacañan, and Magsaysay ordered Cuaderno to grant the allocation. Embassy officials admired Pepsi's pluck, but worried that other firms would follow suit and bankrupt the Central Bank. None did, largely because Pepsi's victory proved fleeting. In 1960, the company was still fighting off suits stemming from the incident. After 1956, American companies, for the most part, stopped bucking the system and found that cooperating with the Filipinos offered the best chance of success.[31]

Controls succeeded in preventing Chinese dominance of manufacturing, or at least in driving investment underground. In 1949, one-third of newly registered enterprises had Chinese owners; by 1955, only 17 percent of new businesses were Chinese-owned; and by 1969, only 3¼ percent of the new businesses registered under Chinese ownership. The once-dominant Chinese share of imports shrank into insignificance. Philippine success is most visible when measured against efforts of other Southeast Asian states to restrict Chinese investment. Indonesia, Malaysia, and Thailand employed state corporations and governmental discrimination against Chinese in the 1950s and 1960s, but in those countries, Chinese capital today predominates over native capital. The Philippines is the only capitalist country in Southeast Asia where native investors own a majority of the manufacturing capital.[32]

Nacionalista leaders liked the power they could exercise through exchange controls. State Department observers reported that in 1957, "the political allegiance of pressure groups was bought by licensing the use of large amounts of foreign exchange, and dollar allocations were sold to finance the large campaign expenditures of majority party candidates." As inflation separated the official exchange rate from the actual rate (officially worth 50 cents, the peso fetched 28 cents on the black market in 1957 and 25 cents in 1958), the dollar allocation turned into a cash gift. Lucky Filipino manufacturers could double their money simply by exchanging it in Hong Kong or on the black market. "What's the best business in this country?" former finance minister Alfredo Montelibano explained. "Quite simple, just get a dollar allocation and sell it. You don't have to work."[33]

But the decade-long experiment with controls damaged Philippine society in ways that were becoming apparent in 1958. Controls created an uncompetitive, import-dependent manufacturing sector that, instead of solving unemployment and stagnation, burdened more productive sectors of the economy and saddled the government with debt and corruption. The profit motive operated, but the state—not competition—regulated economic activity. Sheltered from competition, inefficient manufacturers profited from shortages created by their low outputs and high costs. Most new manufacturers depended heavily on high-cost, preprocessed imports. Two out of three industries favored with tax breaks did not make anything, but merely imported and repackaged finished goods. Philippine companies found that by packaging, assembling, or mixing a widely accepted American brand, like Colgate toothpaste, Parker ink, or Dutch Boy paints, they could gain tax breaks and licenses and avoid the risks of trying to create and sell an untried Philippine brand. Instead of liberating the Philippines from import dependence, the growth of manufacturing only created a new dependent sector.[34] Industry failed to alleviate dependence on export agriculture. Between 1950 and 1958, the share of national income derived from manufacturing grew from 8 percent to 15 percent, but manufactured goods continued to represent a negligible (less than 1 percent) share of export proceeds. Producing for the domestic market, manufacturers earned no dollars to pay for the goods they imported. They depended on infusions of cash from foreign investors and the earnings of other sectors of the economy, chiefly sugar. Manufacturers thus suffered indirectly from the same international price fluctuations that afflicted the farm economy. High export earnings depended entirely on preferential treatment by the United States. Puerto Rican sugar plantations had twice the yield per acre of Philippine haciendas, and Philippine production of other commodities was substantially below Asian averages. The entire structure of industry rested atop this weak and declining agricultural base.[35]

New manufacturing enterprises failed to solve unemployment. Firms that repackaged imported goods or collected tax breaks created few jobs. Paper companies abounded. One steel firm collected dollar allocations and import licenses for three years without building a plant. Industrial employment failed to absorb the annual increase in unemployment (estimated at 100,000 new jobless persons per year), or even the portion of the unemployed who migrated to cities. In 1956, one-fifth of the labor force was unemployed or underemployed. Real wages for industrial workers declined 10 percent from 1955 to 1960, as incomes of company managers increased and investors took huge profits. Touted as the way to improve living standards for Filipinos, industry only worsened maldistribution of wealth.[36]

The government's preoccupation with industrialization crippled its ability to deal with social problems. Latin American governments abandoned exchange control and import substitution programs in the late 1950s because of pressure from the International Monetary Fund, and because of their endemic corruption, bureaucracy, and high costs. Industrial policy was expensive. In 1956, the Philippine government waived 59 million pesos in taxes for preferred industries, an amount that could have covered a quarter of the annual deficit. The portion of the budget supporting the economic regulatory bureaucracy grew from a minor item in 1953 to surpass defense spending in 1957. The burgeoning bureaucracy failed to stem smuggling or graft. The Philippines lost a tenth of its dollar earnings in 1958 to smugglers. Copra producers in Mindanao and Sulu smuggled their entire crop—sixty thousand tons worth $10 million yearly—to British North Borneo. Imports came in the same way, as well as through Hong Kong, foreign embassies, and U.S. bases. The Garcia administration appointed a commission to examine the problem and, a few months later, assembled a second commission to investigate corruption on the first.[37]

License peddling and graft reached the highest levels of government. President Garcia's wife, Leonila, and his executive secretary, Juan Pajo, headed a ring of officials who sold dollar allocations and used economic policy to punish political enemies. In 1958, Mrs. Garcia and the wife of Garcia's economic coordinator arranged for the Central Bank to withdraw a $150,000 allocation from Senator Gil Puyat's steel mill and grant it to a new mill in Garcia's home province. The move threw 350 people out of work. Graft in the economic council, the Central Bank, and customs produced a raft of investigations and deep cynicism among the electorate, business, and government leaders.[38]

Corruption and stagnation won powerful enemies for Garcia, Cuaderno, and the exchange-control policy. The grossly overvalued peso helped manufacturers but injured sugar producers, and landlord-capitalists who had tolerated the mild overvaluation of the Magsaysay years demanded devaluation and an end to restrictions on barter. The Senate blocked legislation, launched corruption probes, and demanded Cuaderno's resignation. Embassy officials reported "open warfare" between the president and Senate leadership. The crisis took an ominous turn shortly after Indonesia's exchange-control policy provoked an army rebellion.

In November, Garcia charged that officers in the Philippine Army were plotting a coup. Bohlen believed that Garcia had concocted the plot as an excuse to purge the military, but State Department officials noted that many officers had criticized the president. The National Security Council cited the alleged coup as evidence of discontent and instability.[39]

Although U.S. officials dismissed predictions of imminent economic and political collapse, they urged the Garcia government to accept an International Monetary Fund mission to recommend reforms. The State Department had opposed devaluation before 1957, but now regarded the grossly overvalued peso as an impediment to growth. Pentagon officials complained that overvaluation doubled the Philippine payroll. Cuaderno patiently explained to embassy and Treasury Department officials that Garcia could not count on Philippine legislators to raise taxes to cover government losses from devaluation, and that IMF reforms would only trigger a crisis. The mission came and went in March 1959 without persuading the Filipinos to adopt a single recommendation. Garcia defiantly raised import taxes in violation of the Laurel-Langley agreement. Embassy officials worried that economic decline could provoke insurgency, and that this time the United States would be unable to interfere. Filipinos had changed since 1950, an economic officer complained. They no longer heeded or even tolerated economic advice from the United States.[40]

Amid mounting foreign and domestic criticism of its economic policy, the Garcia administration counterattacked with the Filipino First policy. Called a "movement" by its supporters, it consisted chiefly of Central Bank dicta and antiforeign declarations by ranking officials. Juan Pajo and a Central Bank official, Marcelo Balatbat, led the drive, while Garcia praised the movement without identifying himself with it. Anti-Chinese laws had appeal. A poll taken in 1960 revealed that nearly three-fourths of Manilans favored restricting business activities of aliens, and even of naturalized Filipinos. Officials found that antiforeign talk silenced critics, and Pajo did not shrink from linking opponents to foreign business interests. With rising unemployment and discontent, Vice President Macapagal commented, "the Filipino

First drive is made to order." Dismayed embassy observers reported that "public officials, congressmen, and prominent businessmen have espoused the Filipino-First cause."[41]

The Filipino First policy combined the dollar-allocation management pioneered by the Magsaysay administration with a new, threatening rhetoric. Cartoonists depicted "alien business" as a hulking, sloe-eyed figure, unmistakably Chinese, but editorialists did not spare firms owned by white foreigners. In reply to criticism from the U.S. Chamber of Commerce, the *Chronicle* warned that "by misrepresenting the policy and frustrating its logical development, alien business interests are only bringing closer the possibility of more drastic methods." Eleven European and Asian countries issued protests against the Filipino First campaign by mid-1959. The *Wall Street Journal* reported that "the Filipino Firsters [were] out to irritate the U.S." and that their target was business. But as before, Philippine policy aimed only to steer foreign investment away from competition with Philippine capital. "Where local capital and resources are adequate and available, priority will be given to Filipinos," Serrano explained. "Where local capital and resources are available but are either timid or not adequate, joint ventures between local and foreign investors would be favored." And, "where local capital and resources are not at all available it will obviously be an open field for foreign investment."[42]

The Filipino First movement increased pressure on American firms to go along or sell out. "I can see what's coming," observed an American who sold his broadcasting network to Filipinos. "They definitely want to get Americans out of business here." The Garcia administration stepped up the pressure on U.S.-owned utilities. In 1961, General Public Utilities of New Jersey sold the largest utility in the Philippines, the Manila power company, to the Lopez family. American manufacturers were concerned but not alarmed. "I think a great deal of what happens to American companies here will depend on how they conduct themselves," the manager of International Harvester said. Manufacturers opened slots for Filipino managers, seized joint-venture opportunities, and continued to profit.[43]

Established firms like Goodyear, International Harvester, and

First National City Bank regarded Philippine regulations as both a nuisance and an opportunity. A firm with the right connections in the Philippine elite could produce for a protected market, and enjoy low or no taxes. "Despite the frustrations and irritations," one manager told an embassy official, "it's the pay-off that counts and the pay-off is good." Older firms realized that their best chance lay in collaboration, even if small and new firms had to be sacrificed. "We have a constant battle," an International Harvester executive explained, "to keep some American companies, especially the newer ones here, from doing things that will get us all tossed out." Although they complained about dollar allocations, American firms seldom took legal action to enforce the parity clause or sought redress from the embassy.[44]

The United States had ample means to protect investors from the discrimination of economic nationalists. The "parity" clause of the Philippine constitution, imposed by the 1946 trade agreement and reaffirmed in the 1955 treaty, guaranteed American citizens the same legal status as Filipinos in the transaction of business affairs. U.S. officials could use financial levers like the sugar quota, multilateral lending, and aid to enforce parity and assure fair treatment. Yet there is no evidence they did so or even threatened to. Commerce and State department officials felt no need to add to the penalties the market would impose in the form of diminished capital flows. They urged businessmen to work with the Philippine government. They increased the sugar quota, and even pushed multilateral lenders to favor Filipino-owned over American-owned firms. In dealing with nationalism, the Eisenhower administration had to choose its points of resistance, and it ranked business investment below its own investment in the bases.[45]

The State Department and other agencies recognized that the Philippine government discriminated against American firms. The Commerce Department warned investors about "an antiforeign sentiment in the Philippines which is inconsistent with the expressed policy of welcoming foreign investment." The National Security Council noted Philippine violations of the Laurel-Langley agreement. They viewed business's distress with concern—not for the sake of investors, but because diminished capital flows would impair the Filipinos' ability to support their military establishment. The National Security Council thought that the United States had an interest in fostering entrepreneurship and industry, since "it would be unrealistic to expect substantial increases in their military budget until the whole level of the Philippine economy is raised." Embassy officials reported on the intensifying official discrimination against American firms. In 1958, the Securities and Exchange Commission investigated charges that "the Central Bank of the Philippines has adopted regulations designed to cause American stockholders in established Philippine corporations to reinvest the proceeds in speculative oil exploration companies." The State Department, however, took no action to enforce the Laurel-Langley treaty or to discourage discrimination.[46]

A number of businessmen in 1959 complained to the embassy that the government had withdrawn the tax privileges of selected American firms. The State Department sent a letter of protest to Ambassador Romulo, citing discrimination against American firms in violation of treaty. In November, Assistant Secretary of Commerce Henry Kearns met in Manila with Garcia's cabinet to discuss violations of the parity clause. He stressed the disadvantages of the Filipino First policy "from the point of view of the Philippines' own self-interest." Capital had to be wooed, since global demand outstripped supply. Firms that wanted to start operations in the Philippines had gone elsewhere because of poor treatment. Cuaderno and Serrano replied that the compelling need to reduce the excessive alien control of business justified Filipino First policies. They explained that the policy only affected new businesses. They had no intention of discriminating against established firms or against joint ventures like those set up by Goodrich or Firestone, and even welcomed new joint ventures.[47]

Serrano's answers reassured Kearns, who instructed a gathering of businessmen in New York that exchange and import controls were warranted and that businessmen would have to "acquire an understanding of the problems and desires of Filipinos, even of the emotional aspects of Philippine nationalism." Discrimination continued, but the State Department took no actions to curtail aid, loans, or quotas. "It is apparent," an embassy official reported, that Filipinos "do not feel bound under Article VII to accord Americans doing business in the Philippines equal treatment with Filipinos." The Philippine position was fixed, and Serrano was "not prepared seriously [to] consider U.S. views." Nonetheless, Philippine economic requests continued to receive favorable treatment. Despite the Council on Foreign Economic Policy's preference for a regional, export-led strategy, the Export-Import Bank agreed to fund the steel plant at Iligan. Throughout 1958 and 1959, the State Department lobbied lending agencies to grant loans to the Philippines and give special preference to Philippine firms. In 1960, following the elimination of the Cuban sugar quota, the United States increased the Philippine quota by a half-million tons.[48]

U.S. officials had the instruments and the justification to mount a vigorous defense of American business. They did not do so because their primary interest in the Philippines was strategic, not economic. National Security Council documents often contained pronouncements about critical chromite and abaca supplies and the importance of Manila as a base for Far Eastern trade, but when officials called the Philippines a vital interest, they were not thinking about chromite; they were thinking about bases, strategy, and geopolitics. Throughout the Magsaysay and Garcia administrations, the United States was involved in sensitive negotiations to enlarge Clark Field and Subic Bay. The Philippines was virtually the only stable, pro-West country in a region prone to communism, neutralism, and subversion. Eisenhower's advisers saw nationalism as a threat to bases in the Philippines and recognized that the easiest way to arouse a backlash was to use American power on behalf of investors.[49]

For that matter, American businesses seldom wanted pressure exerted on their behalf. Big manufacturers recognized that their surest chance of success lay in cooperating, turning over more authority to Filipino managers, going along with the Central Bank. Filipinos made it possible for cooperative firms to earn handsome returns. Utility and mining interests realized that nothing the embassy could do would save them, and sold out. Trading firms did approach the embassy about individual instances of unfairness, and on a few occasions the embassy intervened with the Central Bank on their behalf. But embassy officials acted only in flagrant cases of discrimination, and their reluctance probably discouraged complaints.[50]

The claim that the United States acted on behalf of business interests to make the Philippines a haven for investment can be found in much of the historical literature. The balance sheet of public and private investments in the Philippines, however, reveals that the largest investment was in the strategic alliance. American firms by 1958 had invested some $164 million in the Philippines. By contrast, between 1944 and 1958 the United States gave the Philippines $854 million in grants and $1.2 billion in loans. Officials supported industry in the Philippines to promote relations with the Philippine leadership and because they hoped it would help make the Philippines stable. Some firms lost and some gained by this policy, but none had a part in making it. They were along for the ride.[51]

In the late 1950s, the United States faced greater difficulties in nearly every area of policy. The Eisenhower administration responded by carefully choosing the issues on which it would take a stand and making concessions on the others. It took other actions as well. The Central Intelligence Agency conducted an array of covert operations to reduce the power of the nationalist elite and place in office "Magsaysay-oriented" politicians. Eisenhower visited the Philippines in 1960 to use his popularity to defuse anti-Americanism. These actions had little effect. The relationship continued to rely on the complementary interests of the two countries: the Philippine need to support a costly, managed economy with aid and trade from the United States, and the U.S. need for a base for operations in Asia.

The CIA failed to restructure Philippine politics. Covert operations in Manila have been described with some embellishment in the memoir of a "top" agent, Joseph Smith, who contends that the United States used the agency as its "principal link with the Philippine political leadership," and that the Manila station, with the grudging consent of Washington, took on three types of operations: propaganda, election tampering, and social action. All three were long on ambition and short on results. The Filipinos who ran the propaganda effort had little agency supervision, and chose subjects "that were not themes we had ordered them to take up or were even interested in their discussing." Smith admits that leaders and the public knew where the propaganda sheets came from and ignored them. The CIA spent a million pesos on the 1959 midterm elections in an attempt to unite reform-minded oppositionists with the Liberal machine, which opposed reform. The result was the Grand Alliance, a shaky coalition of former Magsaysay aides and conservative sugar interests whose chief accomplishment was to boost Ferdinand Marcos—whom the agency opposed—to national prominence as victor of the at-large Senate race. The CIA hedged by bankrolling a variety of candidates without regard to their views or alliances. Smith wondered "just how many deals and what kind I could honestly support in the name of more decent politics."[52]

As with Magsaysay, the CIA overestimated how much its actions shaped events and misjudged motives of Filipinos who sought the agency's help. "These men are not agents," the station chief, Gabriel Kaplan, explained. "They're loyal Filipinos who find us a source of help financially and morally in their efforts to make this country work and free it from corruption. Remember that." In addition to propaganda and election-tampering efforts, the agency had a program to send student activists to the provinces to train barrio leaders independent of landlords and political machines. "We were supporting a social revolution," Smith claims. But as with the propaganda campaign, the agency supported the program without controlling it. The social revolution amounted to an effort to build a political base for Ramon Binamira, whom Kaplan saw as the next Magsaysay. Smith argues that the station had few checks on its activities. The CIA allowed its agents in the field to set their own objectives and report their own success in achieving them. The agents, in turn, allowed their Filipino contacts the same latitude. The agency identified Recto and the nationalists as the enemy, but it had no plan to deal with them. Smith claims that he and Bohlen admired the nationalists more than the feuding politicians who took the agency's money. "We both, in our hearts, thought Recto was right."[53]

Eisenhower visited Manila in June 1960 to instruct Philippine leaders in the advantages of "constructive nationalism." Bohlen urged the president not to go, since the visit would be "made an occasion for presenting a long and emotional bill of complaints against the United States which might be embarrassing and would certainly be infuriating." Trusting his own experience, Eisenhower decided to go anyway, dismissing difficulties with Garcia as "psychological and a matter of pride rather than of great moment." Two million Filipinos turned out to greet the president. In three speeches, Eisenhower concentrated on nationalism and neutralism, pointing out that two-thirds of the world's countries had aligned with the free world and criticizing the minority in some who, "possibly the victim of subversion or bribe . . . oppose even the most obviously profitable associations." The United States, he said, did not want to remake other societies, but to join with them in protecting diversity. He contrasted constructive nationalism, which recognized international obligations, with narrow nationalism, which placed parochial interests first. Serrano was able to present his bill of complaints, requesting more development assistance and military aid.[54]

A personal triumph for the president, the visit had little lasting effect on relations. The euphoric optimism with which Eisenhower's aides had viewed Philippine events in 1953 had been replaced with deep pessimism. The prospects for stability and reform looked bleak in the short and long term. The president recognized that nothing of great moment had changed in the relationship. The Philippine government's political weakness had led it to adopt a hectoring, confrontational stance in dealing with the United States, but it still dealt. In the bases negotiations, the United States achieved more tangible results under Garcia than under Magsaysay. Neither side could point to similar accomplishments in the economic field. GNP increased by 40 percent between the end of the war and Eisenhower's visit, but most growth occurred between 1948 and 1953. In the late 1950s, economic growth failed to keep pace with population, and U.S. officials recognized that only thorough, structural changes in the political economy could reverse the trend toward unemployment and stagnation. The United States could not be the instigator of those reforms. Interference would only provoke a backlash that would prevent reform and endanger the bases.

In its last report on the Philippines, Eisenhower's National Security Council reported that although "political, economic, and military problems in the Philippines continue to exist," the administration should stay the course. Filipinos, too, considered the relationship locked into a pattern that would continue for the foreseeable future. Romulo pointed out that President-elect John F. Kennedy's choice of secretaries of State and the Treasury indicated that the change of administration was "not likely to produce any basic change of approach" toward the Philippines, a prospect Romulo viewed optimistically. "I assure you," he cabled Garcia, "we will be closer to this new administration than to the previous one."[55]

After 1958, negotiations on military bases changed from a periodic event to a permanent feature of the bilateral relationship, a regulator of United States behavior and a source of leverage for Filipinos. Garcia continued the process of circumscribing American prerogatives, compressing the hierarchy of U.S. political, economic, and strategic interests into a single interest: access to military installations. Through nationalist agitation, governmental foot-dragging, and small acts of insubordination, Philippine leaders nudged the United States away from commitments to liberal developmentalism, American companies, and, within a decade, democracy. Successive regimes pushed the United States to declare its bottom line, its minimum expectation of Philippine cooperation, and Filipinos stepped up to the line.

Filipinos had free rein over their economy. They decided how to treat foreign investment, how to use export earnings, which industries to develop, and what strategies to use. The world system imposed constraints, as it did on all developing countries, but Filipinos could make choices about how to deal with those limits, and they could bend them in ways other postcolonial countries could not precisely because of their country's strategic importance to the United States. The Philippine government could negotiate its terms of trade and its creditworthiness. Assured of American help in a crisis, its officials were not even constrained by their own capacity to fail.

By 1960, most of the mechanisms that supported what came to be called "crony capitalism" were in place. A pervasive system of controls allowed the ruling faction to apportion economic benefits to its favored clients, and to punish its rivals. The easy availability of money—foreign aid and loans in the 1960s, and recycled petrodollars in the 1970s—would allow cacique capitalists to profit on an even grander scale in successive decades. The bizarre excesses of the Marcos years differed in degree, not in kind, from the political and economic manipulations of his predecessors. Marcos came to power at a moment when the president enjoyed greater freedom from external constraint and easy access to credit, a situation that summoned all of his, and his wife's, ambition and imagination.

Conclusion

Many illusions were shattered on November 24, 1992, the day the last U.S. warship, the helicopter carrier *Belleau Wood*, sailed from Subic Bay. Just as some American diplomats had refused to believe the Philippine Senate would vote to terminate the treaty, many Filipinos, on both sides of the bases issue, believed until the end that the United States would not really leave. The government of Fidel Ramos had other illusions. It planned for the bases to become what nationalist rhetoricians said they had been all along, little Hong Kongs, "free ports," and "industrial processing zones." A shortage of funds and the objections of competition-shy industrialists and traders have so far blocked the conversion plans. There was talk of foreign developers for the abandoned bases, but the only investors to show interest, from Singapore and Taiwan, were unnerved by the kidnappings of several Chinese businessmen by gangs allegedly allied with the police. The bases have become ghost towns, their buildings stripped of wiring and glass. Even the manhole covers were sold for scrap.[1]

Filipinos were surprised at how swiftly the rest of the U.S. diplomatic, military, and economic presence dissolved. Consulates and economic missions closed; aid dwindled to a fraction of previous levels. The State Department withdrew the embassy's large political section, dispersing its officers among the new states of central Asia and eastern Europe. To some Filipinos, their departure came as a revelation. "We have finally realized that we are truly on our own, and must win our own salvation, or perish by our own hand," one editorialist observed. "It is the most wonderful thing that has happened to this country." A central tenet of nationalist scholarship had been the predominantly economic nature of the relationship, yet without bases, the United States had little interest in business or anything else in the Philippines.[2]

A number of American writers adhered to this tenet as well, observing that without the bases the United States could more aggressively push the Philippine government to reform its economy, using the threat of an aid cutoff to ensure progress. They failed to notice that Japan has been the Philippine government's principal source of aid since 1979. Moreover, without the bases, the United States has little interest in reforming the Philippine economy, and it is unlikely to offer millions of dollars in grants so that it can threaten to cut them later.[3]

From the U.S. point of view, the relationship with the Philippines after 1946 was predominantly strategic. World War II transformed the Philippines from a strategic liability to an asset of vast importance. Pentagon planners considered Philippine bases a key element in the strategy for preventing a single power from dominating Eurasia and challenging the United States. Philippine outposts became vital links in a chain of air and naval bases that allowed the United States to project power into distant trouble spots. Poorly equipped and thinly staffed in the late 1940s, the bases grew into highly sophisticated communications, repair, recreation, and transshipment facilities supporting operations throughout Asia and the Pacific, and employing thousands of American and Filipino workers. The Communist victory in China, the emergence of Soviet nuclear striking power, and deepening U.S. involvement in Southeast Asia enhanced the bases' value in the 1950s.

U.S. officials considered a stable, cooperative Philippines essential to the continued functioning of the bases. They chiefly valued social and political stability—a government that willingly accepted the military presence and could guarantee order—but they recognized that stability required a modicum of economic soundness. The government needed sufficient revenue to support an army and essential services. National income needed to be high enough to prevent unrest.

The United States structured economic and aid policies to assure stability. Making a clear exception to its multilateralist, open-door global economic policy, it gave the Philippines preferred access to American markets to encourage trade and prevent Philippine living standards from sinking to the levels of surrounding Asian countries. In the wake of the Communist victory in China in 1949, the United States launched a $250 million economic aid program and encouraged Philippine leaders to adopt import and exchange controls to rescue the government from economic collapse and peasant rebellion. The Eisenhower administration revised the trade act to appease nationalists who threatened to expel the bases.

Officials in Washington also valued the Philippines as a "showcase of democracy." In good times, they wanted it to serve as an exemplar of orderly decolonization or of successful Asian democracy; in bad times, they feared that political chaos or economic collapse would make it a symbol of the cost of collaboration with the United States. As cold-war battle lines hardened, the Eisenhower administration placed a high value on possessing such symbols and denying them to the enemy. As Eisenhower explained, the United States was painted as an imperialistic seeker of limitless power, using small countries as pawns, exploiting their resources, and relegating them to beggarly dependence. "The existence, the prosperity, the prestige, of the Republic of the Philippines proves the falsity of those charges."[4]

State Department officials believed investment in the Philippines improved living standards and enhanced stability, and they encouraged it. But when forced to decide between protecting investors and guarding their own strategic interests, their priorities were clear. In the late 1950s, the department gave business little protection against increasing official discrimination for fear of arousing nationalist sentiment that might turn on the bases. The United States could have cut aid, lending, or trade quotas, but it preferred not to risk reprisals.

Officials were willing to sacrifice businesses to mollify Philippine nationalism, but they would not sacrifice strategic interests. Kolko observes that "only in nations where there has been a strong Left has the United States sometimes allowed strategic and political considerations to define the form and even the ends of its policies and to minimize, at least temporarily, the central importance of its economic purposes." Filipinos never pushed the issue too far, but it was clear from occasions when they did push that, despite official pronouncements about the commercial advantages of the alliance, U.S. officials valued the Philippines chiefly as a military outpost. As Mitra explained, investments and human rights "are nothing when compared to their military bases."[5]

U.S. preoccupation with strategic issues allowed Filipinos to create room for their own objectives. The quota preferences granted in the Trade Act of 1946 recognized the special status of the Philippines as a military ally. The Interior and War departments persuaded Congress that the strategic significance of the Philippines justified an exception from the multilateral trade policy the State Department advocated for the rest of the world. In 1956, the United States extended nontariff quotas to reward Philippine cooperation in its struggle against communism in Southeast Asia. While granting exceptionally generous terms to Philippine exporters, the United States encouraged the Philippines to erect barriers against American imports. Congress and the State Department recognized that this policy hurt American exporters, but they made the sacrifice to protect their strategic investment.

Economic aid protected the U.S. strategic stake in the Philippines. Between 1945 and 1958, the United States provided over a billion dollars in grants and credits, more economic aid than to any country in the Far East. In addition, it supplied military aid averaging $30 million a year in the 1950s, about half of which went to nonmilitary programs like road-building. Though Filipinos never felt that the aid they received was adequate, grants and credits frequently saved the Philippine government from insolvency and allowed it to support costly efforts to industrialize and Filipinize the economy.[6]

U.S. officials discerned in 1950 that the Huk rebellion could be defeated by shoring up the economy rather than by escalating the war, but they failed to draw correct conclusions from their success. Though often compared to revolutionary nationalists in Vietnam, the Huks had more limited aims. They sought the end of armed repression, the legalization of peasant organizations, and signs that the government cared for their welfare. With American help, Magsaysay met those conditions, not by reforming the patrimonial system, but by making it work smoothly, granting more patronage and pork barrel to rebel areas, mediating individual disputes, and encouraging landlords to disband private armies.

Obsessed by the global contest against the Soviet Union, U.S. officials exaggerated links between the Huks and international communism. Because U.S. agencies and the Philippine government pursued a mixture of conflicting policies toward the rebellion, each agency could see the Huks' demise as vindicting policies it had championed. Psywar and counterinsurgency tactics gained followers in the Defense Department; the CIA placed more emphasis on recruitment of cooperative local strongmen; and the State Department began to see economic aid as a weapon against insurgency. The Philippine experience encouraged policymakers to take on other insurgencies without giving them a strategy.

U.S. officials paid little attention to the motives or intentions of Filipinos who seemed cooperative. Philippine leaders could always claim to be beleaguered allies on the front lines of successive struggles—the Pacific War, Communist subversion, the Taiwan Straits crises, Vietnam—in which the United States had a preeminent stake. Officials too readily accepted these claims. Although they scrutinized the motives of those who opposed their interests, they seldom considered how the ulterior motives of their friends might undermine the usefulness of cooperation.

As manipulators, Philippine leaders of this era lacked the panache of their successor, Ferdinand Marcos, or of their contemporaries, Chiang Kai-shek and Syngman Rhee, but they skillfully employed a variety of tactics to make United States policy conform to their interests. They played agencies off one another, selecting the best option from among a variety of policy prescriptions. They assured the success of programs that suited their purposes, and allowed others to atrophy. They converted the U.S.-imposed machinery for economic regulation into a highly responsive instrument for enriching favored clients and impov-

erishing others. U.S. officials were not blind to this manipulation, but their interest in the Philippine economy seldom extended beyond their need for a stable, reasonably contented country in which to locate airfields and drydocks.

The Philippine government defined its interests largely in economic terms. Its principal aim was to maintain the privileged access to U.S. markets. Earnings from sugar and copra, sold in the
United States at prices well above the world market, provided
most of the Philippine foreign exchange and financed the growth
of Filipino-owned manufacturing. Nontariff quotas for its produce allowed the Philippines to avoid the declining terms of
trade that afflicted other agricultural economies, a problem Latin
American economists have identified as a root cause of underdevelopment. Philippine exporters could sell sugar at 40 percent
above the world price. These profits allowed wealthy landed
clans who controlled the government to retain their status and
to diversify into manufacturing.[7]

The Philippine government needed financial aid. The landed
lawyer-politicians who controlled Congress wanted to industrialize the economy without disturbing the patrimonial social order they dominated. The Philippine-Chinese middle class stood
poised to move capital and talent into new industrial enterprises,
threatening the political and economic dominance of Filipino
landlords. To prevent this, the Philippine government undertook
massive and costly interventions in the economy, building cum-
bersome state corporations and regulatory agencies its feeble revenue bureau could scarcely support.

Powerless to tax its own wealthy constituency, the overbur-
dened state required infusions of money from outside. The coincidence of a strong patrimonial tradition and a weak state forced
Philippine leaders to ensure a constant stream of financial rewards for their clients, an aspect of political culture responsible
for the more bizarre acts of Philippines leaders: Quirino's scheme
to ransom Japanese prisoners of war, Marcos's search for the Ya-
mashita gold hoard, Aquino's expedition to open underwater
vaults supposedly containing the treasure of Imelda Marcos.
More commonly, Philippine leaders did their treasure hunting in
Washington. Failure to obtain outside funding forced the state to

engage in inflationary deficit spending, destabilizing the economy and eroding standards of living for the poor.

The Philippine leadership's policy toward the United States was not simply an exercise in self-enrichment. Landholding politicians feared that the creation of new wealth would undermine their social position and create new power centers. Sometimes depicted as a preserve of freebooting capitalism, the Philippines was nearly the opposite. A web of state regulations kept economic power tightly in the hands of politicians who controlled powerful provincial machines. The political economy sacrificed development and increases in national income, investment, and employment to assure that ethnic Filipinos rather than the indigenous Chinese minority accrued the benefits of growth. This objective had wide popular appeal, not just among the elite, but among the mass of Filipino tenants and urban laborers who also resented Chinese economic power.

Other Southeast Asian states—with revolutionary and socialist governments—likewise made reducing Chinese economic power a principal objective. What distinguished the Philippine effort was the relative absence of violence and the relatively high degree of success. In Vietnam, thousands of ethnic Chinese risked their lives on the open sea rather than endure further discrimination. Malaysia, Indonesia, and Thailand each had elaborate programs aimed at diminishing the disproportionate economic power of their Chinese minorities, yet in each of those countries, Chinese capital still predominates over both native and foreign capital. Filipinization—the regulations, the seizure of thousands of street stalls, the police shakedowns, and the official discrimination—was a reprehensible, costly policy, but it was also one that proved to be an independent, popular act of self-definition. It was nationalism.[8]

With the inadvertent help of the United States, Filipinos were able to reconcile the conflicting impulses that often tear new nations apart. As Clifford Geertz explains, the transition from colony to nation, from subject to citizen, awakens in newly independent peoples two contradictory notions of collective identity: the drive to attain national greatness through industrialization or military might, and the urge to derive a singular identity from a cultural, racial, linguistic, or religious birthright. "The task of nationalist ideologizing," Geertz argues, is to decide the relationship between these two imperatives. One only needs to consult the recent histories of Yugoslavia, Ethiopia, or Sri Lanka to understand the importance of this exercise. Roxas's vision of an industrialized Philippines, militarily allied with the United States, and the Huks' attempt to form a national movement around the grievances of the central Luzon share tenants are at opposite ends of this ideological spectrum. Neither enjoyed broad enough appeal to survive. The nationalism articulated by Recto and implemented by Magsaysay and Garcia proved more durable. It combined the promise of industrialization with the assurance that its benefits would go to tycoons with whom, however falsely, the average Filipino felt a racial and cultural affinity. The United States supplied the aid and the institutions—chiefly the Central Bank—Filipinos needed to carry out their plans without bankrupting the government or resorting to force.[9]

Like all postcolonial elites, the Philippine leadership sought to impose its goals and values within the limits circumscribed by integration into a world community dominated by the United States. In this sense, students have exaggerated the extent to which instruments like the 1946 trade act restricted Philippine autonomy in the economic field. Many studies criticize the United States for reimposing the prewar pattern of trade, but fail to explain how the course of trade might have differed in the absence of the 1946 act, or how that difference would have helped Filipinos. In fact, Filipinos remained free to trade with Japan, Europe, and other countries, and the United States encouraged them to do so. Filipinos chose to trade primarily with the United States because it was the largest market in the world and because they enjoyed special advantages there.

The world market, not legislation, bound the Philippines within a U.S.-centered economic sphere. "The truth of the matter is that the United States would like us to sell more of our products to other countries," Jose Romero, the head of the Philippine Sugar Association, explained. "However, we prefer to sell our products in the United States because for most products it is the best market in the world." The trade act allowed the Philippines to negotiate the terms of its dependency, a luxury few countries enjoyed. Romero observed that "many countries would only be too glad to be 'dependent on the United States market' if only they would be allowed to do so."[10] In return for market privileges, the United States exacted concessions that historians have identified as instruments of neocolonial control: the parity clause, granting American businessmen rights equal to Filipinos; and the currency clause, pegging the peso to the dollar at a fixed rate. These provisions, however, had little coercive effect. The Philippine Central Bank nullified the currency clause in 1949 by imposing exchange controls. Filipinos adhered to or violated parity when it suited them, and the State Department made little effort to enforce it. The Treasury and State departments generally sympathized with the ostensible reasoning behind the violations, the need to conserve exchange. Filipinos welcomed the massive economic intervention of the Bell mission, which enhanced the state's ability to regulate the economy. The Bell mission's intervention supported Philippine objectives. Despite the appearance of control, the United States placed few restrictions on the Philippine government's freedom to shape the domestic economy and, in fact, substantially enlarged that freedom.

Between 1950 and 1956, the golden age of United States–Philippine cooperation, the two countries lived under a bargain that allowed each country autonomy in its primary area of interest. Philippine leaders sought and received U.S. aid and guidance in defeating the Huk rebellion. They applauded the intervention of the Bell mission and the large aid program initiated by the Foster-Quirino agreement. The United States vastly expanded the operations of its Philippine bases to support missions in Vietnam, Taiwan, and East Asia. Under Magsaysay, the Philippine government took vigorous steps to Filipinize manufacturing and the retail trade. The two countries negotiated a new trade agreement, a mutual security pact, and the Southeast Asian treaty. The State Department promoted the Philippines as an exemplar of postcolonial democratic development.

The bargain quickly began to decay, as Filipinos came to regard military bases as endangering the economic system they had created. Filipino manufacturers, whose livelihoods depended on official protection from American competition, paid attention to nationalist claims that U.S. policies hampered industrialization. Nationalists argued that the United States would use its bases to protect American investments and open Philippine ports to U.S. goods, a claim made believable by the thriving black market in goods imported through the bases.

It became more difficult after 1954 to reconcile U.S. strategic interests and Philippine economic interests. As caciques fixed their ambitions on manufacturing, they became more demanding, and more suspicious of the United States, insisting on aid and tariff concessions with fewer conditions. They stalled negotiations on military bases, holding them hostage to their economic demands. Needing to direct aid toward Southeast Asian countries facing immediate threats, the Eisenhower administration grew frustrated with Philippine demands.

Policies toward the United States hardened during the Garcia administration, and the terms of the bargain became more explicit. Filipinos spoke of economic aid as "rent" on the bases and appreciated more than ever that dependency was a two-way street. They recognized the leverage implicit in their country's strategic value and employed it to maximum advantage. Garcia adopted a get-tough policy as a tactical maneuver to obtain more aid, firmer security guarantees, and greater freedom to set economic policy. But although the two nations argued to an impasse on both the bases and the trade agreements, they continued to regard the relationship as essential to their respective interests. The United States had to make larger and larger concessions on its secondary interests—allowing the Philippines to discriminate against U.S. investors and to create a political system that bore less resemblance to the showcase model—in order to protect its primary interest in the bases.

The story of the U.S.-Philippine partnership lends new insights into the sources and nature of United States foreign policy. It reveals how few constraints domestic economic interests placed on foreign policy, and how the United States dealt with tradeoffs between strategic interests, nationalism, and development.

Before World War II, labor and agricultural groups influenced Philippine policy in Congress, but after 1945, a decentralized executive branch devised policy with little interference from Congress. The Treasury advocated import and exchange controls in the late 1940s to avoid asking Congress for funds. The Defense Department released the disastrous Brownell memorandum rather than go before Congress. On those occasions when the Constitution required congressional action, the administration carefully constructed legislation to disguise its economic disadvantages. Both of the trade acts amounted to huge off-budget transfers of funds, multimillion-dollar subsidies for Philippine exporters. The Interior and State departments recognized that disguising aid as trade would help win Congressional approval. To sweeten the deal, both trade acts contained the notorious parity provision, granting U.S. firms special business privileges. Unenforceable and resented by U.S. businessmen and Filipinos alike, parity's sole function was to appease Congress, to provide one quid pro quo for the trade giveaway.

Philippine diplomats were skilled lobbyists, but they preferred to deal with the fragmented foreign policy-making machinery of the executive branch, which presented a smorgasbord of policy prescriptions and viewpoints. The division of authority between the State, Defense, Treasury, and Commerce departments, the National Security Council, the Federal Reserve Board, and multilateral lending agencies provided ample opportunities for what Ambassador Myron Cowen called the "classical Philippine maneuver of playing one part of the American government against another part." Policy implementation was equally fragmented. The United States was represented in Manila not just by an ambassador, but also by a military advisory group, an aid mission, a Federal Reserve advisory group, Agriculture Department advisers, a CIA mission, CINCPAC, the Thirteenth Air Force Command, and visiting trade missions, congressional delegations, and military negotiators.[11]

The sources of the various departmental positions are difficult to isolate. Interior Department actions were informed by the vision of liberal colonialists in the Office of High Commissioner, by Ickes's hostility to the State Department, and to some extent by the department's constituents in the oil industry. The Defense Department responded to the imperatives of planning and the changing missions assigned to U.S. forces, which, in turn, derived from a global strategic vision that would take 689 pages to explain. Some students suggest that the State Department acted on behalf of a "hegemonic bloc" of high-tech manufacturing firms. Many firms identified with the bloc—Westinghouse, General Electric, Ford—had investments in the Philippines. State Department records, however, supply little evidence linking Philippine policy to the influence of these firms, nor do the records suggest indirect influence, through the vehicle of shared ideology. State Department officials acted on apprehensions about military threats, subversion, revolutionary nationalism, poverty, and other contingencies that might allow the Soviet Union to win over the periphery bit by bit. If corporations were concerned about these matters, they concealed their fears in their letters to government officials, congressional testimony, and trade publications.[12]

A number of recent studies have focused on the quality of U.S. diplomacy in the Third World in the 1950s. Amid rising scholarly acclaim for Eisenhower's statesmanship, Robert McMahon has pointed out flaws in the administration's policy toward postcolonial countries, and particularly in its policies regarding nationalism and development. He argues that the administration, preoccupied with the cold war, failed to develop constructive relations with postcolonial regimes, and that that policy was detrimental to newly independent peoples. H. W. Brands defends the Eisenhower revisionists, arguing that Dulles's bombastic criticism of neutralism disguised a subtly crafted policy that satisfied the needs of Third World nationalists without drawing the United States into burdensome commitments.[13]

Several historians link Eisenhower's failings to global war plans that required bases in Pakistan, Egypt, and the Philippines. Peter Hahn and Dennis Merrill find that in Egypt and India, Eisenhower acknowledged the aspirations of nationalists and sought to enlist their support, but failed because of conflicting strategic goals. Burton I. Kaufman takes a similar line in criticizing Eisenhower's development policy. The administration genuinely sought to help industrialize postcolonial countries, he argues, but geopolitical objectives confused policy and led U.S. officials to eschew internal social-reform programs that might have made development aid effective.[14]

The Philippine case supports the argument that strategic imperatives precluded effective policies on nationalism and development. To mollify the nationalists, Eisenhower backed away from policies that might interfere with the Philippine economy or social structure, in effect surrendering the chance to turn aid programs into effective instruments of reform. It does not suggest, however, that freed of strategic constraints, policy would have been more effective. Rather, without the strategic imperative, the United States would have had little interest in reform or nationalism in countries like the Philippines.

The United States does not deserve sole blame for the underdevelopment of the Philippine economy. Filipino historians, who have minimized the significance of their own leaders, need to reexamine the importance of choices made by previous administrations. The structure of the Philippine economy and social order, maldistribution of wealth, and political corruption owe more to Philippine decisions and political economy than current scholarship recognizes. Even as the Philippine leaders took the momentous step of rejecting the 1991 military bases agreement, they seemed scarcely to believe their own strength. "Maybe it is a blessing in disguise," the armed forces chief murmured; "maybe we will learn to take care of ourselves." Philippine leaders have taken care of themselves for some time now, and scholars and journalists need to take heed of that.[15]

It remains an open question whether the end of the special relationship will loosen the grip of cacique capitalists on the Philippine social order. Filipinos have recently shown a distaste for traditional politicians, whom they call *trapos*, a punning abbreviation that means "dirty rags." Voters' preference for actors and military men as candidates may signify the decline of cacique authority, but if past experience shows anything, it is that entrenched power will be resourceful and inventive in defending itself. Since national candidates still depend on local machines, it may be that nontraditional candidates appear different but answer to the same dominant families the *trapos* did. Electoral politics may not open avenues for candidates committed to challenging authority.

The proliferation of nongovernmental organizations—private environmental, health, education, and social-welfare agencies, often funded from abroad—is perhaps a more heartening development. These organizations play important, sometimes central parts in the lives of many rural communities and urban neighborhoods. As United States aid to the Philippine government decreases, nongovernmental agencies will gain importance, giving their leaders a stronger voice in local politics. These organizations could produce a generation of leaders capable of challenging the caciques.

Reference Matter

Notes

Introduction

1. Michael Dueñas, "Mt. Pinatubo Speaks: Yankees Go Home," *Philippines Free Press*, July 6, 1991, pp. 8–9.
2. "Politicians Discuss Senate Bases-Related Bills," DZRH Radio, 0030 GMT, Sept. 13, 1991, in *FBIS Daily Report—East Asia*, Sept. 17, 1991, pp. 38–40; "Salonga Declares Rejection," DZMM Radio, 1129 GMT, Sept. 16, 1991, in ibid., pp. 45–49.
3. Kolko, *Confronting*, p. 25.
4. For the most recent description of the Philippines as a case study of reformist intervention, see MacDonald, pp. 129–84; for Philippine nationalist views, see Constantino and Constantino.
5. See Scott, *Weapons*.
6. As Ashis Nandy explains, the process of colonial acculturation produces models of both conformity and dissent, so that even opposition remains predictable and controlled. Rather than defining themselves as resisters, Asians could "construct a West" they could live with while resisting domination by the real West. Nandy, p. xiv.

Chapter 1

1. E. E. Sayre, "Submarine," pp. 22–23.
2. Brands, *Bound to Empire*, pp. 20–35.
3. Karnow, pp. 136–38.
4. May, *Battle*, pp. 286–89.
5. May, *Social Engineering*, pp. 4–23.
6. Brands, *Bound to Empire*, pp. 61–79.
7. D. Wurfel, *Filipino Politics*, p. 11.
8. For Quezon's early career, see May, *Social Engineering*, pp. 35–38.

9. For the military response to the decision for independence, see Friend, *Between Two Empires*, pp. 161–62. For business views, see Friend, *Blue-Eyed*, pp. 18–20; Karnow, p. 272.

10. Friend, *Between Two Empires*, pp. 95–148, 188.

11. United States, *Statutes*, 47: 456–65; Gunther, pp. 67–68; Hartendorp, pp. 60–61.

12. Stanley, *Nation*, pp. 66–67; B. Anderson, "Cacique Democracy," pp. 9–13; Salamanca, *Filipino Reaction*, pp. 161–62.

13. Friend, "Philippine Sugar Industry," p. 181; D. Wurfel, *Filipino Politics*, pp. 33–36. *Utang na loob*, literally "inner debt," is a debt of honor that can only be repaid by continuous reciprocal giving.

14. Friend, "Philippine Sugar Industry," pp. 184–85.

15. Ibid., p. 187; Friend, *Between Two Empires*, p. 118.

16. For the attributes of patrimonial leadership, see Weber, pp. 346–59; Hutchcroft, "Oligarchs," pp. 415–17; Phelan, pp. 324–26; Gleeck, *American Governors-General and High Commissioners*, pp. 356–57; Friend, *Between Two Empires*, p. 156.

17. Kerkvliet, *Huk Rebellion*, pp. 5–25.

18. Hayden, pp. 379–400; Kerkvliet, *Huk Rebellion*, pp. 36–39; Kerkvliet, "Peasant Society," pp. 172–204; Sturtevant, pp. 199–213.

19. Kerkvliet, *Huk Rebellion*, pp. 54–58; Hayden, pp. 399–400; Taruc, *Born*, pp. 26–51; Friend, *Between Two Empires*, p. 160.

20. Purcell, pp. 493–568. U.S. military authorities, fearing the Philippines, Hawaii, and Cuba would become pathways to California, extended U.S. exclusion laws to occupied areas in 1898. Congress ratified the orders by legislation in 1900 and 1902. Weightman, pp. 30–31; Hayden, pp. 692–99; Steinberg, *The Philippines*, p. 22.

21. Purcell, pp. 540–41; Hayden, pp. 701–4; Weightman, p. 41.

22. Purcell, p. 543; Hayden, p. 704.

23. Hayden, pp. 703–4, 838; Agpalo, *Political Process*, pp. 27–30; OIR, "Government Corporations in the Philippines," May 27, 1953, R & A Reports, USNA, RG 59, no. 6206; Hartendorp, pp. 49–57. Osmeña's sympathy for the Chinese distinguished him from most mestizos. Many of the leading anti-Chinese agitators were themselves of Chinese descent.

24. Friend, *Between Two Empires*, p. 123; Gunther, p. 69.

25. Platt, pp. 17–19; Harrison, p. 176; Karnow, pp. 330–31.

26. United States, *Statutes*, 47: 463; "Philippine Bases Subsequent to Granting Independence," JPS 318/1, November 14, 1943, CCS decimal file, 686.9 Philippine Islands (11-7-43), USNA, RG 218, box 699.

27. Petillo, pp. 54–55, 163–72.

28. Ibid., pp. 179–80; Miller, pp. 59–62.

29. Sherry, p. 32.

30. Karnow, pp. 297–301.

31. Capt. John L. McCrea to Adm. William D. Leahy, Dec. 28, 1942, CCS decimal file, 686.9 Philippine Islands (11-7-43), USNA, RG 218, box 264; "Post War Military Problems with Particular Relation to Air Bases," Mar. 15, 1943, ibid.; "Air Routes across the Pacific and Air Facilities for International Police Force," JCS 183/5, Mar. 25, 1943, ibid.

32. "Air Routes across the Pacific and Air Facilities for International Police Force," JCS 183/6, Apr. 10, 1943, CCS decimal file, 686.9 Philippine Islands (11-7-43), USNA, RG 218, box 264.

33. Arnold to JSSC, "United States Military Requirements for Air Bases, Facilities, and Operating Rights in Foreign Territories," Nov. 8, 1943, CCS decimal file, 686.9 Philippine Islands (11-7-43), USNA, RG 218, box 264; Sherry, p. 55.

34. Sherry, p. 159.

35. "Air Routes across the Pacific and Air Facilities for International Police Force," JCS 183/6, Apr. 10, 1943, CCS decimal file, 686.9 Philippine Islands (11-7-43), USNA, RG 218, box 264.

36. Salamanca, "Quezon, Osmeña and Roxas," pp. 303–6.

37. Harrison, p. 225; Grunder and Livezey, pp. 242–43; Walter Lippmann, "Today and Tomorrow," *Washington Post*, Sept. 28, 1943, p. 11; idem, "Today and Tomorrow," *Washington Post*, Sept. 30, 1943, p. 17.

38. Salamanca, "Quezon, Osmeña and Roxas," pp. 301–8; Watkins, pp. 782–83; *Department of State Bulletin* 9, 216 (Aug. 14, 1943): 91. Roosevelt repeated this grant of "practical independence" on October 6; *Congressional Record*, 78th Cong., 2d sess., p. 8121.

39. "Philippine Bases Subsequent to Independence," JPS 318/1, Nov. 8, 1943, CCS decimal file, 686.9 Philippine Islands (11-7-43), USNA, RG 218, box 700; 138th JCS meeting, Dec. 21, 1943, ibid., box 699; Leahy to Roosevelt, "Philippine Bases Subsequent to Granting Independence," Jan. 1, 1944, ibid.; Converse, pp. 94–95.

40. Robert E. Sherwood to Elmer Davis, Aug. 31, 1943, CCS decimal file, 686.9 Philippine Islands (11-7-43), USNA, RG 218, box 699.

41. House Committee on Appropriations, *Appropriations Bill for 1944*, pp. 260–61, 274; Hayden to Brig. Gen. Bonner Fellers, "United States High Commissioner to the Philippine Islands: Status, Powers, Functions, Activities," Aug. 7, 1944, MacArthur Papers, RG 5, Quezon 143.

42. Joint Preparatory Commission on Philippine Affairs, *Report of May 20, 1938*, 1: 40, 51, 68; and 2: 21; Hartendorp, p. 54.

43. Hainsworth and Moyer, pp. 35–37; Hester, "Outline," p. 81; idem, "Restoration," p. 208.

44. Buss, "What Follows Liberation?" p. 126; Hester, "Outline," p. 81; Harold L. Ickes diaries, Ickes papers, Oct. 3, 1943, p. 8222, and June 17, 1944, p. 8897.

45. Hartendorp, pp. 53, 58–59; Hester, "Restoration," p. 216; idem, "Outline," p. 78.

46. Hester, "Footnotes," pp. 134–36; Joint Preparatory Commission on Philippine Affairs, *Report of May 20, 1938*, 1: 143–44.

47. Kurihara, pp. 6, 33.

48. Elizalde to Quezon, Feb. 9, 1944, Romulo papers, UP, ser. 1, box 1; Elizalde to Quezon, Mar. 3, 1944, Roxas papers, ser. 1(b), box 10.

49. Ickes diaries, Ickes papers, May 22, 1943, p. 7757; Fortas memorandum, Dec. 5, 1942, Ickes papers, box 226; Elizalde to Quezon, Feb. 9, 1944, Romulo papers, UP, ser. 1, box 1; Quezon to Elizalde, Feb. 16, 1944, ibid.; Biedzynski, pp. 84–90; Elizalde to Edward R. Stettinius, Feb. 24, 1944, Romulo papers, UP, ser. 1, box 1; Hull to Elizalde, Mar. 24, 1944, ibid.; Elizalde to Quezon, Apr. 19, 1944, ibid.

50. Osmeña to Elizalde, Aug. 12, 1944, Romulo papers, UP, ser. 1, box 1; Elizalde to Charles Parsons, Dec. 30, 1944, Roxas papers, ser. 1(b), box 8; Ickes diaries, Ickes papers, Sept. 5, 1943, p. 8140.

51. Hayden to Fellers, "Office of the High Commissioner," Aug. 7, 1944, MacArthur Archives, RG 5, Quezon 143.

52. *Department of State Bulletin* 12 (Apr. 8, 1945): 613; Joseph Grew to Roosevelt, "Trade Relations with the Philippines," Mar. 20, 1945, DSDF, USNA, RG 59, 611.11.B31/5-1045.

53. Goodrich, pp. 209–10; Pollard, p. 14. For the evolution of multilateralist policy and the development of international financial institutions, see Eckes and Gardner. For business groups' opinions on multilateralism, see Gardner, pp. 197, 375.

54. The committee, assigned to develop a comprehensive foreign economic policy, included representatives from the Treasury, War, Navy, State, Interior, Commerce, Agriculture, and Labor departments as well as the Tariff Commission, the Bureau of the Budget, and the Foreign Economic Administration.

55. Minutes of the ECEFP, June 26, 1945, OPD decimal file (1942–45), 093.5, USNA, RG 165, sec. 1.

56. Ibid.

57. Patterson to Clayton, June 4, 1945, OPD decimal file (1942–45),

093.5, USNA, RG 165, sec. 1; Neff to Patterson, "Trade Relations with the Philippines," June 27, 1945, ibid.

58. Minutes of the ECEFP, June 26, 1945, OPD decimal file (1942–45), 093.5, USNA, RG 165, sec. 1.

59. "American Interests in Southeast Asia," Mar. 26, 1945, Records of the Philippine and Southeast Asian Division, USNA, RG 59, lot 54D190, box 5; Hester, "Footnotes," p. 139; House Committee on Ways and Means, *Philippine Trade Act of 1945*, p. 52; John F. Cady, "The Importance of the Philippines with Respect to United States Policy in Southeastern Asia," Jan. 11, 1946, Records of the Philippine and Southeast Asian Division, USNA, RG 59, lot 54D190, box 5.

60. Ruggie, p. 396; Gardner, pp. 76–77.

61. Pastor, p. 98; "Economic Policy Shaped in Report," *The New York Times*, Nov. 5, 1944, p. 13.

62. Proceedings of the Committee on Trade Relations of the Filipino Rehabilitation Commission, Apr. 11, 1945, DSDF, USNA, RG 59, 7W611.11B31/4-1145.

63. Col. J. H. Baumann to South West Philippines Theater, Oct. 3, 1944, OPD decimal file, 093.5, USNA, RG 165, box 384; "Press Research," Feb. 28, 1945, OHC papers, USNA, RG 126, box 45; "McNutt Leaves after 11-Day 'Fact' Survey," *Free Philippines*, Aug. 1, 1945, ibid., box 42.

64. Hartendorp, pp. 223–24. Figures are for the Philippines overall. In areas of heavy fighting, the situation was worse. In Leyte, Nueva Viscaya, Bataan, and Cagayan, virtually no concrete or masonry buildings remained standing. UNRRA officials were unable to find one cow in Bataan, and livestock losses in several provinces were 80 to 90 percent. UNRRA, *UNRRA in the Philippines*, pp. 8–14.

65. United States, *Code*, pp. 426–28; Willoughby to Clayton, Apr. 15, 1946, DSDF, USNA, RG 59, 896.50/4-1546.

66. Roxas to Elizalde, Oct. 12, 1945, Roxas papers, ser. 1, box 14; Roxas to McNutt, Oct. 11, 1945, ibid., ser. 1(b), box 8.

67. "Tao Must Get Chance, AHC Says in Talk," *Manila Chronicle*, Jan. 11, 1946, p. 2; McNutt to Lt. C. E. Barnett, Feb. 18, 1946, OHC papers, USNA, RG 126, box 4; McNutt radio address, Jan. 20, 1946, ibid.; message from McNutt to Truman, OHC press release 63, Jan. 27, 1946, McNutt papers.

68. Jenkins, p. 72; Wilcox to Clayton, Nov. 10, 1945, *FRUS, 1945*, 4: 1218.

69. During the debate, Filipino advocates objected more to declining preferences, which they considered ungenerous, than to "parity"

or other restrictions on autonomy. Romulo was the only one openly to criticize parity. Even he, however, came to the "firm opinion that without these provisions, particularly the one relating to American rights, the two bills would not have passed." Romulo to Boguslav, May 2, 1946, Romulo papers, UP, ser. 1, box 2; Constantino to Romulo, May 12, 1945, ibid., box 1; Osmeña to Truman, Nov. 8, 1945, Osmeña papers; Roxas to McNutt, Oct. 11, 1945, Roxas papers, ser. 1(b), box 8; Roxas to Elizalde, Oct. 12, 1945, ibid., box 14; Romulo to Constantino, Mar. 20, 1946, Romulo papers, UP, ser. 1, box 6; Romulo to Osmeña, Aug. 28, 1945, Osmeña papers.

70. Saulo, pp. 47–48; Sumulong, pp. 1–29.

71. House Committee on Ways and Means, *Philippine Trade Act of 1945*, pp. 12, 20, 32.

72. Jenkins, p. 71; Hawes to Roxas, Nov. 8, 1944, Roxas papers, ser. 1, box 8.

73. P. W. Parker to Tydings, Oct. 8, 1945, Tydings papers, ser. 4, box 1; Jenkins, pp. 74, 78. The Philippine-American Chamber of Commerce listed officials from Stanvac, National City Bank, Goodyear, General Foods, and General Mills as members.

74. Jenkins, pp. 89–90, 98; House, Office of the High Commissioner, *Seventh and Final Report*, pp. 37–38; Samuel Rosenman to Truman, Oct. 25, 1945, Rosenman papers, Philippine folder.

75. House Committee on Insular Affairs, *Hearings on the Rehabilitation Act*, p. 18; Romulo to Ricardo C. Galang, Mar. 1, 1946, Romulo papers, UP, ser. 1, box 2.

76. Senate Committee on Finance, *Philippine Trade Act*, pp. 49–50.

77. Romulo to Osmeña, Jan. 2, 1946, Romulo papers, UP, ser. 1, box 2; Anderson to Doughton, Feb. 15, 1946, in House Committee on Ways and Means, *Philippine Trade Act of 1945*, p. 282; Anderson to Truman, Jan. 7, 1946, Rosenman papers, Philippine folder; Ickes to Truman, Jan. 24, 1946, Truman papers, president's secretary's files, box 185; Richmond Keech to Fortas, Feb. 1, 1946, Records of the Office of the Secretary of the Interior, USNA, RG 48, file 9-7-1, box 3692; Willard L. Thorp, memo of conversation with Keech, Feb. 7, 1946, DSDF, USNA, RG 59, FW 896.50/2-146.

78. Senate Committee on Finance, *Philippine Trade Act*, pp. 16, 54–55.

79. Senate Committee on Banking and Currency, *Implementation*, p. 6; Romulo to David Boguslav, May 2, 1946, Romulo papers, UP, ser. 1, box 2; Neal Stanford, "The U.S. Has Kept Its Promise," *Christian Science Monitor*, July 15, 1946, p. 16.

80. Byrnes to Truman, Apr. 18, 1946, *FRUS, 1946*, 8: 873–74; *Department of State Bulletin* 14 (May 12, 1946): 822; Byrnes to Truman, "Philippine Rehabilitation Bill (S. 1610)," Apr. 20, 1946, Truman papers, bill file, Apr. 27–30, 1946.

81. The assumption that business interests spearheaded the revision of Philippine policy pervades the literature. Constantino and Constantino, *Continuing Past*, pp. 199–201; Payer, pp. 51–52.

Chapter 2

1. Wolters, p. 16; Friend, *Blue-Eyed*, p. 86; HRAF, 3: 1195.

2. Filipino nationalists argued in the 1950s that the "unequal treaties" of 1946 and 1947 had been imposed on leaders who "had no choice but to accept." Jose P. Laurel, minutes of the Laurel-Langley talks, Sept. 22, 1954, Laurel papers; see also Constantino and Constantino, *Continuing Past*, p. 193; Karnow, p. 330.

3. Osmeña to Stimson, Oct. 4, 1944, Osmeña papers; Ickes diary, Ickes papers, Oct. 1, 1944, p. 9254.

4. Edgerton, "Politics," p. 136.

5. Ibid., p. 138; State Department, "Current Economic Developments no. 14," Sept. 24, 1945, *CED*; Buss, "Report," p. 134.

6. Edgerton, "Politics," pp. 138–41.

7. Steinberg, *Philippine Collaboration*, p. 58; "Press Research," Feb. 28, 1945, OHC papers, USNA, RG 186, box 45.

8. Owens, p. 105; Paredes-San Diego, pp. 91, 94.

9. Steinberg, *Philippine Collaboration*, pp. 119–20; Edgerton, "Politics," pp. 112–13. For Roxas's activities during the occupation, see Laurel, *War Memoirs*, p. 33. Ickes called Roxas "a collaborator of the highest degree." Ickes to Henry Becker, Nov. 20, 1946, Ickes papers, box 78.

10. Owens, pp. 194–95; James, 2: 691.

11. Kunio, pp. 241–42; Cumings, 2: 144; Schaller, *MacArthur*, pp. 60, 104; Shalom, *United States and the Philippines*, pp. 5–6; Abaya, *Betrayal*, pp. 171–72; James, 2: 691–93. Soriano, Elizalde, and Roxas had been active in the pro-Franco falange in the 1930s. Ickes predicted MacArthur would put the falangists in power after the war. "With MacArthur in control," he wrote, "the collaborationists will be in the saddle." Ickes diary, Ickes papers, Oct. 1, 1944, p. 9254.

12. Osmeña to Stimson, June 3, 1945, Osmeña papers; James, 2: 697. On Ickes's thinking about collaboration, see his preface to Abaya, *Betrayal*. Ickes may have intended to strengthen Osmeña's hand, but his bullying backfired against the president. Renato Constantino to

Romulo, Sept. 17, 1945, Romulo papers, UP, ser. 1, box 1. Jose Zulueta, sponsor of the bill to give Congress four years of back pay, explained to the press, "What if it is immoral? Everything is immoral nowadays."

13. Ickes to Truman, July 17, 1945, OHC papers, USNA, RG 126, box 44; Abaya, *Betrayal*, p. 198.

14. Edgerton, "Politics," pp. 65, 96–101; Abueva, pp. 86–90.

15. Owens, pp. 84–85; Saulo, pp. 45–46; Abaya, *Betrayal*, p. 239; Edgerton, "MacArthur," pp. 435–39; USAFFE Military Intelligence Section, "Resume of the Situation," Jan. 11, 1946, National Security Archive, rec. 39947.

16. Teodoro Locsin, "The Chinese Question," *Philippines Free Press*, Oct. 16, 1946, p. 2; USAFFE Military Intelligence Section, "Resume of the Situation," Jan. 11, 1946, National Security Archive, rec. 39947; Abaya, *Betrayal*, p. 242.

17. Friend, *Between Two Empires*, p. 257; D. Wurfel, *Filipino Politics*, pp. 96–97; Edgerton, "Politics," pp. 258–300.

18. Edward Bernstein to Osmeña, Feb. 6, 1946, Romulo papers, UP, ser. 1, box 2; Lockhart to Vincent, Apr. 29, 1946, DSDF, USNA, RG 59, 896.00/4-2946; V. E. Wurfel, "American Implementation," pp. 206, 447; Abaya, *Betrayal*, p. 251.

19. Abaya, *Betrayal*, pp. 263–64.

20. Neal Stanford, "The U.S. Has Kept Its Promise," *Christian Science Monitor*, July 5, 1946, p. 16; Sumulong, p. 44; Shalom, *The United States and the Philippines*, pp. 51–59.

21. Friend, *Between Two Empires*, p. 260; Margaret Parton, "City in Turmoil," *New York Herald Tribune*, July 4, 1946, p. 4.

22. Lachica, pp. 120–21.

23. Gleeck, *Dissolving*, p. 18; Margaret Parton, "City in Turmoil," *New York Herald Tribune*, July 4, 1946, p. 4; "The New Republic," *Washington Post*, July 4, 1946, p. 9.

24. South West Pacific Area Base Development Plan, Mar. 30, 1945, CCS geographic file, 696.8, USNA, RG 218, box 700; Tydings to Truman, Apr. 25, 1945, Tydings papers, ser. 4, box 1; JCS to MacArthur, Apr. 22, 1945, MacArthur Archives, RG 4, War Department 985, box 17; Marshall to MacArthur, Apr. 25, 1945, ibid.; Stimson, *Diaries*, Apr. 18, 1945, reel 9; MacArthur to War Department, Apr. 26, 1945, OPD decimal file 093.5, USNA, RG 165, box 384; "Negotiations for the Retention of American Bases in the Philippines after Independence," JCS 1027/5, Sept. 20, 1945, *Records of the Joint Chiefs of Staff*, reel 12.

25. Stimson, *Diaries*, May 8, 1945, reel 9; "Preliminary Statement

of General Principles Pertaining to the United States Military and Naval Base System in the Philippines," May 14, 1945, *FRUS, 1945*, 6: 1208–9.

26. Roxas to Romulo, Nov. 16, 1946, Roxas papers, ser. 1(b), box 10.

27. Roxas to Elizalde, Oct. 30, 1946, Roxas papers, ser. 1(b), box 5.

28. Ibid.

29. Allan O'Gorman to Roxas, May 23, 1946, Romulo papers, UP, ser. 1, box 2; John C. Vincent to Acheson, June 6, 1946, *FRUS, 1946*, 8: 881.

30. Paul McNutt to Dean Acheson, Sept. 25, 1946, *FRUS, 1946*, 8: 919; C. Quirino, *Apo Lakay*, p. 86.

31. McNutt to Acheson, Sept. 7, 1946, *FRUS, 1946*, 8: 907–9; Roxas to Joaquin Elizalde, Oct. 30, 1946, Roxas papers, ser. 1(b), box 5; O. Zabozlayeva, "The 'Independent' Philippines," *Pravda*, Oct. 10, 1946, *Soviet Press Translations* 1, 3 (Nov. 30, 1946): 8–11.

32. Shalom, *United States and the Philippines*, pp. 51–59; Friend, *Blue-Eyed*, pp. 254–55; Frank P. Lockhart to Vincent, Sept. 25, 1946, DSDF, USNA, RG 59, FW 811.24596/9-2546. The turnout for parity was low because none of the regional machines cared enough to furnish the customary election-day inducements. Platt, pp. 124–25, 133.

33. Eisenhower to MacArthur, Nov. 9, 1946, MacArthur Archives, RG 9, WD 1839; MacArthur to Eisenhower, Nov. 10, 1946, ibid., WD 1842.

34. Leffler, *Preponderance*, p. 147.

35. Nimitz to Eisenhower, Nov. 12, 1946, Secretary of War papers, CD 27-1-8, USNA, RG 330, box 120; John H. Hilldring to McNutt, Dec. 13, 1946, *FRUS, 1946*, 8: 936–37; James Byrnes to McNutt, Dec. 18, 1946, ibid., 8: 939; McNutt to Byrnes, Dec. 23, 1946, ibid., p. 939.

36. Paez, pp. 384–89; War Department Planning Office to MacArthur, Jan. 11, 1947, MacArthur Archives, RG 9, WD 1905; Kenneth Royall to James Forrestal, Mar. 4, 1948, Records of the Secretary of Defense, CD 27-1-8, USNA, RG 330, box 120; William Leahy to Forrestal, July 13, 1948, ibid.

37. Ely to Vincent, Feb. 19, 1947, DSDF, USNA, RG 59, 811.24596/2-1947; McNutt to Acheson, Mar. 14, 1947, *FRUS, 1947*, 6: 1109; Department of State, *Treaties*, 11: 55–73.

38. Roxas to McNutt, July 29, 1946, McNutt papers; Paez, p. 11; O'Gorman to Roxas, May 23, 1946, Romulo papers, UP, ser. 1, box 2; Platt, p. 134; Shalom, *United States and the Philippines*, p. 62; Karnow, p. 330. Some writers criticize the terms of the 1947 treaty,

comparing them to NATO agreements signed in the 1950s, but by the relevant standard, treaties in force in 1947, Filipino negotiators obtained substantial improvements. Karnow concludes that "American negotiators did indeed force Filipino leaders to accept onerous conditions on the bases agreement as the price for freedom." U.S. officials had a different opinion. They worried that the treaty terms were so generous that "stronger" countries like Australia and Britain would seek similar concessions.

39. Simbulan, p. 118; Berry, p. 66; Shalom, *United States and the Philippines,* p. 63.

40. Edgerton, "Politics," p. 365.

41. Paredes-San Diego, p. 104; Golay, *The Philippines,* p. 29; Jenkins, p. 120.

42. Beyster Corporation, p. 72; Hartendorp, p. 238; McNutt to Clayton, Sept. 14, 1946, *FRUS, 1946,* 8: 917; Department of State, "Current Economic Developments no. 14," Sept. 24, 1945, *CED.*

43. Roxas to McNutt, Oct. 11, 1945, Roxas papers, ser. 1(b), box 8; NAC minutes, July 2, 9, and 15, 1946, Secretary of the Treasury papers, NAC records, USNA, RG 56, box 1.

44. NAC minutes, July 2, 9, and 15, 1946, Secretary of the Treasury papers, NAC records, USNA, RG 56, box 1.

45. Agpalo, *Political Process,* pp. 27–42; Filipinas Foundation, p. 90; C. Quirino, *Philippine Tycoon,* pp. 173–74; McBeath, p. 33. Memorandum of conversation by Ellsworth C. Carlson, Dec. 10, 1946, *FRUS, 1946,* 8: 936; minutes of technical discussions on the Treaty of Friendship, Commerce and Navigation, July 2, 1948, Quirino papers, PHILCUSA file; *Sunday Post Magazine* (Nov. 3, 1946), quoted in Edgerton, "Politics," p. 354.

46. Hartendorp, pp. 56–61; Department of Commerce and Industry, *Second Annual Report,* p. 29; Hester to Ely, Nov. 14, 1949, DSDF, USNA, RG 59, 896.50/11-1449; Stevens to Quirino, Aug. 9, 1949, Quirino papers, Trips, USA 1949–1950; State Department, *Report of the Economic Survey Mission,* p. 24; Ray Cromley, "ECA-Type Plan to Put Philippine Islands on Their Feet Is Failing," *Wall Street Journal,* June 17, 1949, p. 1.

47. McNutt, "Democracy," p. 364; Hartendorp, p. 241; Cuaderno, *Problems,* pp. 1–2; Beyster Corporation, p. 23.

48. Wolters, p. 16; Lachica, p. 121; Pomeroy, "Philippine Peasantry," p. 508; James J. Halsema, "Taruc Answers Roxas," *Manila Chronicle,* Feb. 7, 1947, p. 2. Landlords sometimes amassed huge private armies. The commander of the largest civil guard brigade, Pam-

Notes to Pages 64–69 207

panga governor Jose B. Lingad, could field a force of three battalions, 1,000 men. Lockett to George Marshall, Aug. 15, 1948, DSDF, USNA, RG 59, 896.00/8-1548.

49. Lachica, p. 122; Kerkvliet, *Huk Rebellion*, pp. 120–21; Halsema, "Taruc Answers Roxas," *Manila Chronicle*, Feb. 7, 1947, p. 1; Pomeroy, "Philippine Peasantry," pp. 511–12; Edgerton, "Politics," p. 387.

50. Nathaniel Davis to George Marshall, "The Two Party System in the Philippines," Feb. 1, 1947, DSDF, USNA, RG 59, 896.00/2-147; Ely to Vincent, Feb. 13, 1947, ibid.; memorandum of conversation by Ellsworth C. Carlson, Dec. 10, 1946, *FRUS, 1946*, 8: 936.

51. A series of articles in the Scripps-Howard papers in late 1946 alleged the presence of Russian nationals among the Huks. Julius Edelstein to Byrnes, July 17, 1946, DSDF, USNA, RG 59, 896.00/7-1746; Emmett O'Neal to Marshall, Jan. 15, 1948, ibid., 896.00/1-1548; O'Neal, "Estimated Strength of Hukbalahaps on Luzon," Feb. 19, 1948, ibid., 896.00/2-948; Ely to W. Walton Butterworth, "Possible Disturbance in the Philippines," Jan. 2, 1948, ibid., 896.00/1-248; Ely to Vincent, Mar. 3, 1947, ibid., 896.00/2-1047.

52. United States Army Forces, Pacific, Military Intelligence Summary no. 1377, Jan. 11, 1946, and no. 121-1369, Jan. 3, 1946, National Security Archive, recs. 39947 and 39952.

53. NAC minutes, July 2 and 15, 1946, Secretary of the Treasury papers, NAC records, USNA, RG 56, box 1.

54. Ibid.

55. Edgar Crossman to Truman, Aug. 19, 1947, Snyder papers; House, *Report and Recommendations*, pp. 31–40, 65.

56. House, *Report and Recommendations*, pp. 67–68, 49–51. The report suggested that the Philippine government take its time in acquainting itself with the administration of controls because "in the absence of proper safeguards, excessive profits can be made by those granted licenses."

57. Thomas Hibben, "Philippine Economic Development: A Technical Memorandum," in House, *Report and Recommendations*, pp. 151–222; Romulo to Roxas, Feb. 4, 1947, Romulo papers, UP, ser. 1, box 2; Hartendorp, pp. 260–62; Beyster Corporation.

58. Hartendorp, pp. 657, 669–71.

59. State Department, "Current Economic Developments no. 256," May 29, 1950, *CED*; Julius Edelstein to McNutt, Feb. 6, 1947, McNutt papers.

60. House, *Report and Recommendations*, p. 70; Campbell, p. 268.

61. Roxas to Elizalde, May 17, 1947, Roxas papers, ser. 1(b), box 5; Hartendorp, p. 273. Philippine economist Elpidio R. Sta. Romana explains the perverse effect of regulation under a weak state. In each new regulated sector, the government loses control of regulation to its own clients. Sta. Romana, "Philippine State's Hegemony," p. 197; Hartendorp, p. 261; Golay, *The Philippines*, p. 350.

62. House, *Report and Recommendations*, p. 53; ECAFE, *Economic Survey*, pp. 123–37; idem, *Mobilization*, pp. 15–22; David Grove to J. Burke Knapp, Feb. 23, 1948, Federal Reserve Board records, Philippine Islands—Central Bank.

63. Jenkins, p. 117; Hartendorp, pp. 248, 252; C. Quirino, *Apo Lakay*, pp. 95–96.

64. Saulo, p. 49; William T. T. Ward, "Death of a President," Thirteenth Air Force Office of History Special Study, Aug. 25, 1976, pp. 13–14, Thirteenth Air Force Historical Office.

Chapter 3

1. B. Anderson, "Cacique Democracy," p. 15; Acheson, *Present*, p. 727.

2. CIA, "The Death of Philippine President Roxas," Apr. 16, 1948, *DDRS*, 1990: 1254; C. Quirino, *Apo Lakay*, pp. 30–45; Julius Edelstein to Roxas, May 22, 1947, Roxas papers, ser. 1(b), box 4; Romulo and Romulo, *Philippine Presidents*, pp. 81–89.

3. Coquia, p. 101; "Quirino Must Break with Avelino Is Consensus," *Manila Evening Chronicle*, Jan. 17, 1949, p. 1; C. Quirino, *Apo Lakay*, p. 99; CIA, "The Current Situation in the Philippines," Mar. 30, 1949, in CIA, *CIA Research Reports*, reel 5.

4. Thomas Lockett to George Marshall, Aug. 18 and Sept. 13, 1948, *FRUS, 1948*, 6: 632–34; Emmett O'Neal to Marshall, Apr. 24, 1948, DSDF, USNA, RG 59, 896.00/4-2248; Kerkvliet, *Huk Rebellion*, pp. 200–202; Lachica, p. 122; Saulo, p. 52; Lockett to Marshall, Sept. 7, 1948, DSDF, USNA, RG 59, 896.00/9-748.

5. T. Wanamaker to the State Department, Mar. 29, 1950, DSDF, USNA, RG 59, 896.00/3-2950; C. Quirino, *Apo Lakay*, p. 117; State Department, *Report of the Economic Survey Mission*, pp. 19, 22; Tolentino, pp. 95–96; CIA, "The Current Situation in the Philippines," Mar. 30, 1949, in CIA, *CIA Research Reports*, reel 5.

6. Maj. Gen. A. F. Jones to Ruperto Kangleon, Nov. 2, 1948, JUSMAG file, Quirino papers; Pach, pp. 124–29, 157–59; Quirino memoirs, Quirino papers, pp. 308, 346.

7. Ohno, pp. 10–25; Schaller, "Securing," pp. 393–95; Schonberger,

"Japan Lobby," pp. 327–59; Edelstein to Roxas, July 10, 1947, Roxas papers, ser. 1(b), box 4; Elizalde to Quirino, May 17, 1949, Quirino papers, Elizalde special correspondence file.

8. One Philippine general requested depth charges to deal with subs. Lockett to Marshall, Nov. 18, 1948, DSDF, USNA, RG 59, 896.00/11-1848; Elizalde to Quirino, Oct. 17, 1949, Quirino papers, Elizalde special correspondence file; Elizalde to Quirino, June 9, 1948, ibid.; Jones to Kangleon, Nov. 2, 1948, ibid.; Elizalde to Quirino, Sept. 17, 1948, ibid.; Lockett to Marshall, Sept. 13, 1948, *FRUS, 1948*, 6: 633–34.

9. E. Quirino, *New Philippine Ideology*, pp. 255–56; "The Business View," *American Chamber of Commerce Journal* (Jan. 1949): 20; Knoke to E. Gottesman, Sept. 14, 1949, United States Federal Reserve records, country files, Philippine Islands; Lopez, p. 147; Myron Cowen to W. Walton Butterworth, Nov. 28, 1949, DSDF, USNA, RG 59, 896.50/11-2849; Hester to Dept. of State, "Opposition to the Philippine Trade Act," Aug. 10, 1950, ibid., 411.9631/8-1050; Acheson to Manila embassy, Dec. 30, 1949, ibid., 696.116/12-2849.

10. Hartendorp, pp. 657, 669–71; Lovett to Manila, Jan. 18, 1948, DSDF, USNA, RG 59, 696.006/1-1249; Melby to Robert Stokes, Dec. 20, 1949, ibid., 696.006/12-1249; Tolentino, p. 105; Abaya, *Betrayal*, p. 170. In 1946, Elizalde and Co. said it represented Westinghouse, DeSoto Motors, Sharp and Dohme (drugs), Union Oil, Seagram and Sons, and "other United States industries to be announced later."

11. Acheson to Manila embassy, Dec. 30, 1949, DSDF, USNA, RG 59, 696.116/12-2849; Edward E. Rice to Melby, Aug. 29, 1949, Melby papers, personal correspondence.

12. Tolentino, p. 88; Webb to Manila, Oct. 3, 1949, DSDF, USNA, RG 59, 696.006/10-349.

13. May, *Social Engineering*, p. 54; D. Wurfel, *Filipino Politics*, p. 35; Scott, *Comparative*, p. 149.

14. Maj. Gen. J. W. Anderson to Quirino, Jan. 3, 1950, Quirino papers, JUSMAG file.

15. Dingman, "Diplomacy of Dependency," pp. 307–21; Dobbs, pp. 29–42; Romulo to Quirino, July 14, 1949, Quirino papers, Romulo file; Acheson to diplomatic offices, July 20, 1949, *FRUS, 1949*, 7: 1170; Acheson, *Present*, p. 502; W. Fitzmaurice, "Philippines: An Odyssey for Dollars and Votes," *Newsweek* (Aug. 22, 1949): 19. For Acheson's aims in China, see Tucker.

16. Richard Ely, memo of conversation, Aug. 9, 1949, *FRUS, 1949*, 7: 597–99.

17. Butterworth to Acheson, Aug. 9, 1949, Acheson papers, memoranda of conversation, box 64; Melby to Philip Jessup, Aug. 31, 1949, Melby papers, Philippine file, box 6; OIR, "The Problem of Agrarian Reform in the Philippines," Dec. 20, 1949, ibid.; idem, "Communist Party of the Philippines," May 1950, ibid.; CIA, "The Current Situation in the Philippines," Mar. 30, 1949, in CIA, *CIA Research Reports*, reel 5; Joint Intelligence Group, "Intelligence Estimate of the Internal Security Situation in the Philippines," May 23, 1950, Office of the Secretary of Defense papers, USNA, RG 330, CD 22-2-23, box 99; Melby to Lacy, "Chinese Communist Party Aims in Southeast Asia," Mar. 27, 1950, Melby papers, Philippine file, box 7; Melby to Cowen, Jan. 11, 1950, ibid.

18. Kenneth Royall to Louis Johnson, May 5, 1949, "Defense Commitments, Policies and Operations in Support thereof with Respect to the Philippines," Office of the Secretary of Defense papers, USNA, RG 330, box 81, CD 5-2-8; Johnson to Acheson, Sept. 16, 1949, ibid., CD 18-2-29.

19. On the position of Southeast Asia in global strategy, see Rotter; Borden; Schaller, *American Occupation*; Leffler, *Preponderance*, p. 300; Charlton Ogburn, memo of conversation, May 17, 1949, *FRUS, 1949*, 7: 27; Policy Planning Staff 51, "United States Policy Toward Southeast Asia," Mar. 29, 1949, *FRUS, 1949*, 7: 1132–33.

20. Lockett to Marshall, June 10, 1948, DSDF, USNA, RG 59, 896.00/6-1048; Lockett to Marshall, Aug. 11, 1948, ibid., 896.00/8-448; Lockett to Marshall, Feb. 24, 1949, ibid., 896.00/2-2449; Sumulong, p. 70; Taruc, *He Who Rides the Tiger*, p. 60.

21. Cuaderno, *Problems*, p. 23; Cowen to Butterworth, Nov. 28, 1949, DSDF, USNA, RG 59, 896.50/111-2849; Department of State, "Current Economic Developments no. 259," June 19, 1950, *CED*; Howard Shepherd (National City Bank) to Acheson, June 7, 1950, DSDF, USNA, RG 59, 896.131/6-750.

22. Hartendorp, pp. 293–95.

23. The Lava memorandum is discussed in Lachica, pp. 124–28; Taruc, *He Who Rides the Tiger*, pp. 72–74; and Saulo, pp. 55–56.

24. Joint Intelligence Group, "Intelligence Estimate of the Internal Security Situation in the Philippines," May 23, 1950, Office of the Secretary of Defense papers, USNA, RG 330, box 99, CD 22-2-23.

25. Melby to Livingston Merchant, Sept. 6, 1949, Melby papers, Philippine file, box 6; Merchant to Acheson, Jan. 26, 1950, DSDF, USNA, RG 59, 896.00/1-2650.

26. Acheson to Truman, Apr. 20, 1950, DSDF, USNA, RG 59,

896.00/4-1450; Butterworth to Acheson, Mar. 23, 1950, ibid., 896.00/3-2350.

27. Elizalde to Quirino, Apr. 17, 1950, Quirino papers, Elizalde file; Acheson to Truman, Apr. 20, 1950, DSDF, USNA, RG 59, 896.00/4-1450.

28. Butterworth to Acheson, Mar. 23, 1950, DSDF, USNA, RG 59, 896.00/3-2350; Acheson to Manila, Mar. 24, 1950, *FRUS, 1950,* 6: 1425–26; "Report of the Philippine Council for United States Aid for the Year Ending June 30, 1952," Quirino papers, PHILCUSA file; Fifield, *Diplomacy,* p. 101; Romulo to Quirino, Mar. 14, 1950, Quirino papers, Romulo file.

29. Melby to Acheson, Jan. 26, 1950, DSDF, USNA, RG 59, 896.00/1-2650; [U.S.] President, *Public Papers,* p. 506.

30. Romulo to Quirino, Sept. 29, 1950, Romulo papers, UP, ser. 1, box 4; Cumings, 2: 628.

31. State Department, *Report of the Economic Survey Mission,* p. 20; Acheson to Truman, Aug. 31, 1950, Truman papers, president's secretary's files, box 185; D. Wurfel, "Bell Report and After," p. 123.

32. State Department, *Report of the Economic Survey Mission,* p. 14; Dos Santos, p. 233.

33. State Department, *Report of the Economic Survey Mission,* pp. 55–56.

34. Ibid., pp. 15, 61.

35. Acheson, memo of conversation, Sept. 11, 1950, *FRUS, 1950,* 6: 1483; Romulo to Quirino, Sept. 10, Sept. 18, and Oct. 11, 1950, Quirino papers, Romulo file; State Department, *Report of the Economic Survey Mission,* pp. 55–56, 70–71.

36. State Department, *Report of the Economic Survey Mission,* pp. 4–5; Truman to Acheson, Sept. 2, 1950, Truman papers, president's secretary's files, box 185. Foster engineered the ECA's takeover of Philippine aid during the absence of top State Department officials at the Wake Island conference in October. Acheson was not pleased. Romulo to Quirino, Nov. 2, 1950, Quirino papers, Romulo file.

37. Cuaderno, *Problems,* p. 32; Romulo to Quirino, Oct. 11, 1950, Quirino papers, Romulo file; State Department, *Report of the Economic Survey Mission,* p. 4; Bell to Snyder and Acheson, Aug. 1, 1950, *FRUS, 1950,* 6: 1471; NAC minutes, Oct. 31, 1950, Secretary of the Treasury papers, NAC records, USNA, RG 56, box 2.

38. D. Wurfel, "Bell Report and After," pp. 139–40; Cuaderno, *Problems,* p. 32; State Department, *Report of the Economic Survey Mission,* pp. 61–71; "Report of the Special Committee on Industries,"

Nov. 5, 1950, Quirino papers, Bell report and Bell trade act file; PHILCUSA, "The Philippines and ECA Assistance," June 30, 1952, Quirino papers, PHILCUSA file.

39. Memo of conversation, Dec. 27, 1950, Acheson papers, memoranda of conversation, box 65; "Summary of Philippine Stand on the Bell Report as Made by His Excellency the President," Nov. 12, 1950, Quirino papers, Bell Mission file; Romulo to Quirino, Sept. 28, 1950, ibid., Romulo file; Felino Neri to Romulo, Nov. 10, 1950, Romulo papers, UP, ser. 1, box 5.

40. D. Wurfel, "Bell Report and After," pp. 147, 166; Lopez, p. 93; Golay, *The Philippines*, pp. 83–84.

41. David Ferber to William Lacy, Sept. 6, 1950, DSDF, USNA, RG 59, 896.00/9-650; Eugene Clay, memorandum of conversation, Sept. 22, 1950, *FRUS, 1950*, 6: 1492.

42. Saulo, p. 58; Lachica, pp. 128–30; Ralph E. Doty to Gen. Anderson, Mar. 31, 1950, Quirino papers, JUSMAG file; Abueva, p. 168.

43. Lachica, p. 131; Kerkvliet, *Huk Rebellion*, pp. 255–56.

44. Truman to Acheson, Feb. 15, 1951, Truman papers, White House central files, box 26; Abueva, p. 181; Kerkvliet, *Huk Rebellion*, p. 207.

45. Kerkvliet, *Huk Rebellion*, pp. 238–39; Hartendorp, pp. 500–501; Starner, pp. 91–93.

46. Cable, p. 63. For a list of studies, see Greenberg, pp. 151–54.

47. Central Bank of the Philippines, *Second Annual Report, 1950*, p. 28; Golay, *The Philippines*, pp. 80–81.

48. T. Locsin, "It Must NOT Happen Again," *Philippines Free Press*, Nov. 12, 1950, p. 3; "The Expansion of the ECA," *Manila Chronicle*, Aug. 3, 1951, p. 4; ECA, *Strength for the Free World*, p. 4; Senate Committee on Appropriations, *Mutual Security Appropriations*, pp. 329–92.

49. "US-PI Governments Sign Investment Guaranty Pact," *Philippines Newsletter*, Mar. 15, 1952, p. 1. For items on joint ventures, see *Philippines Newsletter*, June 1951–Dec. 1952; "U.S.-P.I. Pact Heartening," *Manila Bulletin*, Aug. 30, 1951, p. 1.

50. Sicat, pp. 5–6; "The U.S. Opportunity," *Fortune* (June 1947): 191; "Time Magazine on Soriano," *Philippines Free Press*, Sept. 1, 1951, p. 14; "Lacson Hits L.P. Wealth Formula," *Manila Bulletin*, Oct. 5, 1953, p. 2.

51. Department of State, "Recent Progress in the Philippine Manufacturing Industry," State Department R & A Reports, USNA, RG 59, no. 7488; Rivera, pp. 134–36.

52. Leffler, *Preponderance*, pp. 393–94; Brands, "United States," pp.

387–401; Dingman, "Diplomacy of Dependency," pp. 307–21; Ohno, pp. 47–51.

53. Francisco Umali to Romulo, Apr. 11, 1951, Romulo papers, UP, ser. 1, box 5; "Just an Interpretation," *Manila Chronicle*, July 22, 1951, p. 4; Ohno, pp. 124, 32–33.

54. JCS to Johnson, Sept. 6, 1950, ibid., 6: 1486; Cowen to Rusk, June 1, 1950, *FRUS, 1950*, 6: 1456.

Chapter 4

1. Pérez, p. 103; see also Frank.
2. Scott, *Weapons*, p. xvi.
3. "The People's Choice," *Time* (Nov. 23, 1953): 36–37.
4. James Webb to Harry Truman, Dec. 6, 1951, Truman papers, official file, box 1573.
5. Recto, *My Crusade*, pp. 74–76; Jose P. Laurel, "The Defense of Our Freedom," [undated], Laurel papers, ser. 5, box 6.
6. Starner, p. 37; "The People's Choice," *Time* (Nov. 23, 1953): 36–37; J. P. McEvoy, "Ramon Magsaysay: Dynamic Example for Asia," *Reader's Digest* (Sept. 1954): 109; R. A. Smith, p. 152. "I don't know why Monching continues giving the impression that we were poor," his sister Concepcion Magsaysay wondered. "We were not millionaires, but we were well off." Quoted in C. Quirino, *Magsaysay*, p. 2.
7. J. B. Smith, p. 101; Kahin, p. 70.
8. Cable, p. 65.
9. "Magsaysay indeed performed as 'America's Boy,' " according to Shalom, welcoming capital and closely following the foreign policy dictates handed down from Washington. William Pomeroy summed him up as "the most notorious U.S. puppet of all." MacDonald writes that "Magsaysay was an American liberal reformer's dream come true. A dynamic, charismatic, honest, and compassionate leader, . . . he was one of the best allies the United States ever had in the Third World." Filipino scholars of the nationalist school stress his use of propaganda and loyalty to the United States, minimizing his role in engineering his own rise or formulating his administration's policy. Under Magsaysay, according to Constantino, "United States control over the country was complete." Earlier monographs take a different view. Based on oral histories, Abueva's 1971 biography describes Magsaysay's extensive ties to political and economic interests. He portrays U.S. influence as a contributing rather than a decisive factor in Magsaysay's rise to power. A 1961 study by Frances Starner stresses the decisive influence of Magsaysay's political alliances on the 1953 elec-

tion. Pomeroy, *American-Made Tragedy*, p. 18; MacDonald, p. 183; Constantino and Constantino, *Continuing Past*, p. 262; Shalom, *United States and the Philippines*, pp. 92–93.

10. Abueva, pp. 35–64.

11. Edgerton, "Politics," pp. 99–100; Abueva, p. 93; Abueva's notes of interview with L. de Rosario, May 28, 1961, Magsaysay papers.

12. Abueva, p. 154.

13. Currey, p. 71; C. Quirino, *Apo Lakay*, pp. 128–29; E. Quirino, *Memoirs*, pp. 200–201; Abueva, p. 154; Lansdale, p. 33.

14. J. B. Smith, p. 95. *The New York Times* remarked, "We need men of integrity, imagination, courage and simplicity. Mr. Magsaysay is that sort of leader." *Time* called him the "Eisenhower of the Pacific," and the *New York Herald Tribune* found him "a pillar of democratic government and an extraordinarily vivid and commanding personality." Abueva, p. 213.

15. Abueva, p. 164; Myron Cowen to Quirino, Sept. 22, 1950, Quirino papers, U.S. ambassadors file; E. Quirino, *Memoirs*, p. 203.

16. Currey, p. 98; Lansdale, pp. 58, 78; Department of National Defense, "The EDCOR Plan," [undated], Eisenhower papers, White House office files, OCB subject file, Southeast Asia; Hartendorp, pp. 500–501; Starner, pp. 91–93.

17. For the roots of the Huk rebellion, see Kerkvliet, *Huk Rebellion*, pp. 1–25; Lansdale, p. 59; Starner, p. 26.

18. "General Magsaysay New PAL Board Chairman," *Philippines Newsletter*, Oct. 1, 1951, p. 2; Abueva, p. 205. Abueva notes that Magsaysay "multiplied his patronage and resources for repaying his 'debts' to the legislators themselves. Now he could help local politicians all over the country." Abueva, p. 159.

19. C. Quirino, *Apo Lakay*, pp. 13, 183; Lopez, p. 140.

20. Currey, p. 72; Abueva, pp. 164, 190–91.

21. Agerico Palaypay oral history interview, Mar. 24, 1981, Magsaysay papers; Walter Reed Hospital, Abstract Clinical Record of the Hon. Ramon Magsaysay, June 18, 1952, ibid.; Manahan oral history interview, Apr. 14, 1987, ibid.

22. JUSMAG semiannual report, July 18, 1951, JUSMAG records, USNA, RG 334; Lansdale, p. 43.

23. Temple Wanamaker, the Philippine desk officer, observed in late 1952 that "we today can be most thankful that we didn't officially back Quirino in 1949. How will we feel about Magsaysay three years from November 1953 if he should win the presidency with our open support?" Wanamaker left the State Department the following

month. T. Wanamaker to Philip Bonsal, Dec. 5, 1952, *FRUS, 1952–54*, pt. 2, 12: 519.

24. NSC 84/2, "The Position of the United States with Respect to the Philippines," Nov. 9, 1950, *FRUS, 1950,* 6: 1516; Cowen to Department of State, Feb. 15, 1951, *FRUS, 1951,* 6: 1507; Cowen to Acheson, Mar. 27, 1951, ibid., 6: 1526.

25. NSC 135/1, "NSC Staff Study on Reappraisal of United States Objectives and Strategy for National Security," Aug. 22, 1952, *FRUS, 1952–54,* 2: 97.

26. Paul Nitze to Acheson, Mar. 5, 1952, *FRUS, 1952–54,* pt. 1, 12: 68; "113th NSC Meeting," Mar. 5, 1952, ibid., 12: 70; Acheson, *Present,* p. 676; Brands, "From ANZUS to SEATO," p. 265; Hess, *Vietnam,* p. 41.

27. NSC 124/2, "United States Objectives and Courses of Action with Respect to Southeast Asia," June 25, 1952, *FRUS, 1952–54,* pt. 1, 12: 127; "Substance of Discussions at a Department of State–JCS Meeting," Jan. 16, 1952, ibid., 12: 32.

28. Memorandum of discussion, July 25, 1951, *FRUS, 1951,* 6: 229; JCS to George Marshall, Aug. 8, 1951, ibid., 6: 239; Brands, "From ANZUS to SEATO," p. 261.

29. Buell, p. 435; Lacy to Department of State, Mar. 31, 1953, DSDF, USNA, RG 59, 796.00/4-153; Gleeck, *Dissolving,* p. 65.

30. Buell, p. 437.

31. William Lacy to Department of State, Mar. 31, 1953, DSDF, USNA, RG 59, 796.00/4-153; Starner, pp. 128, 19–20, 33–34.

32. Lacy to John M. Allison, Oct. 31, 1952, *FRUS, 1952–54,* pt. 2, 12: 509; R. Spruance to Allison, Dec. 16, 1952, ibid., 12: 525; Sen. Lorenzo Tañada oral history interview, July 2, 1981, Magsaysay papers.

33. NSC 148, Apr. 6, 1953, *FRUS, 1952–54,* pt. 1, 12: 288; summaries prepared by NSC Staff of Project Solarium, [undated], ibid., 2: 409, 429; Charles Ogburn to Allison, Jan. 21, 1953, ibid., 12: 260–61.

34. Kolko, *Confronting,* p. 64; Shalom, *United States and the Philippines,* pp. 87–92; Karnow, pp. 352–53; "Stolen Election Could Mean Revolution Says U.S. Writer," *Manila Bulletin,* Sept. 26, 1953, p. 1; "Isaac Stern Here, Says He Plans to Make Music That'll Not Sway Voters," *Manila Bulletin,* Nov. 6, 1953, p. 4; House Committee on Foreign Affairs, *Executive Session Hearings,* pt. 2, 17: 89; "Charge Liberals with Seeking U.S. Intervention," *Manila Bulletin,* July 4, 1953, p. 1; University of the East, p. 9.

35. I. P. Soliongco, "Seriously Speaking," *Manila Chronicle,* July 2, 1957, p. 4; Teodoro Locsin, "The Inside Story: Why the Nacionalistas

Nominated Ramon Magsaysay in '53," *Philippines Free Press,* Jan. 19, 1957, p. 2; Laurel, quoted in *Philippines Free Press,* Nov. 7, 1953, p. 4; Tolentino, pp. 85, 107.

36. Coquia, p. 25; Ellsbree, p. 6.

37. "Magsaysay Says P.I. Won't Get More U.S. Aid Unless Quirino Is Replaced," *Manila Bulletin,* July 2, 1953, p. 5; "Palace Spokesman Comments on Magsaysay Statement," July 2, 1953, RM file, Quirino papers; Spruance to John F. Dulles, Apr. 9, 1953, DSDF, USNA, RG 59, 796.00/4-953; University of the East, pp. 8–29.

38. House Committee on Foreign Affairs, *Executive Session Hearings,* pt. 2, 17: 88; Alexander Smith to James S. Lay, July 16, 1953, *FRUS, 1952–54,* pt. 2, 12: 539–44; Espinosa Robles, p. 223.

39. D. Wurfel, "Bell Report and After," p. 531; Lacy to Department of State, Nov. 21, 1952, *FRUS, 1952–54,* pt. 2, 12: 514.

40. Ellsbree, p. 6; Lacy to Wanamaker, Apr. 8, 1953, DSDF, USNA, RG 59, 796.00/4-853.

41. Lopez, pp. 148–51; D. Wurfel, "Bell Report and After," p. 48.

42. Lopez, pp. 142–43; Ellsbree, p. 12; "Joint Pastoral Letter on Elections," *Philippines Herald,* Sept. 16, 1953, p. 2; Spruance to Department of State, Sept. 18, 1953, DSDF, USNA, RG 59, 796.00/9-1853; Abueva, p. 213. In the early 1950s, the Church worked hand in glove with the United States. In 1952, Quirino asked the Vatican to recall its nuncio, Edigio Vagnozzi, because of his meddling in the schools. At Vagnozzi's request, the State Department urged Spellman to intercede with the Holy See on his behalf. The maneuver succeeded, and the nuncio, whom Lacy considered a friend of the United States, stayed. Lacy to Allison, Nov. 19, 1952, *FRUS, 1952–54,* pt. 2, 12: 513.

43. Spruance to Department of State, "Local Chinese Reactions Toward Recent Philippine Acts of Venality and Ineptitude," Apr. 1, 1953, DSDF, USNA, RG 59, 796.00/4-153; Ravenholt, p. 15.

44. "Magsaysay," *Manila Bulletin,* Nov. 7, 1953, p. 11; "The People's Choice," *Time* (Nov. 23, 1953): 36–37.

45. Currey, p. 106; "Where NAMFREL and Other Allied Organizations Are Getting Funds," [undated], Quirino papers, RM file.

46. Wanamaker to Bonsal, Dec. 5, 1952, *FRUS, 1952–54,* pt. 2, 12: 517; Bohannon oral history interview, Mar. 10, 1981, Magsaysay papers; Allison to Lacy, Dec. 2, 1952, *FRUS, 1952–54,* pt. 2, 12: 514; D. Wurfel, "Bell Report and After," p. 49; Starner, pp. 62–64.

47. D. Wurfel, "Bell Report and After," pp. 198–200, 261–64; Abueva, p. 346.

48. D. Wurfel, "Bell Report and After," pp. 166, 224; Hartendorp, p. 346.

49. Jose E. Romero to the Philippine Sugar Association, Aug. 30, 1954, Romulo papers, UP, ser. 1, box 8.

50. CIA, *Current Intelligence Weekly*, June 5, 1953, National Security Archive, rec. 38148; Smith to Lay, "Third Progress Report on NSC 84/2," *FRUS, 1952–54*, pt. 2, 12: 541; "Yanks Here Warned on Poll Interference," *Manila Times*, Mar. 14, 1953, p. 1; "US Neutrality Stressed in Spruance's US Stay," *Daily Mirror* (Manila), Oct. 16, 1953, p. 1; "US Keeps Silent on Elizalde Blast," *Daily Mirror* (Manila), Nov. 6, 1953, p. 2.

51. Lansdale to Cowen, June 11, 1953, Cowen papers; Teodoro Locsin, "A Bloodless Revolution," *Philippines Free Press*, Feb. 2, 1957, p. 3; Currey, pp. 120–21; Elizalde, "A Statement on the Philippine Situation," Nov. 3, 1953, Quirino papers; James Bell, memo of conversation, Dec. 8, 1953, DSDF, USNA, RG 59, 796.00/12-853. Lansdale had Spruance's backing, but, he recalled, JUSMAG chief Albert Pierson "treated me real dirty."

52. Lansdale to Spruance, Oct. 3, 1953, *FRUS, 1952–1954*, pt. 2, 12: 551; Bohannon oral history interview, Mar. 10, 1981, Magsaysay papers; Abueva, p. 265; Lacy to Bell, Dec. 2, 1953, DSDF, USNA, RG 59, 896.00/12-253; "The Bi-Partisan Effort," *Manila Bulletin*, Nov. 4, 1953, p. 12. The CIA intelligence digest distributed to the State Department and the White House the week before the election gave credence to the coup story and named Magsaysay and Laurel as principal organizers. CIA, *Current Intelligence Weekly*, Nov. 6, 1953, *DDRS*, 1986: 14.

53. Philippine Commission on Elections, *Report* (1954), p. 142; "Troops Rush to Pasay," *Manila Times*, Nov. 11, 1953, p. 1; "Violence in Isolated Areas Listed," *Manila Chronicle*, Nov. 11, 1953, p. 1; "Philippines Election," *Christian Science Monitor*, Nov. 12, 1953, p. 26; "Magsaysay in Big Philippines Lead," *Los Angeles Times*, Nov. 11, 1953, p. 1; House Committee on Foreign Affairs, *Special Study Mission*, p. 83; Dulles to Spruance, Nov. 20, 1953, DSDF, USNA, RG 59, 796.00/11-2053; Department of State to NSC, Jan. 14, 1954, *FRUS, 1952–54*, pt. 2, 12: 577; Spruance to Dulles, Nov. 24, 1953, DSDF, USNA, RG 59, 796.00/11-2453.

54. Department of State to NSC, Jan. 14, 1954, *FRUS, 1952–54*, pt. 2, 12: 576–77; Sheehan, p. 132; NSC 5413/1, Apr. 5, 1954, Eisenhower papers, NSC policy papers, box 12.

55. "New Guy," *Time* (Jan. 11, 1954): 21; Abueva, p. 296; Starner, pp. 143, 179–99; D. Wurfel, "Bell Report and After," p. 88.

56. Kaufman, "Eisenhower's Foreign Economic Policy," p. 113; "Mutual Security Program, Philippines," [undated], Eisenhower papers, White House Central Files, subject ser., box 43; Golay, *The Philippines*, p. 188; telephone conversation between Dulles and Nixon, May 11, 1956, in Department of State, *FRUS, 1955–57*, 22: 648.

57. Starner, pp. 127–43, 265, 143, 132; Bell to Bonsal, Aug. 12, 1954, Records of the Officer in Charge of Philippine Affairs, State Department lot file 58D312, USNA, RG 59, box 2.

58. Starner, pp. 143, 132; Bell to Bonsal, Aug. 12, 1954, Records of the Officer in Charge of Philippine Affairs, State Department lot file 58D312, USNA, RG 59, box 2; discussion at the 248th NSC meeting, May 12, 1955, *DDRS*, 1986: 3380.

59. Homer Ferguson to Department of State, Aug. 12, 1955, *FRUS, 1955–57*, 22: 601; discussion at the 248th meeting of the NSC, May 12, 1955, *DDRS*, 1986: 3380; memorandum of discussion at a Department of State—Joint Chiefs of Staff meeting, Jan. 14, 1955, *FRUS, 1955–57*, 22: 581; Charles R. Burrows to Bell, Apr. 11, 1956, Records of the Officer in Charge of Philippine Affairs, State Department lot file 58D312, USNA, RG 59, box 1.

60. Dulles to Department of State, Mar. 16, 1956, *FRUS, 1955–57*, 22: 642; discussion at 280th NSC meeting, Mar. 23, 1956, Eisenhower papers, Whitman file, NSC ser., box 7; J. V. Cruz, "The Guy and I," *Manila Chronicle*, July 4, 1957, p. 15; Charles R. Burrows to Bell, Apr. 11, 1956, Records of the Officer in Charge of Philippine Affairs, State Department lot file 58D312, USNA, RG 59, box 1.

61. Department of State to NSC, Jan. 14, 1954, *FRUS, 1952–54*, 22: 577; Spruance to Dulles, Nov. 24, 1953, DSDF, USNA, RG 59, 796.00/11-2453; Dingman, "John Foster Dulles," pp. 409–612; "Recto Cautions PI to Fit Voice to Size," *Daily Mirror* (Manila), July 28, 1954, p. 1; "Recto Backs Mag on Aims," *Daily Mirror* (Manila), Aug. 19, 1954, p. 1; "Progress Report on the Philippines," Aug. 21, 1957, Eisenhower papers, NSC policy papers, box 10. The Philippines recognized South Vietnam in late 1956, when Recto announced he would challenge Magsaysay for the presidency.

62. Operations Coordinating Board, "Progress Report on the Philippines," Aug. 21, 1957, Eisenhower papers, NSC policy papers, box 10.

63. J. V. Cruz, "The Guy and I," *Manila Chronicle*, July 2, 1957, p. 1.

Chapter 5

1. For criticism of Eisenhower's handling of nationalism, see McMahon, "Eisenhower," and Kaufman, *Trade and Aid.*

2. NSC 162/2, Oct. 31, 1953, *FRUS 1952–54,* pt. 1, 2: 577–604; D. L. Anderson, pp. 20–21; Dulles, pp. 108–9.

3. "Magsaysay Defines Foreign Policy He Would Pursue If He Is Elected," *Manila Bulletin,* Nov. 6, 1953, p. 1.

4. Spruance to Department of State, Dec. 15, 1953, *FRUS, 1952–54,* pt. 2, 12: 566–67; Department of State to NSC, "Current Situation in the Philippines," Jan. 14, 1954, ibid., 12: 575–79.

5. Department of State to NSC, "Current Situation in the Philippines," Jan. 14, 1954, *FRUS, 1952–54,* pt. 2, 12: 575–79; Acheson to Manila embassy, Apr. 18, 1952, ibid., 12: 492–93.

6. Gaddis, pp. 134–35; Kaufman, *Trade and Aid,* pp. 13–20; Rostow, *Eisenhower, Kennedy and Foreign Aid,* pp. 84–108; idem, *Diffusion,* pp. 88–90.

7. Senate Committee on Appropriations, *Mutual Security Appropriations,* pp. 329–92.

8. "New Guy," *Time* (Jan. 11, 1954): 21; Abueva, p. 296.

9. Ferguson to Department of State, Aug. 22, 1955, *FRUS, 1955–57,* 22: 603; Starner, p. 143.

10. "U.S. to Boost Aid to Asians," *Christian Science Monitor,* Oct. 9, 1954, p. 10; "Goal of Our Foreign Policy," *Department of State Bulletin* (Dec. 13, 1954): 893; discussion at the 230th NSC meeting, Jan. 5, 1955, *FRUS, 1955–57,* 19: 18; NSC 5501, Jan. 7, 1955, *FRUS, 1955–57,* 19: 35; Rostow, *Eisenhower, Kennedy and Foreign Aid,* pp. 114–20; Kaufman, "Eisenhower's Foreign Economic Policy with Respect to East Asia," p. 113; U.S. aid figures from "Mutual Security Program, Philippines," [undated], Eisenhower papers, White House Central files, subject ser., box 43; spending figures from Golay, *The Philippines,* p. 188; Harry Brenn, "U.S. Aid Program in the Philippines," Dec. 1956, United States Council on Foreign Economic Policy recs., box 2.

11. Ferguson to Department of State, Aug. 22, 1955, *FRUS, 1955–57,* 22: 603; Ferguson to Department of State, Aug. 26, 1955, ibid., p. 605; telephone conversation between Dulles and Nixon, May 11, 1956, ibid., p. 648; Dulles to Magsaysay, Apr. 25, 1956, ibid., p. 646; Cuaderno, *Problems,* p. 54.

12. Seidman, "Enterprise," p. 21; Sicat, pp. 5–6; Rivera, pp. 72–73; Department of State, "Recent Progress in the Philippine Manufacturing Industry," Apr. 22, 1957, State Department, R & A Reports, USNA, RG 59, no. 7488.

13. Kunio, pp. 154, 157, 159–61; Doronila, p. 111.

14. For the origins of other Asian nationalisms, see B. Anderson, *Imagined Communities*. For the treatment of the Chinese under the Americans, see Weightman and Jensen. For figures on Chinese control of business, see Seidman, p. 180.

15. For simplicity, I will use the terms "Filipino," "alien," and "Chinese" as Filipinos used them. For Philippine citizenship laws, see Golay, "The Philippines," pp. 46–47.

16. Carlos Palanca, "the alcohol king of Tondo," was the type of Chinese entrepreneur Filipinos feared. Born in Fukien, he opened a dry-goods store in Manila in the 1930s, perfected the manufacture of rubbing alcohol from molasses in the 1940s, and bought the enormous Binalbagan-Isabela sugar estate in the 1950s. Kunio, p. 187.

17. Agpalo, *Political Process*, pp. 65–71, 111; McBeath, p. 32; Rivera, pp. 128–29; B. Anderson, "Cacique Democracy," p. 8.

18. Braddock to Department of State, Feb. 3, 1954, DSDF, USNA, RG 59, 796.00/2-354; Agpalo, *Political Process*, pp. 92–104.

19. Paez, pp. 173–74; Newman to Brand, Dec. 19, 1957, Records of the Officer in Charge of Philippine Affairs, State Department lot file 58D312, USNA, RG 59, box 1.

20. "U.S. Town of 7,672, at Far East Base," *The New York Times*, July 31, 1955, p. 5; Marshall to Truman, July 12, 1948, DSDF, USNA, RG 59, 811.24596/7-1248.

21. CINCPAC to CNO, Sept. 15, 1955, JCS geographic file, USNA, RG 218, box 27; memorandum of conversation, Oct. 24, 1955, *FRUS, 1955–57*, 22: 620; "U.S. to Transfer $7.4M to Philippines," *Daily Mirror* (Manila), Jan. 16, 1957, p. 2; " 'Isolation' Living Hits U.S. in East," *The New York Times*, Aug. 21, 1955, p. 12.

22. "U.S. Armed Forces in the Philippines," July 5, 1951, Records of the Officer in Charge of Philippine Affairs, State Department lot file 58D312, USNA, RG 59, box 2; Cdr. Wharton to Capt. Aurand, Sept. 30, 1958, *DDRS*, 1986: 1437.

23. House Committee on Foreign Affairs, *Special Study Mission*, p. 49; Futrell, p. 31; Billings-Yun, "Ike and Vietnam," pp. 13–19.

24. Billings-Yun, *Decision Against War*, pp. 49, 109, 120; D. L. Anderson, p. 26; Young, *Vietnam Wars*, p. 33.

25. Memo of conversation by Cutler, May 28, 1954, *FRUS, 1952–54*, pt. 1, 12: 522.

26. Dingman, "Atomic Diplomacy," p. 87; Trachtenberg, "Strategic Thought"; Watson, p. 25; Ambrose, pp. 224–25; Billings-Yun, *Decision Against War*, p. 18; Gallicchio, "Best Defense," p. 63.

27. Horace Smith to Charles Bohlen, May 11, 1957, Records of the Officer in Charge of Philippine Affairs, State Department lot file 58D312, USNA, RG 59, box 1.

28. Ad Hoc Interdepartmental Committee on Military Bases, Philippines, "Action Summary," Oct. 16, 1953, Records of the Officer in Charge of Philippine Affairs, State Department lot file 58D312, USNA, RG 59, box 2; Walter B. Smith to Eisenhower, July 15, 1953, Eisenhower papers, Whitman file, international ser., box 40; "U.S. Sinks Billions in Bases," *U.S. News and World Report* (Feb. 27, 1952): 15.

29. Walter S. Robertson to Dulles, "Military Bases Negotiations with the Philippines," Nov. 29, 1954, Records of the Officer in Charge of Philippine Affairs, State Department lot file 58D312, USNA, RG 59, box 2; Robertson to Bonsal, Oct. 27, 1953, ibid.

30. Over the objection of his American attorneys, Roxas had left the issue unsettled during the 1947 negotiations in the belief that the treaty's 99-year lease replaced other claims. Dulles to Eisenhower, Dec. 23, 1953, *FRUS, 1952–54*, pt. 2, 12: 569–70; "Chronological History of Question of Method of Approach to Philippine Government on Title to U.S. Bases," Mar. 24, 1954, Records of the Officer in Charge of Philippine Affairs, State Department lot file 58D312, USNA, RG 59, box 2.

31. Telephone conversation, Dec. 24, 1953, J. F. Dulles papers, Eisenhower Library, telephone calls, box 10; "Chronological History of Question of Method of Approach to Philippine Government on Title to U.S. Bases," Mar. 24, 1954, Records of the Officer in Charge of Philippine Affairs, State Department lot file 58D312, USNA, RG 59, box 2.

32. Manuel Salientes and Rigoberto Atienza to Magsaysay, "Suggested Outline for Conversations by the President with U.S. Ambassador Spruance Regarding Military Bases," [undated, probably Feb. 1954], Magsaysay papers, VVM, box 2.

33. "Proposal Submitted to PI Panel," *Manila Times*, Mar. 15, 1954, p. 1; "US Bares Stand on PI Bases," *Daily Mirror* (Manila), Mar. 16, 1954, p. 1; "Differences Threshed out in Next Meet," *Manila Times*, Mar. 16, 1954, p. 1; Bell to Bonsal, Mar. 25, 1954, *FRUS, 1952–54*, pt. 2, 12: 586–87; "Refutes American Argument," *Manila Times*, Mar. 17, 1954, p. 1.

34. Constantino, *Making*, p. 201; "Refutes American Argument," *Manila Times*, Mar. 17, 1954, p. 1.

35. "PI to Spurn Barter of Territory," *Manila Times*, Mar. 25, 1954,

p. 1; "AFP Clarifies Washington Story on Trade-Bases," *Manila Times*, Mar. 28, 1954, p. 2; Abueva, p. 462.

36. I. P. Soliongco, "Seriously Speaking," *Manila Chronicle*, Jan. 1, 1957, p. 4; Recto, *Recto Reader*, pp. 50–51, 71–72, 77, 100.

37. Nufer to Department of State, Aug. 27, 1956, *FRUS, 1955–57*, 22: 677; Dulles to Department of State, Mar. 16, 1956, ibid., p. 642; discussion at 280th NSC meeting, Mar. 23, 1956, Eisenhower papers, Whitman file, NSC ser., box 7; Tolentino, p. 151.

38. Clarence B. Randall, "Report on Foreign Economic Policy Discussions," Eisenhower papers, Randall ser., trips subseries, box 2; Del Carmen, p. 45; Seidman, p. 17.

39. Golay, *The Philippines*, pp. 250–51; Hutchcroft, "Situating," p. 42; Higgins, pp. 166–69; Baldwin, pp. 12–132; Kunio, p. 106.

40. NSC 5413/1, Aug. 12, 1954, Eisenhower papers, OCB central files, box 52.

41. D. L. Anderson, pp. 26–39, 65–80; Watson, pp. 254–55; Brands, "From ANZUS to SEATO," pp. 250–69; Hess, "American Search," pp. 272–95.

42. "Magsaysay Defines Foreign Policy He Would Pursue If He Is Elected," *Manila Bulletin*, Nov. 6, 1953, p. 1; Salvador P. Lopez to Carlos P. Garcia, Apr. 1, 1954, Romulo papers, UP, ser. 1, box 7; Lopez to Garcia, Mar. 23, 1954, "Implications of the 'New Look' Defense Policy of the United States on the Security of the Philippines," ibid.

43. Laurel, "The Nature of Philippine-American Relations," Oct. 14, 1954, Laurel papers, ser. 5, box 6; Garcia to Romulo, May 31, 1954, Romulo papers, UP, ser. 1, box 7; "SEATO," *Philippines Free Press*, Aug. 14, 1954, pp. 2, 70; the 1951 Mutual Defense Treaty committed the United States to respond to an armed attack "in accordance with its constitutional processes."

44. Filipino historians identify SEATO as one of the four "unequal treaties" through which the United States imposed neocolonial control after granting flag independence. Roger Dingman disagrees, calling the Philippines one of the authors of SEATO. By increasing military aid and including the Pacific Charter, he argues, the United States made substantial concessions to the Philippine view. Neither rendering fully explains the Philippine motives, which in large part were unrelated to the issues before the conference. Cf. Simbulan, p. 82; Dingman, "John Foster Dulles," pp. 409–612.

45. Memo of conversation by Cutler, May 28, 1954, *FRUS, 1952–54*, pt. 1, 12: 522; "Peking on Preparation for War," *The Times* (London), Sept. 4, 1954, p. 6; "Moscow Suspicions," *The Times*, Sept.

6, 1954, p. 6; "PI for 100,000-Man SEATO 'Standby' Army," *Daily Mirror* (Manila), Aug. 23, 1954, p. 1; "See PI Bid for Huge Arms to Back Up SEATO," *Daily Mirror*, Sept. 4, 1954, p. 1.

46. "War Jitters," *Philippines Free Press*, Sept. 11, 1954, p. 1; "Recto Cautions PI to Fit Voice to Size," *Daily Mirror* (Manila), July 28, 1954, p. 1; "Recto Backs Mag on Aims," *Daily Mirror*, Aug. 19, 1954, p. 1.

47. "Automatic Reaction," *Philippines Free Press*, Sept. 11, 1954, p. 3; "The President's Speech," *Manila Times*, Sept. 7, 1954, p. 2; "Speech of Vice President Garcia," *Manila Times*, Sept. 7, 1954, p. 2; Fourth Plenary Session of the Manila Conference, Sept. 7, 1954, *FRUS, 1952–54*, pt. 1, 12: 891.

48. Telephone conversation, Dulles to Merchant, Aug. 30, 1954, *FRUS, 1952–54*, pt. 1, 12: 821; "Compromise Leads to Agreement," *Manila Times*, Sept. 8, 1954, p. 1; University of the Philippines, Division of Research and Law Reform, *Philippine Treaty Series*, 3: 355–62.

49. "Report on Foreign Economic Policy Discussions Between United States Officials in the Far East and Clarence B. Randall," Dec. 1956, U.S. Council on Foreign Economic Policy records, Randall ser., trips subseries, box 2; Golay, *The Philippines*, p. 48; "Report of the Panel of Experts on Revision of the Philippine Trade Act," Aug. 17, 1954, Laurel papers, Final Report, app. A; Jose E. Romero to the Philippine Sugar Association, Aug. 30, 1954, Romulo papers, UP, ser. 1, box 8; Abueva, pp. 341–50; Adrienne Fousek and Edna Erlich, "The Philippines and 'Selective Free Trade,' " Nov. 19, 1953, Federal Reserve Board records, country files, Philippine Islands, banking, general; Leonard S. Tyson to Kenneth Young, Oct. 28, 1954, *FRUS, 1952–54*, pt. 2, 12: 635–36.

50. Styles Bridges of New Hampshire, chairman of the Senate Appropriations Committee, pushed Langley's appointment on the State Department. Langley to Laurel, May 3, 1956, Laurel papers, ser. 5, box 5; Langley to Robertson, Oct. 25, 1954, *FRUS, 1952–54*, pt. 2, 12: 638–40; Baldwin to Robertson, Oct. 25, 1954, ibid., pp. 640–41; Dulles to Manila Embassy, Nov. 17, 1954, ibid., pp. 641–42; memo of conversation, Dec. 8, 1954, ibid., pp. 645–46; House Committee on Ways and Means, *Philippine Trade Agreement*, p. 36.

51. "Opening Statement of Hon. Jose P. Laurel," Sept. 20, 1954, Laurel papers, bound vol. 1; Pedro R. Sabido, "Observations on the Mission's Work," Oct. 17, 1954, Laurel papers, ser. 5, box 6.

52. Although Recto later criticized foreign investment, in 1954 he welcomed it, observing in July that "there can be no question that

U.S. investments here should be further encouraged." "The Transformation of the Philippines," *Philippines Free Press*, July 31, 1954, p. 3; Recto to Laurel, Nov. 18, 1954, Laurel papers, ser. 5, box 3; Langley to Robertson, Oct. 25, 1954, *FRUS, 1952–54*, pt. 2, 12: 638; Cuaderno to Laurel, Dec. 9, 1954, Laurel papers, ser. 5, box 5; Golay, *Revised Trade Agreement*, pp. 52–53.

53. Constantino and Constantino, *Continuing Past*, pp. 291–93; Golay, *Revised Trade Agreement*, pp. 15–17; "Report to the President of the Philippines by the Philippine Economic Mission to the United States," Feb. 1955, p. 108, Laurel papers.

54. Laurel to Magsaysay, Nov. 16, 1954, Laurel papers, ser. 5, box 3; Valencia to Magsaysay, Mar. 10, 1955, ibid., box 6; House Committee on Ways and Means, *Philippine Trade Agreement*, pp. 78, 87, 70, 110.

55. Dulles to Department of State, Mar. 16, 1956, *FRUS, 1955–57*, 22: 642.

56. Golay, *The Philippines*, pp. 179–81; Hutchcroft, "Situating," pp. 46–47.

57. "Report on Foreign Economic Policy Discussions Between United States Officials in the Far East and Clarence B. Randall," Dec. 1956, U.S. Council on Foreign Economic Policy records, Randall ser., trips subseries, box 2; Brand to William Walker, Oct. 1, 1956, *FRUS, 1955–57*, 22: 687.

58. "US Concedes Philippine Ownership," *Manila Times*, July 4, 1956, p. 1; Pelaez, pp. 8–23; memorandum of conversation, Dec. 14, 1956, *FRUS, 1955–57*, 22: 708; editorial note, *FRUS, 1955–57*, 22: 684.

59. Horace Smith to Boland, May 11, 1957, Records of the Officer in Charge of Philippine Affairs, State Department lot file 58D312, USNA, RG 59, box 1; Joint Logistics Plans Committee, "U.S. Base Requirements Overseas," JCS decimal file 360, USNA, RG 218, box 99; J. B. Smith, pp. 252–53.

60. Magsaysay to Romulo, Apr. 12, 1956, Magsaysay papers, ser. 1, box 82; Lansdale, pp. 168–70, 178–79, 234–35; Kerima Polotan, "Orendain's Historic Mission to Vietnam," *Philippines Free Press*, Jan. 19, 1957, p. 20; J. B. Smith, p. 252.

61. J. B. Smith, p. 251; Armstrong to Dulles, Mar. 18, 1957, *FRUS, 1955–57*, 22: 714.

62. Rabe, p. 176; Kaufman, *Trade and Aid*, p. 208.

63. Holsti, p. 71. Some dependency theorists have turned away from the concept of a transnational "pact of class domination" in favor of more flexible definitions of dependent relationships that allow for reciprocity and even dependency reversal. See Packenham.

Chapter 6

1. W. V. Turnage, Division of Intelligence and Research, to Mann, Jan. 20, 1958, DSDF, USNA, RG 59, 896.00/1-2058; William Walker to Dulles, July 15, 1957, ibid., 796.00/7-1557; D. Wurfel, "Philippine Elections," p. 61; "After Magsaysay, What?" *Time* (Oct. 28, 1957): 36; 338th NSC meeting, Oct. 2, 1957, Eisenhower papers, Whitman file, NSC ser., box 9.

2. Walker to Department of State, July 16, 1957, DSDF, USNA, RG 59, 796.00/7-1657; Philippine Commission on Elections, *Report* (1958), p. 207; "The Philippine Elections, Results and Prospects," Nov. 15, 1957, DSDF, USNA, RG 59, 796.00/11-1557.

3. "President Asks for P1.1-B Budget," *Manila Chronicle*, Feb. 9, 1958, p. 1.

4. Meyer, p. 256; Koren to Department of State, Dec. 23, 1958, DSDF, USNA, RG 59, 796.00/12-2358; "Foreign Sources of Financial Support for Postwar Philippine Rehabilitation and Economic Development," May 19, 1958, State Department R & A Reports, USNA, RG 59, no. 8020.

5. Memo of conversation between President Eisenhower and President Garcia, June 18, 1958, Eisenhower papers, Whitman file, international ser., box 40; Garcia inaugural address, Dec. 30, 1957, Garcia papers, ser. 4, box 1; Robert M. Macy, Bureau of the Budget, to Clarence Randall, "Regional Economic Development," Jan. 2, 1959, Council on Foreign Economic Policy Records, policy papers ser., box 11; Randall to Elmer Staats, May 13, 1958, ibid., chronological file, box 2; Recto to Garcia, Jan. 15, 1959, Garcia papers, ser. 1, box 78.

6. Romulo speech to the Los Angeles Press Club, Jan. 7, 1959, Garcia papers, box 82; Romulo to Garcia, Feb. 24, 1959, ibid.; Serrano, pp. 39–41; Meyer, p. 253.

7. Koren to Department of State, Oct. 16, 1959, DSDF, USNA, RG 59, 796.00/10-1659.

8. Dulles to Bohlen, Nov. 7, 1957, *FRUS, 1955–57*, 22: 732.

9. Operations Coordinating Board, "Report on the Philippines," Apr. 2, 1958, Eisenhower papers, Whitman file, files of the National Security Adviser, box 10; CINCPAC to CNO, Nov. 23, 1957, JCS geographic file, 686.9 Philippine Islands, USNA, RG 218, box 15.

10. JCS, "The Military Importance of the U.S. Base System in the Philippines," Nov. 6, 1958, JCS geographic file, 686.9 Philippine Islands, USNA, RG 218, box 157.

11. Discussion at the 393rd NSC meeting, Jan. 15, 1959, *DDRS*, 1990: 875; Nathan F. Twining to Neil McElroy, secretary of defense,

Mar. 12, 1959, JCS central file, 9146/4920 Philippines, USNA, RG 59, box 134.

12. Operations Coordinating Board, "Report on the Philippines," Nov. 26, 1958, Eisenhower papers, Whitman file, NSC policy papers, box 25; "Base Survey, the Philippines," Apr. 25, 1957, Records of the Officer in Charge of Philippine Affairs, State Department lot file 58D312, USNA, RG 59, box 1; Pelaez, p. 16.

13. "Base Survey, the Philippines," Apr. 25, 1957, Records of the Officer in Charge of Philippine Affairs, State Department lot file 58D312, USNA, RG 59, box 1; "PI-US Bases Pact Change Agenda Ok'd," *Manila Chronicle*, Nov. 13, 1958, p. 5.

14. Healy, pp. 287–98; Gleeck, *Dissolving*, pp. 105–9.

15. Tolentino, p. 152.

16. Gleeck, *Dissolving*, p. 108; Bohlen, *Witness*, p. 475. Adm. Felix B. Stump, CINCPAC, to Twining, Nov. 22, 1958, JCS geographic file, CCS 686.9 Philippine Islands 1958, USNA, RG 218, box 157. Stump declared that "prompt payment of civil claims will continue to be the effective practical answer" to incidents on the bases.

17. I. P. Soliongco, "Seriously Speaking," *Manila Chronicle*, Nov. 24, 1958, p. 4.

18. Meyer, pp. 258–59; Serrano, pp. 119–29; John N. Irwin, Asst. Sec. of Defense, to Serrano, Oct. 8, 1958, Romulo papers, UP, ser. 1, box 10; Lt. Gen. Manuel F. Cabal to Romulo, Jan. 8, 1960, ibid.; Operations Coordinating Board, "Report on the Philippines," Nov. 26, 1958, Eisenhower papers, Whitman file, NSC policy papers, box 25.

19. "US Signs Accord with Philippines," *The New York Times*, Oct. 13, 1959, p. 7; University of the Philippines, Division of Research and Law Reform, *Philippine Treaty Series*, 4: 5–24; Serrano, pp. 30, 36.

20. Meyer, p. 257; "Guards Agreed on in Manila," *The New York Times*, Nov. 28, 1959, p. 6, Operations Coordinating Board, "Report on the Philippines," Mar. 30, 1960, Eisenhower papers, Whitman file, National Security advisers' papers, box 6; Sylvia Mendez Ventura, pp. 145–49.

21. Leon O. Ty, "Dr. Jose C. Locsin: Father of the 'Filipino First' Policy," *Philippines Free Press*, Feb. 6, 1960, p. 4; Constantino and Constantino, *Continuing Past*, p. 303; "No Sale? Nationalists Decry Apathy of Filipinos," *Philippines Free Press*, Oct. 10, 1959, p. 4.

22. OIR, "Recent Progress in the Philippine Manufacturing Industry," Apr. 22, 1957, R & A Reports, USNA, RG 59, no. 7488; Recto, *Recto Reader*, p. 42. Wolters describes the social imperatives driving landowners to diversify; see pp. 188–89.

23. Teodoro Locsin, "Filipino First—or Last," *Philippines Free Press*, Sept. 19, 1959, pp. 2–3; Recto, *Recto Reader*, p. 50. For Philippine state corporations, see OIR, "Government Corporations in the Philippines," May 27, 1953, R & A Reports, USNA, RG 59, no. 6206.

24. Teodoro Locsin, "Filipino Last?" *Philippines Free Press*, Sept. 19, 1959, p. 74; "No Sale? Nationalists Decry Apathy of Filipinos," *Philippines Free Press*, Oct. 10, 1959, p. 7.

25. Because stagnating sectors are the first to seek government protection, attempts to suppress an economically successful minority through legislation often push the minority into more dynamic sectors, thereby assuring its continued success. See Eitzen. Chinese kinship networks and firm structure also conferred an entrepreneurial advantage (Seidman, p. 183). Horace Smith, "Report on Foreign Economic Policy Discussions with Clarence B. Randall and Associates," Dec. 1956, *DDRS*, 1990: 445.

26. Higgins, p. 167; Henry Gemmill, "Orient Investment," *Wall Street Journal*, May 14, 1957, p. 1.

27. Golay, "Entrepreneurship," p. 83; Pizer and Cutler, p. 20; Golay, "The Philippines," p. 89.

28. Committee on Interior and Insular Affairs, *Critical Materials*, pp. 37–38; Department of Commerce, *Investment*, p. 6.

29. For anti-Chinese use of exchange, see Braddock to Department of State, Feb. 3, 1954, DSDF, USNA, RG 59, 796.00/2-354. For a description of the No Dollar Import Law, see "Political and Economic Prospects for the Philippine Republic," Jan. 6, 1957, State Department R & A Reports, USNA, RG 59, no. 7412; Golay, "The Philippines," pp. 92–95; OIR, "Recent Progress in the Philippine Manufacturing Industry," Apr. 22, 1957, R & A Reports, USNA, RG 59, no. 7488.

30. "Manila's Controls," *Fortune* (Apr. 1957): 98; Brodie to Department of State, Oct. 10, 1956, DSDF, USNA, RG 59, 896.13/10-1056. In 1955, Cuaderno, then chairman of the International Monetary Fund, asked U.S. Secretary of the Treasury George Humphrey to "intervene with President Magsaysay to insist that the President of the Philippines take only Cuaderno's advice." The State Department agreed to do its best. Kenneth Young to Walter Robertson, Sept. 22, 1955, DSDF, USNA, RG 59, 896.131/9-2255. During the Magsaysay administration, State Department officials knew Cuaderno was "generally considered by Filipino politicians to be strongly backed by the U.S." "Political and Economic Prospects for the Philippine Republic," Jan. 6, 1957, State Department R & A Reports, USNA, RG 59, no. 7412.

31. Manila to secretary of state, "Weekly Economic Report," July 13, 1956, DSDF, USNA, RG 59, 796.00(w)/7-1356; Manila to secretary of state, "Weekly Economic Report," July 7, 1956, ibid., 796.00(w)/7-656.

32. For comparisons of Chinese capital in various Southeast Asian economies, see Kunio, pp. 51–52; Del Carmen, p. 45.

33. "The Philippine Economic Austerity Program," May 9, 1958, State Department R & A Reports, USNA, RG 59, no. 7716; Igor Organesoff, "Philippine Turmoil," Wall Street Journal, Mar. 25, 1959, p. 11.

34. Golay, "The Philippines," p. 34; Napoleon G. Rama, "The New and Necessary Importers," Philippines Free Press, Aug. 9, 1958, p. 4; Golay, "Entrepreneurship," p. 84; "Recent Progress in the Philippine Manufacturing Industry," Apr. 22, 1957, State Department R & A Reports, USNA, RG 59, no. 7488.

35. "Recent Progress in the Philippine Manufacturing Industry," Apr. 22, 1957, State Department R & A Reports, USNA, RG 59, no. 7488; Golay, The Philippines, pp. 37, 45, 105.

36. Higgins, pp. 165–66; Golay, The Philippines, p. 395; Baldwin, p. 147.

37. Collings, pp. 274–86; Rabe, p. 113; Napoleon G. Rama, "The New and Necessary Importers," Philippines Free Press, Aug. 9, 1958, p. 4; Golay, The Philippines, pp. 151, 202; Napoleon G. Rama, "Our Fearful Businessmen," Philippines Free Press, Aug. 23, 1958, p. 29.

38. Leon O. Ty, "Furor over the Bohol Steel Mill," Philippines Free Press, Aug. 23, 1958, pp. 4–5; Bohlen to secretary of state, July 25, 1958, DSDF, USNA, RG 59, 796.00(w)/7-2558.

39. For the devaluation dispute, see "Decontrol Battle," Philippines Free Press, Sept. 6, 1958, pp. 34–35; "Political and Economic Prospects for the Philippine Republic," Jan. 6, 1957, State Department R & A Reports, USNA, RG 59, no. 7412; R. Gordon Arneson, State Department Bureau of Intelligence and Research, to Robertson, Nov. 15, 1957, DSDF, USNA, RG 59, 796.00/11-1557; H. K. Koren, first secretary–Manila embassy, to Department of State, Dec. 23, 1958, ibid., 796.00/12-235. For the coup story, see "The General and the Congressman," Philippines Free Press, Nov. 8, 1958, p. 1; Bohlen to Dulles, Nov. 8, 1958, DSDF, USNA, RG 59, 796.00/11-858; Bohlen to Dulles, Nov. 12, 1958, ibid., 796.00/11-1258.

40. William Brewster, "Annual Economic Assessment 1958," Mar. 5, 1959, DSDF, USNA, RG 59, 896.00/3-559; Michael Cross, Treasury Attaché to Department of State, Oct. 27, 1958, ibid., 896.10/10-2758;

Brewster, "Quarterly Economic Summary," Apr. 24, 1959, ibid., 896.00/4-2459; H. L. Koren to Department of State, Dec. 23, 1958, ibid., 796.00/12-2358.

41. Del Carmen, p. 45; Igor Organesoff, "Philippine Turmoil," *Wall Street Journal*, Mar. 25, 1959, p. 11; Teodoro Locsin, "Filipino First—or Last," *Philippines Free Press*, Sept. 19, 1959, pp. 2–3; Brewster, "Annual Economic Assessment, 1958," Mar. 5, 1959, DSDF, USNA, RG 59, 896.00/3-559.

42. "Filipino First and Alien Interests," *Manila Chronicle*, Nov. 6, 1958, p. 4; Meyer, p. 231; Igor Organesoff, "Philippine Turmoil," *Wall Street Journal*, Mar. 25, 1959, p. 11; Serrano, pp. 45–46.

43. Igor Organesoff, "Philippine Turmoil," *Wall Street Journal*, Mar. 25, 1959, p. 11; Golay, "The Philippines," p. 93; "Step-up in Filipino First Policy Feared by American Companies," *The New York Times*, Mar. 21, 1960, p. 39.

44. Horace Smith, "Report to Clarence B. Randall and Associates," Dec. 1956, *DDRS*, 1990: 445; "Step-up in Filipino First Policy Feared by American Companies," *The New York Times*, Mar. 21, 1960, p. 39.

45. Shalom (*United States and the Philippines*, pp. 131–33, 138–43) describes the instruments through which the United States could protect investment and observes that, as a general policy, the United States aimed to protect U.S. investments abroad. He does not reveal *how* or *if* the United States protected American investments in the Philippines. Constantino and Constantino (*Continuing Past*, pp. 334–35) assert that U.S. pressure made the Philippines a "haven for U.S. investors."

46. Department of Commerce, *Investment*, p. 6; Operations Coordinating Board, "Progress Report on the Philippines," Aug. 21, 1957, Eisenhower papers, Whitman file, NSC policy papers, box 10; idem, "Report on the Philippines," Nov. 26, 1958, ibid., box 25; Henry Heller, Securities and Exchange Commission, to William V. Tarnage, Department of State, Dec. 2, 1958, DSDF, USNA, RG 59, 896.00/12-1258.

47. John M. Leddy, U.S. Department of State, to Romulo, May 11, 1959, Garcia papers, ser. 1, box 82; Abbott to Herter, Nov. 26, 1959, DSDF, USNA, RG 59, 896.131/11-2659.

48. "Sympathy Asked for Manila's Aim," *The New York Times*, Jan. 21, 1960, p. 7; Abbott to Herter, Dec. 3, 1959, DSDF, USNA, RG 59, 896.131/12-359; Samuel C. Waugh, president, Export-Import Bank, to Romulo, Dec. 7, 1959, Romulo papers, UP, ser. 1, box 10; Walter S. Robertson to C. Douglas Dillon, Jan. 17, 1959, DSDF, USNA, RG 59,

896.10/1-1759; Garcia, State of the Nation, Jan. 23, 1961, Garcia papers, ser. 4, box 3.

49. On the importance of U.S. bases, see JCS, "The Military Importance of the U.S. Base System in the Philippines," Nov. 6, 1958, JCS geographic file, 686.9 Philippine Islands, USNA, RG 218, box 157.

50. See DSDF, 1955–58, 896.13 (Philippines, monetary policy), USNA, RG 59.

51. U.S. Department of Commerce, *Survey of Current Business* (Aug. 1959): 30; "Foreign Sources of Financial Support for Postwar Philippine Rehabilitation and Economic Development," May 19, 1959, State Department R & A Reports, USNA, RG 59, no. 8020.

52. J. B. Smith, pp. 265–321.

53. Ibid.

54. Bohlen, memo of conversation with Eisenhower, Feb. 11, 1959, Eisenhower papers, Whitman file, Office of the Staff Secretary, box 12; "Ike Says PI-US 'Rift' Just a 'Matter of Pride,' " *Manila Times*, Feb. 20, 1959, p. 1; "President Eisenhower's Address to Congress," *Manila Times*, June 16, 1960, p. 1; "PI-US Ties Reaffirmed," *Manila Times*, June 16, 1960, p. 1; "Economy, Defense Threshed," *Daily Mirror* (Manila), June 15, 1960, p. 1; "Ike Speech at the Luneta," *Manila Times*, June 17, 1960, p. 1.

55. Operations Coordinating Board, "Report on the Philippines," Mar. 30, 1960, Eisenhower papers, Whitman file, OCB subject ser., box 6; Romulo to Garcia, Dec. 17, 1960, Romulo papers, UP, ser. 1, box 10; Romulo to Garcia, Nov. 17, 1960, ibid.

Conclusion

1. Donald Goertzen, "Withdrawal Trauma," *Far Eastern Economic Review*, Jan. 30, 1992, p. 10; William McGurn, "Traveler's Tales," *Far Eastern Economic Review*, Dec. 17, 1992, p. 30.

2. " 'Benign Neglect' Is Fine," *Malaya*, Dec. 20, 1992, p. 4.

3. Bartholomew Lahiff, "Good-bye Admiral Dewey," *America*, Dec. 7, 1991, pp. 436–37; William McGurn, "Yankees Go Home," *American Spectator* (Jan. 1992): 42; MacDonald, pp. 282–83; Habu, p. 311.

4. "President Eisenhower's Address to Congress," *Manila Times*, June 16, 1960, p. 1.

5. Kolko, *Confronting*, p. 292.

6. "Foreign Sources of Financial Support for Philippine Rehabilitation and Economic Development," May 19, 1959, State Department R & A Reports, USNA, RG 59, no. 8020; "Mutual Security Program,

Philippines," [undated], Eisenhower papers, Whitman file, subject ser., box 43.

7. Golay, *The Philippines*, p. 75.

8. For the history of anti-Chinese legislation in other Southeast Asian countries, see Purcell.

9. Geertz, pp. 238–49.

10. Jose Romero to the Philippine Sugar Association, Aug. 30, 1954, Romulo papers, UP, ser. 1, box 8.

11. Cowen, quoted in Welch, p. 290.

12. For details on the hegemonic bloc of high-tech firms, see Cumings, 2: 18–20; and Ferguson.

13. McMahon, "Eisenhower," pp. 453–73; Brands, *Specter.*

14. See Hahn; Merrill; Kaufman, *Trade and Aid.*

15. "Abadia on Bases Rejection," *FBIS Daily Report—East Asia,* Sept. 19, 1991, p. 53.

Bibliography

Manuscript Collections

Abilene, Kansas

Eisenhower Library
Edward Beach Papers
Joseph M. Dodge Papers
John Foster Dulles Papers
Draper Committee Records
Dwight D. Eisenhower Papers
  • White House Central Files (Whitman File)
  • White House Office, NSC Staff Papers
  • White House Office, Special Assistant for National Security Affairs Records
  • White House Office, Staff Secretary Records: International Series
Leland Hobbs Papers
Carl McCardle Papers
Neil McElroy Papers
Randall Commission Records
Thomas E. Stephens Records
U.S. Council on Foreign Economic Policy Records

Angeles City, Philippines

Thirteenth Air Force Historical Office

Bloomington, Indiana

Lilly Library
Paul V. McNutt Papers

Charlottesville, Virginia

Alderman Library
Louis Johnson Papers
Edward Stettinius Papers

College Park, Maryland
  University of Maryland Library
    Millard E. Tydings Papers

Independence, Missouri
  Harry S Truman Library
    Dean Acheson Papers
    Myron Cowen Papers
    Nathaniel P. Davis Papers
    George M. Elsey Papers
    J. Weldon Jones Papers
    John Melby Papers
    Samuel Rosenman Papers
    John Snyder Papers
    Harry S Truman Papers
      • Official File
      • President's Secretary's Files
      • White House Central File
    United States Economic Survey Mission to the Philippines Records
    Frank A. Waring Papers

Manila, Philippines
  American Historical Collection
  Ayala Museum
    Elpidio Quirino Papers
    Carlos P. Romulo Papers
  Laurel Foundation
    Jose P. Laurel Papers
  Magsaysay Foundation
    Ramon Magsaysay Papers
  National Library (Aklatan Pambansa)
    Carlos P. Garcia Papers
    Sergio Osmeña Papers
    Manuel Roxas Papers

Norfolk, Virginia
  MacArthur Memorial
    Douglas MacArthur Papers

Quezon City, Philippines
  University of the Philippines Library
    Miguel Cuaderno Papers
    Federico Mahangas Papers

Carlos P. Romulo Papers
Vicente Sinco Papers
Lopez Museum
    Chronicle Collection
Washington, D.C.
Library of Congress
Harold Ickes Papers
National Archives
General Records of the Department of State, RG 59
JUSMAG Records, RG 334
Records of the Division of Territories and Island Possessions, RG 126
Records of the Joint Chiefs of Staff, RG 218
Records of the Office of the Secretary of Defense, RG 330
Records of the Office of the Secretary of the Interior, RG 48
Records of the Secretary of the Treasury, Records of the National Advisory Council on International Monetary and Financial Policies (NAC), RG 56
Records of the Senate Committee on Territories, RG 46
Records of the War Department General and Special Staffs, Records of the Office of the Director of Plans and Operations, RG 165
State Department Lot Files, RG 59
    • Records of the Bureau of Far Eastern Affairs, lot 58D238
    • Records of the Officer in Charge of Philippine Affairs, lot 58D312
    • Records of the Philippine and Southeast Asian Affairs Division, lot 54D190
Records of the Office of High Commissioner to the Philippine Islands, RG 126
National Security Archive
Ray Bonner Files
United States Federal Reserve
Country Files, Philippines

Government Publications, Philippines

Baguio Conference. *Final Act and Proceedings of the Baguio Conference of 1950.* Baguio: Secretariat of the Baguio Conference, 1950.
Central Bank of the Philippines. *Second Annual Report, 1950.* Manila: Bureau of Printing, 1951.
Commission on Elections. *Report of the Commission on Elections.* Manila: Bureau of Printing, 1954.
———. *Report of the Commission on Elections.* Manila: Bureau of Printing, 1958.

Department of Commerce and Industry. *The Nationalization of Retail Trade.* Manila: Bureau of Printing, 1950.
———. *Second Annual Report.* Manila: Bureau of Printing, 1952.
University of the Philippines, Division of Research and Law Reform. *Philippine Treaty Series.* Vols. 3 and 4. Quezon City: University of the Philippines Law Center, 1970.

Government Publications, United States

Central Intelligence Agency (CIA). *CIA Research Reports: Japan, Korea, and the Security of Asia.* Edited by Paul Kesaris. Frederick, Md.: University Publications of America, 1983. 5 reels.
Department of Commerce. *Investment in the Philippines.* Washington, D.C.: Government Printing Office, 1955.
———. *Selected Data on U.S. Direct Investment Abroad, 1950–1976.* Washington, D.C.: Government Printing Office, 1982.
Department of State. *Current Economic Developments, 1952–1954: Foreign Relations of the United States Microfiche Publication.* Washington, D.C.: U.S. Department of State, 1987.
———. *Foreign Relations of the United States, 1945.* Vol. 6. Washington, D.C.: Government Printing Office, 1969.
———. *Foreign Relations of the United States, 1946.* Vols. 1, 8. Washington, D.C.: Government Printing Office, 1971–72.
———. *Foreign Relations of the United States, 1947.* Vol. 6. Washington, D.C.: Government Printing Office, 1972.
———. *Foreign Relations of the United States, 1948.* Vol. 6. Washington, D.C.: Government Printing Office, 1974.
———. *Foreign Relations of the United States, 1949.* Vols. 1, 7. Washington, D.C.: Government Printing Office, 1975–76.
———. *Foreign Relations of the United States, 1950.* Vols. 1, 6. Washington, D.C.: Government Printing Office, 1976–77.
———. *Foreign Relations of the United States, 1951.* Vols. 1, 6. Washington, D.C.: Government Printing Office, 1977–79.
———. *Foreign Relations of the United States, 1952–1954.* Vols. 1–2, 12–13. Washington, D.C.: Government Printing Office, 1982–84.
———. *Foreign Relations of the United States, 1955–1957.* Vols. 1, 21–22. Washington, D.C.: Government Printing Office, 1985–89.
———. *Report of the Economic Survey Mission to the Philippines.* Washington, D.C.: Government Printing Office, 1950.
———. *Treaties and Other International Agreements of the United States, 1776–1949.* 11 vols. Washington, D.C.: Government Printing Office, 1974.

Economic Cooperation Administration, Special Economic and Technical Mission to the Philippines. *Strength for the Free World from the United States of America: ECA in the Philippines.* Manila: Economic Cooperation Administration, 1951.

House. Committee on Appropriations. *Appropriations Bill for 1944.* Pt. 1. 78th Cong., 1st sess., 1943.

————. *Department of State Appropriations Bill for 1948.* 80th Cong., 1st sess., 1947.

————. *Department of State Appropriations for 1951.* 81st Cong., 2nd sess., 1950.

House. Committee on Banking and Currency. *Financial Aid to the Republic of the Philippines.* 79th Cong., 2nd sess., 1946.

House. Committee on Foreign Affairs. *Selected Executive Session Hearings of the Committee, 1951–56.* Vol. 17, *United States Policy in the Far East.* 99th Cong., 1st sess., 21 vols., 1980–87.

————. *Special Study Mission to Southeast Asia and the Pacific.* 83rd Cong., 2nd sess., 1954.

House. Committee on Insular Affairs. *Establishing the Filipino Rehabilitation Commission.* 78th Cong., 2nd sess., report 1507, 1944.

————. *Hearings on the Rehabilitation Act.* 79th Cong., 1st sess., 1946.

House. Committee on International Relations. *Selected Executive Session Hearings of the Committee, 1943–1950.* 94th Cong., 2nd sess., 8 vols., historical series, 1976.

House. Committee on Ways and Means. *Philippine Trade Act of 1945.* 79th Cong., 2nd sess., report 1089, 1946.

————. *Philippine Trade Agreement Revision Act of 1955.* 84th Cong., 1st sess., 1955.

————. *Taxes on Income Derived in the Philippines.* 80th Cong., 2nd sess., 1948.

House. Office of the High Commissioner to the Philippines. *Seventh and Final Report of the High Commissioner to the Philippines.* 80th Cong., 1st sess., 1946.

House. *Report and Recommendations of the Joint Philippine-American Finance Commission.* 80th Cong., 1st sess., 1947.

Joint Chiefs of Staff (JCS). *Records of the Joint Chiefs of Staff.* Pt. 1, *1942–45.* Frederick, Md.: University Press of America, 1973. [Microfilm.]

Joint Preparatory Committee on Philippine Affairs. *Report of May 20, 1938.* 3 vols. Washington, D.C.: Government Printing Office, 1938.

President. *Public Papers of the Presidents, Harry S. Truman, 1950.* Washington, D.C.: Government Printing Office, 1965.

Senate. Committee on Appropriations. *Mutual Security Appropriations for 1954.* 83rd Cong., 1st sess., 1953.

Senate. Committee on Banking and Currency. *Implementation of the Financial Agreement Between the United States and the United Kingdom.* 79th Cong., 2nd. sess., report 1144, 1946.

Senate. Committee on Finance. *Philippine Trade Act of 1946.* 79th Cong., 2nd sess., 1946.

Senate. Committee on Foreign Relations. *Economic, Social and Political Changes in the Underdeveloped Countries and Its Implications for United States Policy.* 86th Cong., 2nd sess., 1960.

———. *Executive Sessions of the Senate Foreign Relations Committee.* 82nd Cong., 1st sess., 3 vols., historical series, 1976.

———. *Military Assistance Program, 1949.* 81st Cong., 1st sess., historical series, 1974.

———. *Mutual Security Act of 1954.* 83rd Cong., 2nd sess., 1954.

———. *Reviews of the World Situation: 1949-1950.* 81st Cong., 1st and 2nd sess., historical series, 1974.

Senate. Committee on Interior and Insular Affairs. *Critical Materials: Factors Affecting Self-Sufficiency Within Nations of the Western Hemisphere.* 84th Cong., 1st sess., 1956.

United States. *Code of Federal Regulations, 1943-48.* Washington, D.C.: Government Printing Office, 1957.

———. *Statutes at Large, 1933-1934.* Vol. 47. Washington, D.C.: Government Printing Office, 1934.

Wile, Annadel, ed. *Declassified Documents Reference System.* Washington, D.C.: Carrolton Press, 1976-91. [Microfiche.]

International Organizations

United Nations Economic Commission for Asia and the Far East (ECAFE). *Economic Survey for 1948.* Lake Success, N.Y.: ECAFE Department for Economic Affairs, 1949.

———. *Mobilization of Domestic Capital in Certain Countries in Asia and the Far East.* Bangkok: ECAFE, 1951.

United Nations Relief and Rehabilitation Administration. *UNRRA in the Philippines, 1946-1947.* Washington, D.C.: United Nations Relief and Rehabilitation Administration, April 1948.

Other Cited Sources: Primary and Secondary

Abaya, Hernando J. *Betrayal in the Philippines.* New York: A.A. Wyn, 1946.

————. *The Making of a Subversive: A Memoir.* Quezon City: New Day, 1984.

Abelarde, Pedro E. *American Tariff Policy Toward the Philippines: 1896–1946.* New York: Oriole Editions, 1974.

Abueva, Jose Veloso. *Ramon Magsaysay: A Political Biography.* Manila: Solidaridad Publishing House, 1971.

Acheson, Dean. *Present at the Creation: My Years in the State Department.* New York: Norton, 1969.

Agpalo, Remigio E. "The Philippine Political System in the Perspective of History." *Philippine Journal of Public Administration* 15 (1971): 239–58.

————. *The Political Process and the Nationalization of the Retail Trade in the Philippines.* Quezon City: University of the Philippines Office of Coordinator of Research, 1962.

Albertini, Rudolf von. *Decolonization: The Administration and Future of the Colonies, 1919–1960.* Garden City, N.Y.: Doubleday, 1971.

Ambrose, Stephen. *Eisenhower: The President.* New York: Simon and Schuster, 1985.

Anderson, Benedict. "Cacique Democracy in the Philippines: Origins and Dreams." *New Left Review* 169 (May/June 1988): 3–31.

————. *Imagined Communities: Reflections on the Origin and Spread of Nationalism.* London: Verso, 1983.

Anderson, David L. *Trapped by Success: The Eisenhower Administration and Vietnam, 1953–1961.* New York: Columbia University Press, 1991.

Ando, Hirofumi. "A Study of Voting Patterns in the Philippines Presidential and Senatorial Elections, 1946–1965." *Midwest Journal of Political Science* 13 (1969): 567–86.

Andrade, Pio, Jr. *The Fooling of America: The Untold Story of Carlos P. Romulo.* Manila: By the author, 1985.

Appleton, S. "Communism and the Chinese in the Philippines." *Pacific Affairs* 32 (1959): 376–91.

Averch, Harvey A., and John Koehler. *The Huk Rebellion in the Philippines: Quantitative Approaches.* Santa Monica, Calif.: Rand, 1970.

Averch, Harvey A., John C. Koehler, and Frank H. Danton. *The Matrix of Policy in the Philippines.* Princeton: Princeton University Press, 1971.

Bacho, Peter. "U.S.-Philippine Relations in Transition: The Issue of the Bases." *Asian Survey* 28 (June 1988): 650–60.

Baldwin, Robert E. *Foreign Trade Regimes and Economic Development: The Philippines*. New York: Columbia University Press, 1975.

Baliga, Bantval M. "The American Approach to Imperialism in Southeast Asia—the Attitude of the United States Government in the Philippines, Indochina, and Indonesia, 1945–1958." Ph.D. diss., Southern Illinois University, 1961.

Barr, Robert J., ed. *American Trade with Asia and the Far East*. Milwaukee: Marquette University Press, 1959.

Bauzon, Leslie. *Philippine Agrarian Reform, 1880–1965: The Revolution That Never Was*. Occasional Paper 31. Singapore: Institute for South-East Asian Studies, 1975.

Bernstein, David. *The Philippine Story*. New York: Farrar, Straus, 1947.

Berry, William E., Jr. *U.S. Bases in the Philippines: The Evolution of the Special Relationship*. Boulder, Colo.: Westview, 1989.

Beyster Corporation. *Proposed Program for Industrial Rehabilitation and Development of the Republic of the Philippines*. Manila: Benipayo, 1947.

Biedzynski, James C. "Quezon's Views on Post-War Philippine-American Relations." *Bulletin of the American Historical Collection* 18, 1 (Jan. 1990): 84–90.

Billings-Yun, Melanie. *Decision Against War: Eisenhower and Dien Bien Phu, 1954*. New York: Columbia University Press, 1988.

———. "Ike and Vietnam." *History Today* 38 (Nov. 1988): 13–19.

Blake, Israel George. *Paul V. McNutt: Portrait of a Hoosier Statesman*. Indianapolis: Central Publishing, 1966.

Blum, Robert M. *Drawing the Line: The Origin of American Containment Policy in East Asia*. New York: Norton, 1982.

Bohlen, Charles E. *Witness to History*. New York: Norton, 1973.

Borden, William S. *The Pacific Alliance: United States Foreign Economic Policy and Japanese Trade Recovery*. Madison: University of Wisconsin Press, 1984.

Borg, Dorothy, and Waldo Heinrichs, eds. *Uncertain Years: Chinese-American Relations, 1947–1950*. New York: Columbia University Press, 1980.

Brands, Henry W. *Bound to Empire: The United States and the Philippines*. New York: Oxford University Press, 1992.

———. "From ANZUS to SEATO: United States Strategic Policy Toward Australia and New Zealand." *International History Review* 9 (May 1987): 250–70.

———. *The Specter of Neutralism: The United States and the Emer-*

gence of the Third World, 1947–1960. New York: Columbia University Press, 1989.

———. "The United States and the Emergence of an Independent Japan." *Pacific Affairs* 59 (1986): 387–401.

Buell, Thomas A. *The Quiet Warrior.* Annapolis, Md.: Naval Institute Press, 1987.

Buhite, Russel D. *Soviet-American Relations in Asia, 1945–1954.* Norman: University of Oklahoma Press, 1981.

Buss, Claude A. "Independence, Collaboration Issues Splitting Philippine People." *Commonweal* 21 (July 23, 1945): 149–50.

———. "Nationalization in the Philippines." *Fortune* (Feb. 1989): 80–81.

———. "Report from Manila." *Fortune* (July 1945): 134–39.

———. *The United States and the Philippines: Background for Policy.* Washington, D.C.: American Enterprise Institute for Public Policy Research, 1977.

———. "Waking from a Dream." *Wilson Quarterly* 10, 3 (1986): 106–15.

———. "What Follows Liberation." *Fortune* (Dec. 1944): 126–29.

Cable, Larry E. *Conflict of Myths: The Development of American Counterinsurgency Doctrine and the Vietnam War.* New York: New York University Press, 1986.

Calderon, Aurelio B. *The Laurel-Langley Agreement: A Critically Annotated and Selected Bibliography.* Manila: De La Salle University Press, 1979.

Campbell, John C. *The United States in World Affairs, 1947–1948.* New York: Council on Foreign Relations, 1948.

Cannon, M. Hamlin. *Leyte: The Return to the Philippines.* Washington, D.C.: Government Printing Office, 1954.

Castro, Amado A. "Philippine Export Development, 1950–1965." In *Economic Interdependence in Southeast Asia,* ed. Theodore Morgan and Nyle Spoelstra, pp. 181–200. Madison: University of Wisconsin Press, 1969.

Chand, Attar. *Southeast Asia and the Pacific: A Select Bibliography, 1947–1977.* New Delhi: Sterling, 1979.

Chay, John, ed. *The Problems and Prospects of American-East Asian Relations.* Boulder, Colo.: Westview, 1977.

Christobal, Adrian E., and Gregor A. James. "The Philippines and the United States: A Short History of the Security Connection." *Comparative Strategy* 6, 1 (1987): 61–89.

Collings, F. d'A. "Recent Progress in Latin America Toward Eliminating Exchange Restrictions." *International Monetary Fund Staff Papers* 9, 2 (May 1961): 274–86.

Constantino, Renato. *The Making of Filipino.* Quezon City: By the author, 1987.

Constantino, Renato, and Letizia Constantino. *The Continuing Past.* Quezon City: Foundation for Nationalist Studies, 1978.

Converse, Elliott V. "United States Plans for a Postwar Overseas Military Base System, 1942–1948." Ph.D. diss., Princeton University, 1984.

Coquia, Jorge R. *The Philippine Presidential Election of 1953.* Manila: University Publishing Co., 1955.

Corpuz, Onofre D. *The Bureaucracy in the Philippines.* Manila: University of the Philippines Institute of Public Administration, 1957.

Crowther, William. "Philippine Authoritarianism and the International Economy." *Comparative Politics* 18, 3 (1986): 339–46.

Cuaderno, Miguel. "Is Politics a Necessary Factor to Economic Growth?" *Philippine Economy Review* (Jan.-Feb. 1960): 28–30.

———. *Problems of Economic Development.* Manila: By the author, 1964.

Cullather, Nick. "The Limits of Multilateralism: Making Policy for the Philippines, 1945–1950." *International History Review* 13, 1 (Feb. 1991): 70–95.

Cumings, Bruce. *The Origins of the Korean War.* Vol. 2. Princeton: Princeton University Press, 1990.

Currey, Cecil B. *Edward Lansdale: The Unquiet American.* Boston: Houghton Mifflin, 1988.

Del Carmen, Rolando V. "The Chinese in the Philippines: Integration Revisited." *Asian Forum* 6, 2 (Apr. 1974): 43–53.

Dingman, Roger. "Atomic Diplomacy During the Korean War." *International Security* 13, 3 (Winter 1988–89): 50–91.

———. "The Diplomacy of Dependency: The Philippines and Peacemaking with Japan, 1945–1952." *Journal of Southeast Asian Studies* 17 (1986): 307–21.

———. "John Foster Dulles and the Creation of the South-East Asia Treaty Organization in 1954." *International History Review* 11, 3 (1989): 409–612.

———. "Strategic Planning and the Policy Process: American Plans for War in East Asia, 1945–1950." *Naval War College Review* 32 (1979): 4–21.

Dobbs, Charles M. "The Pact That Never Was: The Pacific Pact of 1949." *Journal of Northeast Asian Studies* 3, 4 (1984): 29–42.

Doronila, Amando. *The State, Economic Transformation, and Political Change in the Philippines, 1946–1972*. Singapore: Oxford University Press, 1992.

Dos Santos, Theotonio. "The Structure of Dependence." *American Economic Review* 60, 2 (May 1970): 231–33.

Dulles, John Foster. "The Evolution of Foreign Policy." *Department of State Bulletin* (Jan. 25, 1954): 108–9.

Eckes, Alfred E. *A Search for Solvency: Bretton Woods and the International Monetary System, 1941–1971*. Austin: University of Texas Press, 1975.

Edgerton, Ronald K. "General Douglas MacArthur and the American Military Impact in the Philippines." *Philippine Studies* 25, 4 (1977): 420–40.

——. "The Politics of Reconstruction in the Philippines: 1945–1948." Ph.D. diss., University of Michigan, 1975.

Eisenhower, Dwight D. *Mandate for Change, 1953–1956*. New York: Doubleday, 1963.

Eitzen, D. Stanley. "Two Minorities, the Jews of Poland and the Chinese of the Philippines." In *Philippine-Chinese Profile: Essays and Studies*, ed. Charles T. McCarthy, pp. 107–28. Manila: Pagkakaisa sa Pag-unlad, 1974.

Ellsbree, Willard H. "The 1953 Philippine Presidential Election." *Pacific Affairs* 27, 1 (Mar. 1954): 3–15.

Ely, Richard R. "The Bell Trade Act." *American Chamber of Commerce Journal* 29 (1953): 268–73.

Espinosa Robles, Raissa. *To Fight Without End*. Manila: Ayala Foundation, 1990.

Etzold, Thomas H. *Aspects of Sino-American Relations since 1784*. New York: New Viewpoints, 1978.

Etzold, Thomas H., and John L. Gaddis. *Containment: Documents on American Policy and Strategy, 1945–1950*. New York: Columbia University Press, 1978.

Fauni, Manuel Nato. "The Philippine Commonwealth Government in Exile." M.A. thesis, Manuel L. Quezon Educational Institution Graduate School, 1953.

Ferguson, Thomas. "From Normalcy to New Deal: Industrial Structure, Party Competition, and American Public Policy in the Great Depression." *International Organization* 38, 1 (Winter 1984): 41–94.

Ferrell, Robert H. *Off the Record: The Private Papers of Harry S Truman*. New York: Harper and Row, 1980.

Fifield, Russel H. *Americans in Southeast Asia: The Roots of Commitment.* New York: Crowell, 1973.

———. *The Diplomacy of Southeast Asia, 1945–1958.* New York: Harper and Brothers, 1958.

———. "The Hukbalahap Today." *Far Eastern Survey* 20 (Jan. 24, 1951): 4–21.

Filipinas Foundation. *Philippine Majority-Minority Relations and Ethnic Attitudes.* Makati: Filipinas Foundation, 1975.

Forrestal, James. *The Forrestal Diaries.* New York: Viking, 1951.

Frank, André Gunder. *Lumpenbourgeoisie, Lumpendevelopment: Dependence, Class and Politics in Latin America.* New York: Monthly Review Press, 1972.

Friend, Theodore. *Between Two Empires.* New Haven: Yale University Press, 1965.

———. *The Blue-Eyed Enemy: Japan Against the West in Java and Luzon, 1942–1945.* Princeton: Princeton University Press, 1988.

———."The Philippine Sugar Industry and the Politics of Independence." *Journal of Asian Studies* 22, 2 (Feb. 1963): 179–92.

Futrell, Robert F. *The United States Air Force in Southeast Asia: The Advisory Years to 1965.* Washington, D.C.: Office of Air Force History, 1981.

Gaddis, John L. *Strategies of Containment: A Critical Appraisal of Postwar American National Security Policy.* New York: Oxford University Press, 1982.

Gallicchio, Marc S. "The Best Defense Is a Good Offense: The Evolution of American Strategy in East Asia, 1953–1960." In *The Great Powers in East Asia, 1953–1960,* ed. Warren Cohen and Akira Iriye, pp. 63–85. New York: Columbia University Press, 1990.

Garcia, Ed. *The Sovereign Quest: Freedom from Foreign Military Bases.* Quezon City: Claretian Publications, 1988.

Garcia, Enrique Voltaire. *U.S. Military Bases and Philippine-American Relations.* Quezon City: Bookman Printing House, 1968.

Gardner, Richard N. *Sterling-Dollar Diplomacy: The Origins and Prospects of Our International Economic Order.* New York: McGraw-Hill, 1969.

Garnell, H. J. "Interpretation of the Philippine Election of 1953." *American Political Science Review* 48 (1954): 1129–31.

Garson, R. A. "The Origins of the Cold War in Asia." *Review of International Studies* 12, 4 (1986): 293–300.

Geertz, Clifford. *The Interpretation of Cultures.* New York: Basic Books, 1973.

Gleeck, Lewis E., Jr. *The American Governors-General and High Commissioners in the Philippines.* Quezon City: New Day, 1986.
———. *Dissolving the Colonial Bond.* Quezon City: New Day, 1988.
Golay, Frank H. "Entrepreneurship and Economic Development in the Philippines." *Far Eastern Survey* 29, 6 (1960): 81–86.
———, ed. *Philippine-American Relations.* Manila: Solidaridad, 1966.
———. *The Philippines: Public Policy and National Economic Development.* Ithaca, N.Y.: Cornell University Press, 1961.
———. "The Philippines." In *Underdevelopment and Economic Nationalism in Southeast Asia,* ed. Frank H. Golay et al., pp. 21–109. Ithaca, N.Y.: Cornell University Press, 1969.
———. *The Revised United States–Philippine Trade Agreement of 1955.* Ithaca, N.Y.: Cornell Southeast Asia Program, 1956.
Goodrich, Leland M., ed. *Documents on American Foreign Relations.* Vol. 4, *July 1941–June 1942.* Boston: World Peace Foundation, 1942.
Gormly, James L. *The Collapse of the Grand Alliance, 1945–1948.* Baton Rouge: Louisiana State University Press, 1987.
Greenberg, Lawrence M. *The Hukbalahap Insurrection.* Washington, D.C.: U.S. Army Center for Military History, 1986.
Greene, Fred, ed. *The Philippine Bases: Negotiating the Future.* New York: Council on Foreign Relations, 1988.
Gregor, A. James, and Virgilio Agnan. *The Philippine Bases: U.S. Security at Risk.* Washington, D.C.: Ethics and Public Policy Center, 1987.
Gripaldo, Rolando M. "The Quezon-Winslow Correspondence: A Friendship Turned Sour." *Philippine Studies* 32, 2 (1984): 129–62.
Grunder, Garel A., and William A. Livezey. *The Philippines and the United States.* Norman: University of Oklahoma Press, 1951.
Gunther, John. "Manuel Quezon." *The Atlantic* (Jan. 1939): 59–70.
Habu, Nagaho. "The Philippines' New Start and Japan." *Japan Quarterly* 39, 3 (July-Sept. 1992): 311–20.
Hahn, Peter L. *The United States, Great Britain, and Egypt, 1945–1956.* Chapel Hill: University of North Carolina Press, 1991.
Hainsworth, Reginald G., and Raymond T. Moyer. *Agricultural Geography of the Philippine Islands.* Washington, D.C.: U.S. Department of Agriculture, 1945.
Harrington, Fred Harvey. " 'Europe First' and Its Implications for the Far Eastern Policy of the United States." In *Redefining the Past: Essays in Diplomatic History in Honor of William Appleman Williams,* ed. Lloyd C. Gardner, pp. 105–20. Corvallis: University of Oregon Press, 1985.
Harrison, Francis Burton. *Origins of the Philippine Republic: Extracts*

from the Diaries and Records of Francis Burton Harrison. Edited by Michael P. Onorato. Ithaca, N.Y.: Southeast Asia Program, Cornell University, 1974.

Hartendorp. A.V.H. *History of Industry and Trade of the Philippines.* Manila: American Chamber of Commerce of the Philippines, 1958.

Hayden, Joseph Ralston. *The Philippines: A Study in National Development.* New York: Macmillan, 1942.

Hayes, Samuel P., ed. *The Beginnings of American Aid to Southeast Asia: The Griffin Mission of 1950.* Lexington, Mass.: Heath Lexington Books, 1971.

Healy, Gerald W. "The Question of Jurisdiction: American Military Personnel in the Philippines." *Philippine Studies* 5, 3 (Sept. 1957): 287–98.

Hess, Gary. "The American Search for Stability in Southeast Asia: The SEATO Structure of Containment." In *The Great Powers in East Asia, 1953–1960,* ed. Warren I. Cohen and Akira Iriye, pp. 272–95. New York: Columbia University Press, 1990.

———. *Vietnam and the United States.* Boston: Twayne, 1990.

Hester, Evett D. "Footnotes to Philippine Economics." *Philippine Social Science Review* 12, 2 (1940): 131–41.

———. "Outline of Our Recent Political and Trade Relations with the Philippine Commonwealth." *Annals of the American Academy of Political and Social Science* 226 (1943): 73–85.

———. "Restoration of the Philippine Economy and Trade." In *Report of the 31st National Foreign Trade Convention, October 9–11, 1944,* pp. 204–16. New York: National Foreign Trade Convention, 1945.

Higgins, Benjamin. "Development Problems in the Philippines: A Comparison with Indonesia," *Far Eastern Survey* 26, 11 (Nov. 1957): 161–69.

Holsti, Ole R. "International Relations Models." In *Explaining the History of American Foreign Relations,* ed. Michael J. Hogan and Thomas G. Paterson, pp. 57–88. New York: Cambridge University Press, 1991.

Human Relations Area Files, Inc. *Subcontractor's Monograph: The Philippines.* 4 vols. New Haven: Human Relations Area Files, 1956.

Hutchcroft, Paul. "Oligarchs and Cronies in the Philippine State: The Politics of Patrimonial Plunder." *World Politics* 43, 3 (Apr. 1991): 414–50.

———. "Situating the Philippine Political Economy: Import Substitution Industrialization in Comparative Perspective." *Kasarinlan* 4, 4 (1989): 39–56.

Iriye, Akira. *The Cold War in Asia: A Historical Introduction.* Englewood Cliffs, N.J.: Prentice Hall, 1974.

Iriye, Akira, and Yonosuke Nagai, eds. *The Cold War in Asia.* New York: Columbia University Press, 1977.

James, D. Clayton. *The Years of MacArthur.* Vol. 2, *1941–1945.* Boston: Houghton Mifflin, 1975.

Jenkins, Shirley. *American Economic Policy Toward the Philippines.* Stanford, Calif.: Stanford University Press, 1954.

Jensen, Irene Khin Myint. *The Chinese in the Philippines During the American Regime, 1898–1946.* San Francisco: R and E Research Associates, 1975.

Jordan, Amos A. *Foreign Aid and the Defense of Southeast Asia.* New York: Praeger, 1962.

Kahin, George McT. *Intervention: How America Became Involved in Vietnam.* New York: Knopf, 1986.

Karnow, Stanley. *In Our Image: America's Empire in the Philippines.* New York: Random House, 1989.

Kaufman, Burton I. "Eisenhower's Foreign Economic Policy with Respect to East Asia." In *The Great Powers in East Asia, 1953–1960,* ed. Warren I. Cohen and Akira Iriye, pp. 104–20. New York: Cornell University Press, 1990.

———. *Trade and Aid: Eisenhower's Foreign Economic Policy, 1953–1961.* Baltimore: The Johns Hopkins University Press, 1982.

Kerkvliet, Benedict. *The Huk Rebellion.* Quezon City: New Day, 1989.

———. "Peasant Society and Unrest Prior to the Huk Revolution." *Asian Studies* 9 (Aug. 1971): 172–204.

Kessler, Richard J. *Rebellion and Repression in the Philippines.* New Haven: Yale University Press, 1989.

Kolko, Gabriel. *Confronting the Third World: United States Foreign Policy, 1945–1980.* New York: Pantheon, 1988.

Kolko, Gabriel, and Joyce Kolko. *The Limits of Power: The World and United States Foreign Policy, 1945–1954.* New York: Harper and Row, 1972.

Krasner, Stephen D. *Defending the National Interest: Raw Materials, Investments, and U.S. Foreign Policy.* Princeton: Princeton University Press, 1978.

———. "State Power and the Structure of International Trade." *World Politics* 27, 3 (1976): 317–47.

———. *Structural Conflict: The Third World Against Global Liberalism.* Berkeley: University of California Press, 1985.

Kunio, Yoshihara. *The Rise of Ersatz Capitalism in South-East Asia.* Quezon City: Ateneo de Manila University Press, 1988.

Kurihara, Kenneth K. *Labor in the Philippine Economy.* Stanford, Calif.: Stanford University Press, 1945.

Lachica, Eduardo. *Huk: Philippine Agrarian Society in Revolt.* Manila: Solidaridad, 1971.

Landé, Carl H. *Leaders, Factions and Parties: The Structure of Philippine Politics.* Monograph Series 6. New Haven: Yale University Southeast Asia Area Studies, 1966.

———. "Politics in the Philippines." Ph.D. diss., Harvard University, 1958.

Lansdale, Edward Geary. *In the Midst of Wars: An American's Mission to Southeast Asia.* New York: Harper and Row, 1972.

Laurel, Jose P. *Bread and Freedom.* Manila: By the author, 1953.

———. *The War Memoirs of Dr. Jose P. Laurel.* Manila: Jose P. Laurel Memorial Foundation, 1962.

Leffler, Melvyn P. "The American Conception of National Security and the Beginnings of the Cold War, 1945–48." *American Historical Review* 89 (1984): 346–400.

———. *A Preponderance of Power: National Security, the Truman Administration, and the Cold War.* Stanford, Calif.: Stanford University Press, 1992.

Lichuaco, Alejandro. *The Lichuaco Paper: Imperialism in the Philippines.* New York: Monthly Review Press, 1973.

———. *Nationalist Economics: History: Theory and Practice.* Quezon City: Institute for Rural Industrialization, 1988.

Lichuaco, Marcial P. *Roxas.* Manila: Kiko Printing, 1952.

Lim Joo-Jock and Vani Shanmuginarantnam, eds. *Armed Communist Movements in Southeast Asia.* New York: St. Martin's Press, 1984.

Lopez, Salvador P. *Elpidio Quirino: The Judgment of History.* Manila: President Elpidio Quirino Foundation, 1990.

Lundestad, Geir. "Empire by Invitation? The United States and Western Europe, 1945–1952." *Journal of Peace Research* 23, 3 (1986): 263–77.

MacArthur, Douglas. *Reminiscences.* New York: McGraw Hill, 1964.

McBeath, Gerald A. *Political Integration of the Philippine Chinese.* Berkeley: University of California Center for South and Southeast Asian Studies, 1983.

McCarthy, Charles T., ed. *Philippine-Chinese Profile: Essays and Studies.* Manila: Pagkakaisa sa Pag-unlad, 1974.

McCormick, Thomas J. *America's Half Century: United States For-*

eign Policy in the Cold War. Baltimore: The Johns Hopkins University Press, 1989.

MacDonald, Douglas J. *Adventures in Chaos: American Intervention for Reform in the Third World.* Cambridge, Mass.: Harvard University Press, 1992.

Machado, K. G. "Continuity and Change in Philippine Factionalism." In *Faction Politics: Political Parties and Factionalism in Comparative Perspective,* ed. Frank Belloni and Dennis C. Beller, pp. 193–218. Santa Barbara, Calif.: ABC-Clio, 1978.

McMahon, Robert. *Colonialism and Cold War: The United States and the Struggle for Indonesian Independence, 1945–1949.* Ithaca, N.Y.: Cornell University Press, 1981.

———. "Eisenhower and Third World Nationalism: A Critique of the Revisionists." *Political Science Quarterly* 101 (1986): 453–73.

———. "Hegemony and Its Problems." *Reviews in American History* 19, 1 (1991): 136–41.

McNutt, Paul V. "America's Role in the Orient." *Annals of the American Association of Political and Social Science* 258 (1948): 53–56.

———. "Democracy on Trial in the Orient." *Vital Speeches* (Apr. 1, 1946): 362–66.

———. "The Philippines: Its Strategic, Economic, and Ideological Importance." *Far East Advertiser* (Apr. 1947): 32–35.

———. "The Task Ahead." *American Federationist* (Jan. 1943): 5–6.

Maxfield, Sylvia, and James H. Nolt. "Protectionism and the Internationalization of Capital: U.S. Sponsorship of Import Substitution Industrialization in the Philippines, Turkey and Argentina." *International Studies Quarterly* 34 (1990): 49–81.

Maxwell, Richard S. "A Historical Study of the Office of United States High Commissioner to the Philippine Islands, 1935–1946." M.A. thesis, The American University, 1966.

May, Glenn Anthony. *Battle for Batangas: A Philippine Province at War.* New Haven: Yale University Press, 1991.

———. *A Past Recovered.* Quezon City: New Day, 1987.

———. *Social Engineering in the Philippines.* Quezon City: New Day, 1984.

Meadows, Martin. "Recent Development in Philippine American Relations: A Case Study in Emergent Nationalism." *Asian Survey* 5 (1965): 305–18.

———. "Theories of External-Internal Political Relationships: A Case Study of Indonesia and the Philippines." *Asian Studies* 6 (1968): 297–324.

Merrill, Dennis. *Bread and the Ballot: The United States and India's Economic Development, 1947–1963.* Chapel Hill: University of North Carolina Press, 1990.

Meyer, Milton Walker. *A Diplomatic History of the Philippine Republic.* Honolulu: University of Hawaii Press, 1965.

Mill, Edward W. "The Conduct of Philippine Foreign Relations." Ph.D. diss., Princeton University, 1954.

Miller, Edward S. *War Plan Orange: The U.S. Strategy to Defeat Japan, 1897–1945.* Annapolis, Md.: Naval Institute Press, 1991.

Millikan, Max F., and W. W. Rostow. *Proposal: Key to an Effective Foreign Policy.* New York: Harper, 1957.

Mitchell, Edward J. "Some Econometrics of the Huk Rebellion." *American Political Science Review* 63 (1969): 1159–71.

Moore, T. J. "The Hukbalahap in the Philippines." *Australian Outlook* 1 (June 1947): 24–41.

Morton, Louis. "War Plan ORANGE: Evolution of a Strategy." *World Politics* 11 (1959): 221–50.

Nandy, Ashis. *The Intimate Enemy: Loss and Recovery of Self Under Colonialism.* Delhi: Oxford University Press, 1983.

National Foreign Trade Council. *Reconstruction Studies, No. 1.* New York: National Foreign Trade Council, December 1942.

———. *Report of the Thirty-Seventh National Foreign Trade Convention.* New York: National Foreign Trade Council, 1950.

Ohno, Takushi. *War Reparations and Peace Settlement.* Manila: Solidaridad Publishing House, 1986.

Onorato, Michael. *A Brief Review of American Interest in the Philippines and Other Essays.* Manila: MCS Enterprises, 1972.

Owen, Norman G., ed. *The Philippine Economy and the United States.* Ann Arbor: University of Michigan Center for South and Southeast Asian Studies, 1983.

Owens, William A. *Eye-Deep in Hell: A Memoir of the Liberation of the Philippines.* Dallas: Southern Methodist University Press, 1989.

Pach, Chester J. *Arming the Free World: The Origins of the United States Military Assistance Program, 1945–1950.* Chapel Hill: University of North Carolina Press, 1991.

Packenham, Robert A. *Holistic Dependency and Analytic Dependency: Two Approaches to Dependency and Dependency Reversal.* Stanford: Stanford-Berkeley Joint Center for Latin American Studies, 1984.

Paez, Patricia Ann. *The Bases Factor.* Manila: Center for Strategic and International Studies of the Philippines, 1985.

Paredes-San Diego, Lourdes. *Don Quentin of Abra*. Manila: By the author, 1985.

Pastor, Robert A. *Congress and the Politics of U.S. Foreign Economic Policy, 1929–1976*. Berkeley: University of California Press, 1980.

Payer, Cheryl. *The Debt Trap: The IMF and the Third World*. London: Penguin, 1974.

Pelaez, Emmanuel. "The Military Bases in the Philippines: The Past and the Future." *Foreign Relations Journal* 1, 1 (Jan. 1986): 1–39.

Pérez, Louis A., Jr. "Dependency." In *Explaining the History of American Foreign Relations*, ed. Michael J. Hogan and Thomas G. Paterson, pp. 99–110. New York: Cambridge University Press, 1991.

Petillo, Carol Morris. *Douglas MacArthur: The Philippine Years*. Bloomington: Indiana University Press, 1981.

Petras, James, and Morris Morley. *U.S. Hegemony Under Seige: Class, Politics and Development in Latin America*. London: Verso, 1990.

Phelan, John Leddy. *The Kingdom of Quito in the Seventeenth Century*. Madison: University of Wisconsin Press, 1967.

Pizer, Samuel, and Frederick Cutler. "Capital Outlays Abroad by U.S. Companies: Rising Plant Expansion in Manufacturing." *Survey of Current Business* 40, 10 (Oct. 1960): 19–23.

Platt, Donald L. "A Sovereignty of Sorts: Filipino-American Relations During the Truman Administration, 1945–1951." Ph.D. diss., University of Toledo, 1988.

Pollard, Robert A. *Economic Security and the Origins of the Cold War, 1945–1950*. New York: Columbia University Press, 1985.

Pomeroy, William J. *An American-Made Tragedy: Neocolonialism and Dictatorship in the Philippines*. New York: International Publishers, 1974.

———. *American Neo-Colonialism: Its Emergence in the Philippines and Asia*. New York: International Publishers, 1970.

———. *The Forest: A Personal Record of the Huk Guerrilla Struggle in the Philippines*. New York: International Publishers, 1963.

———. "The Philippine Peasantry and the Huk Revolt." *Journal of Peasant Studies* 5 (1978): 497–517.

———. "United States Military Bases in the Philippines." *Eastern World* (Feb. 1965): 7–9.

Purcell, Victor. *The Chinese in Southeast Asia*. London: Oxford University Press, 1965.

Quirino, Carlos. *Apo Lakay*. Manila: Total Book World, 1987.

———. *Magsaysay of the Philippines*. Manila: Carmelo and Baurmann, 1964.

———. *Philippine Tycoon: The Biography of an Industrialist, Vicente Madrigal.* Manila: Vicente Madrigal Memorial Foundation, 1987.
Quirino, Elpidio. *The Memoirs of Elpidio Quirino.* Manila: National Historical Institute, 1990.
———. *The New Philippine Ideology.* Manila: Bureau of Printing, 1949.
Rabe, Stephen G. *Eisenhower and Latin America.* Chapel Hill: University of North Carolina Press, 1988.
Rafferty, Kathryn E. *Foreign Policy Making in the Philippines.* McLean, Va.: Research Analysis Corporation, 1968.
Ravenholt, Albert. "Chinese in the Philippines—An Alien Business and Middle Class." *American Universities Field Staff Reports,* Southeast Asia series (Dec. 9, 1955).
Recto, Claro M. *My Crusade.* Manila: Pio C. Colica and Nicanor Corag, Publishers, 1955.
———. *The Recto Reader: Excerpts from the Speeches of Claro M. Recto.* Edited by Renato Constantino. Manila: Recto Memorial Foundation, 1965.
Richardson, Jim. "The Huk Rebellion." *Journal of Contemporary Asia* 8, 2 (1978): 231–37.
Rivera, Temerio Campos. "Class, the State, and Foreign Capital: The Politics of Philippine Industrialization, 1950–1986." Ph.D. diss., University of Wisconsin–Madison, 1991.
Romana, Elpidio R. Sta. "The Philippine State's Hegemony and Fiscal Base." *Developing Economies* 27, 2 (June 1989): 185–97.
———. *State Hegemony and the Fiscal Basis of the State in the Philippines, 1950–1985.* Quezon City: Social Weather Station, 1988.
Romulo, Carlos P. "GIs and Asian Justice." *The Nation* (July 17, 1957): 510–14.
———. *I See the Philippines Rise.* Garden City, N.Y.: Doubleday, 1946.
———. *I Walked With Heroes.* New York: Holt, Rinehart, and Winston, 1961.
Romulo, Carlos P., and Beth Day Romulo. *The Philippine Presidents: Memoirs.* Quezon City: New Day, 1988.
Ronquillo, Bernardino. "The Life of the Peso." *The Philippines Quarterly* 1, 2 (Sept. 1951): 36.
Rostow, Walt W. *The Diffusion of Power: 1957–1972.* New York: MacMillan, 1972.
———. *Eisenhower, Kennedy and Foreign Aid.* Austin: University of Texas Press, 1985.
Rotter, Andrew J. *The Path to Vietnam: Origin of the American Com-*

mitment to Southeast Asia. Ithaca, N.Y.: Cornell University Press, 1987.

Ruggie, John Gerard. "International Regimes, Transactions and Change: Embedded Liberalism in the Postwar Economic Order." *International Organization* 36, 2 (Spring 1982): 379–415.

Saito, Shiro. *Philippine-American Relations: A Guide to Manuscript Sources in the United States.* Westport, Conn.: Greenwood Press, 1982.

Salamanca, Bonifacio S. *The Filipino Reaction to American Rule, 1901–1913.* Quezon City: New Day, 1984.

———. "Quezon, Osmeña and Roxas and the American Military Presence in the Philippines." *Philippine Studies* 37 (1989): 301–16.

Saulo, Alfredo B. *Communism in the Philippines: An Introduction.* Manila: Ateneo Publications Office, 1969.

Sayre, Elizabeth E. "Submarine from Corregidor." *The Atlantic* (Aug. 1942): 22–28.

Sayre, Francis. *Glad Adventure.* New York: MacMillan, 1957.

Schaller, Michael. *The American Occupation of Japan.* New York: Oxford University Press, 1985.

———. *Douglas MacArthur: The Far Eastern General.* New York: Oxford University Press, 1989.

———. "Securing the Great Crescent: Occupied Japan and the Origins of Containment in Southeast Asia." *Journal of American History* 69, 2 (Sept. 1982): 392–414.

Schirmer, Daniel B., and Stephen R. Shalom, eds. *The Philippine Reader: A History of Colonialism, Neocolonialism, and Dictatorship.* Boston: South End Press, 1987.

Schonberger, Howard B. "The Cold War and the American Empire in Asia." *Radical History Review* 33 (1985): 139–54.

———. "The Japan Lobby in American Diplomacy, 1947–1952." *Pacific Historical Review* 46 (Aug. 1977): 327–59.

Scott, James C. *Comparative Political Corruption.* Englewood Cliffs, N.J.: Prentice-Hall, 1972.

———. *Weapons of the Weak: Everyday Forms of Peasant Resistance.* New Haven: Yale University Press, 1985.

Seidman, Samuel N. "Enterprise and Entrepreneurship in the Philippine Republic, 1949–1959." Ph.D. diss., New York University, 1963.

Serrano, Felixberto. *Crisis after Crisis.* Manila: By the author, 1973.

Shalom, Stephen R. *A Comparative Analysis of Dependency in the Philippines and Eastern Europe.* Honolulu: Western Conference of the Association for Asia Studies, 1983.

———. "The Implications of the Pre-War Philippine Experience for Peace Research." *Journal of Peace Research* 26, 1 (Feb. 1989): 19–26.

———. "Philippine Acceptance of the Bell Trade Act of 1946: A Study of Manipulatory Democracy." *Pacific Historical Review* 49, 3 (Aug. 1980): 499–517.

———. *The United States and the Philippines: A Study of Neocolonialism.* Quezon City: New Day, 1986.

Shaplen, Robert. "Letter from Manila." *The New Yorker* (Apr. 7, 1951): 96.

Sheehan, Neil. *A Bright Shining Lie: John Paul Vance and America in Vietnam.* New York: Random House, 1988.

Sherry, Michael S. *Preparing for the Next War: America's Plans for Postwar Defense, 1941–1945.* New Haven: Yale University Press, 1977.

Sicat, Gerardo P. *Economic Policy and Philippine Development.* Quezon City: University of the Philippines Press, 1972.

Simbulan, Roland G. *The Bases of Our Insecurity.* Manila: BALAI Fellowship, 1985.

Smith, Joseph B. *Portrait of a Cold Warrior.* Quezon City: Plaridel Books, 1976.

Smith, Perry McCoy. *The Air Force Plans for Peace, 1943–1945.* Baltimore: The Johns Hopkins University Press, 1970.

Smith, Robert Aura. *Philippine Freedom, 1948–1958.* New York: Columbia University Press, 1958.

Stanley, Peter. *A Nation in the Making: The Philippines and the United States, 1899–1921.* Cambridge, Mass.: Harvard University Press, 1974.

———, ed. *Reappraising an Empire: New Perspectives on Philippine-American History.* Cambridge, Mass.: Harvard University Press, 1984.

Starner, Frances. *Magsaysay and the Philippine Peasantry: The Agrarian Impact on Philippines Politics, 1953–1956.* Berkeley: University of California Press, 1961.

Stauffer, Robert B. *The Manila-Washington Connection: Continuities in the Transnational Political Economy of Philippine Development.* Sydney: Transnational Corporations Research Project, University of Sydney, 1983.

Steinberg, David Joel. *Philippine Collaboration in World War II.* Ann Arbor: University of Michigan Press, 1967.

———. *The Philippines: A Singular and a Plural Place.* Boulder, Colo.: Westview, 1971.

Stettinius, Edward R., Jr. *The Diaries of Edward R. Stettinius, Jr.,* *1943–1946.* Edited by Thomas M. Campbell and George C. Herring. New York: New Viewpoints, 1975.

Stimson, Henry L. *Diaries of Henry Lewis Stimson.* New Haven: Yale University, 1973. [Microfilm.]

Sturtevant, David R. "Sakdalism and Philippine Radicalism." *Journal of Asian Studies* 21 (Feb. 1962): 199–213.

Sumulong, Lorenzo. *My Years in Public Service.* Manila: By the author, 1981.

Sung Yong Kim. *United States-Philippine Relations, 1946–1956.* Washington, D.C.: Public Affairs Press, 1968.

Tan, Antonio S. "Five Hundred Years of Anti-Chinese Prejudice in the Philippines." Unpublished paper, Philippine Social Science Council Library, Quezon City.

Taruc, Luis. *Born of the People.* New York: International Publishers, 1953.

————. *He Who Rides the Tiger: The Story of an Asian Guerrilla Leader.* New York: Praeger, 1967.

Thompson, Helen M. "The Asian-African Conference at Bandung, Indonesia." M.A. thesis, University of the Philippines, 1956.

Tolentino, Arturo. *Voice of Dissent.* Quezon City: Phoenix Publishing House, 1990.

Trachtenberg, Marc. "Strategic Thought in America, 1952–1966." *Political Science Quarterly* 104 (1989): 301–84.

Truman, Harry S. *Memoirs.* 2 vols. New York: Doubleday, 1955.

Tucker, Nancy B. *Patterns in the Dust: Chinese-American Relations and the Recognition Controversy.* New York: Columbia University Press, 1983.

University of the East. *The 1953 Issues: Major Speeches Delivered by the Presidential Candidates.* Manila: University of the East, 1953.

University of the Philippines Library. *Ramon Magsaysay: A Bibliography.* Manila: University of the Philippines, 1957.

Urgal, Elizabeth T., and Mamorta Q. Caguimbal. *U.S. Military Bases in the Philippines: An Annotated Bibliography, 1947–1988.* Quezon City: University of the Philippines Asian Center, 1990.

Valeriano, Napoleon, and Charles T. R. Bohannon. *Counter Guerrilla Operations: The Philippine Experience.* New York: Praeger, 1961.

Van der Kroef, Justus. *Communism in Southeast Asia.* London: Macmillan, 1981.

Ventura, Mamerto S. "Philippine Postwar Recovery: A Record of United States-Philippine Cooperation and Cross-Purposes." Ph.D. diss., Southern Illinois University, 1966.

Ventura, Sylvia Mendez. *Mauro Mendez: From Journalism to Diplomacy.* Quezon City: University of the Philippines Press, 1978.
Watkins, T. H. *Righteous Pilgrim: The Life and Times of Harold L. Ickes, 1874-1952.* New York: Henry Holt, 1990.
Watson, Robert J. *History of the Joint Chiefs of Staff: The Joint Chiefs of Staff and National Policy, 1953-1954.* Washington, D.C.: JCS Historical Division, 1986.
Weber, Max. *The Theory of Social and Economic Organization.* New York: Free Press, 1947.
Weightman, George Henry. "The American Colonial Policy Toward the Chinese: A Legacy and a Problem for the Commonwealth." *Pilipinas* 7 (Fall 1986): 29-43.
Welch, Richard E., Jr. "America's Philippine Policy in the Quirino Years: A Study in Patron-Client Diplomacy." In *Reappraising an Empire: New Perspectives on Philippine-American History,* ed. Peter W. Stanley, pp. 285-306. Cambridge, Mass.: Harvard University Press, 1984.
Wilgus, Walter. "Economic Outlook for the Philippines." *Foreign Policy Reports* 21 (Oct. 1, 1945): 201-8.
Wolf, Charles, Jr. *Foreign Aid: Theory and Practice in Southeast Asia.* Princeton: Princeton University Press, 1960.
Wolters, Willem. *Politics, Patronage and Class Conflict in Central Luzon.* Quezon City: New Day, 1984.
Wurfel, David. "The Bell Report and After: A Study of the Political Problems of Social Reform Stimulated by Foreign Aid." Ph.D. diss., Cornell University, 1960.
———. *Filipino Politics: Development and Decay.* Ithaca, N.Y.: Cornell University Press, 1988.
———. "The Philippine Elections: New Trends." *Foreign Policy Bulletin* (Jan. 1, 1951): 61-64.
Wurfel, Violet E. "American Implementation of Philippine Independence." Ph.D. diss., University of Virginia, 1951.
Young, Marilyn. *The Vietnam Wars: 1945-1990.* New York: Harper Collins, 1991.

Index

In this index an "f" after a page number indicates a separate reference on the next page, and an "ff" indicates separate references on the next two pages. A continuous discussion over two or more pages is indicated by a span of page numbers, e.g., "pp. 57–59." *Passim* is used for a cluster of references in close but not consecutive sequence.

Library of Congress Cataloging-in-Publication Data

Cullather, Nick
Illusions of influence : the political economy of United
States–Philippines relations, 1942–1960 / Nick Cullather.
    p.   cm. — (Modern America)
Includes bibliographical references and index.
ISBN 0-8047-2280-3 (paper) :
    1. United States—Foreign economic relations—Philip-
pines. 2. Philippines—Foreign economic relations—United
States. 3. Philippines—Economic policy. 4. Philippines—Poli-
tics and government—1946– 5. United States—Colonies—
Asia—Economic policy. 1. Title. 11. Series: Modern America
(Stanford, Calif.)
HF1456.5.P6C85 1994
337.730599—dc20   93-36104
                                                              CIP

Printed and bound by CPI Group (UK) Ltd, Croydon, CR0 4YY

16/04/2025

14658401-0002